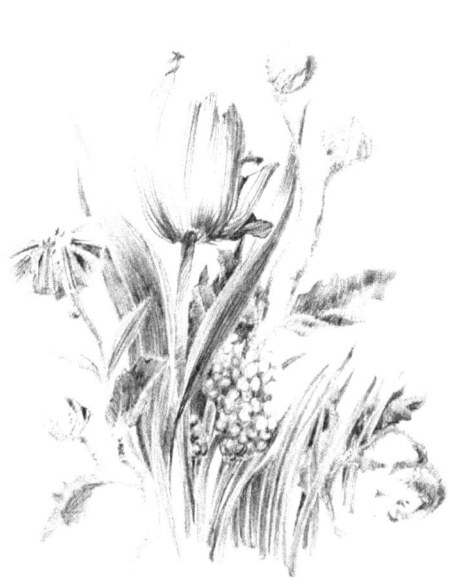

Copyright © Kathryn I. W. Sparks 2014.
All rights reserved.

This book may not be reproduced, in whole or in part, including illustrations, in any form (beyond that copying permitted by Sections 107 and 108 of the U.S. Copyright Law and except by reviewers for the public press), without written permission from the author.

All text, artworks, photos, digital images and graphic design in this book are the work of Kathryn I. W. Sparks.

MISS KITTY'S FABULOUS EMPORIUM OF
MAGICAL THINKING

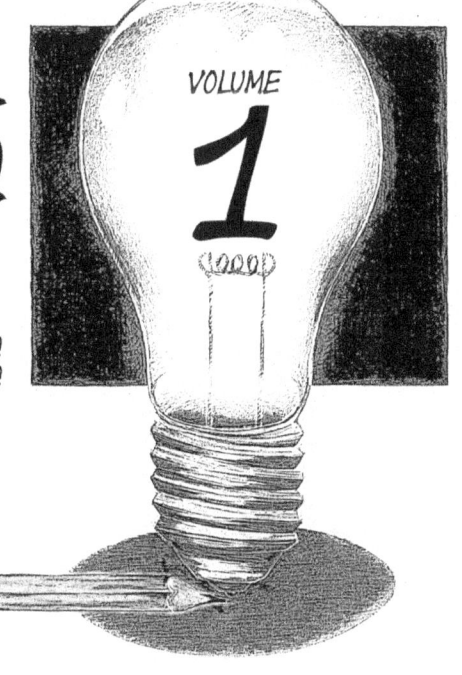

VOLUME 1

DRAWINGS & OTHER ARTWORKS
TALL TALES & WEIRD CREATURES

Kathryn I. W. Sparks

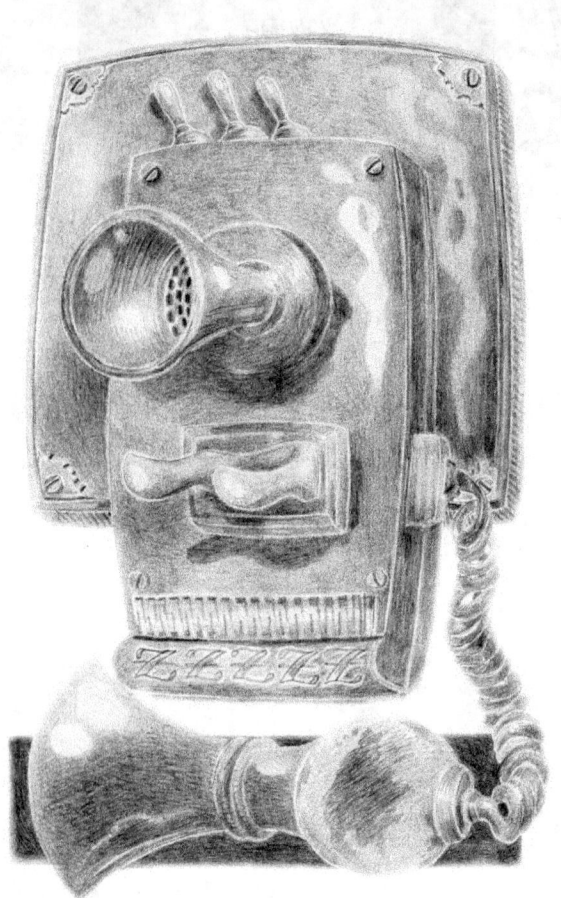

Hello, Earth Calling

Hello, hello, whoever you are
that perch upon a shooting star
And occupy the passing time
by listening for a tune sublime,
But hear instead the sounds of us
who people the earth and make a fuss
Of all the ridiculous things we do,
as though there were any value to
Our petty, silly, arcane lives
as we buzz about in our busy hives
A big production of each breath—
must bore you listeners half to death!—
Our self-obsession, navel-bound,
with every miniscule human sound,
Is foolish, yes, but while it is so,
we send you, too, a great big Hello.

Here's Watching You

Knocking on the inside
of my teeming little skull,
A thousand wriggling creatures
with wild eyes begin their sport
Of twisting through my cranium,
a dazzling cohort
Made up of all the crazy thoughts
with which my mind is full—
And when they've had their playtime,
as expressed upon my face
As mystifying consternation,
oddly pleased, bemused,
And mindful that I'm being watched:
I hope they are amused
Who gaze upon me from the stars
in deepest distant space.

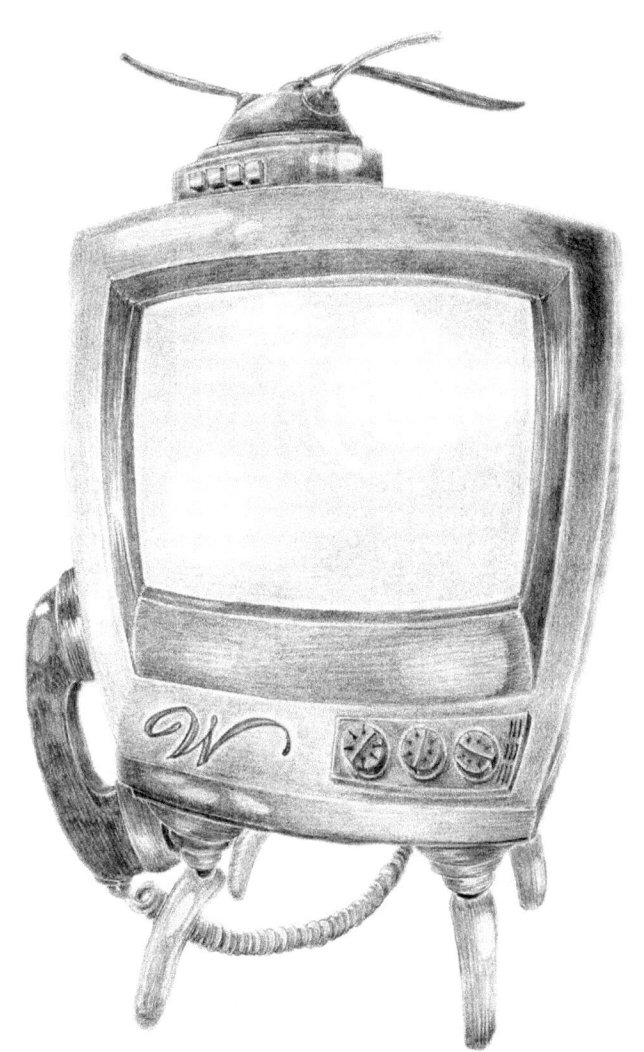

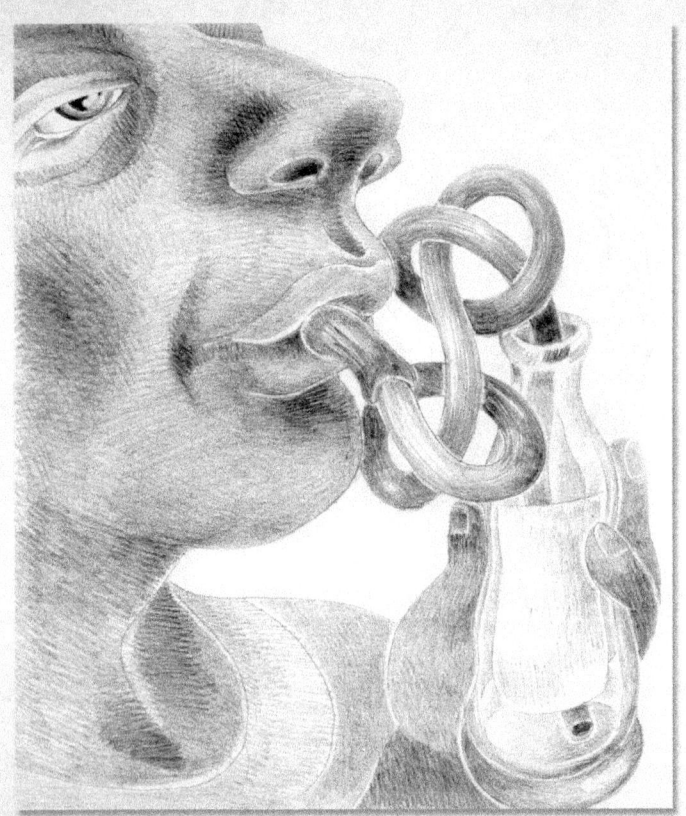

Beastly Discovery

The mild-mannered Ste-Hilaire
Went out one night to take the air
And came home newly sharp and snarky
(Full of mischief and malarkey);
I think maybe in the park, he
Might have met a succulent
Voracious, wild and truculent,
That bit his elbows (left and right),
Infecting him that very night
(As you'd imagine, quite a sight)
With psychedelic thoughts to itch
Him to a highly fevered pitch
Wherein he met another world
And in its vortex, seeing swirled
(The way such rarities are hurled)
Strange creatures in bizarre parade,
He loosed the window, threw the shade
Upon it open just to share
With us the beastly thoughts in there
(Effects of which you're now aware).

When Invited to Dinner by a Basilisk

The basilisk in yonder cavern,
Gore depending from its lips,
Nabbed its supper near a tavern
After many frothy sips
Whilst they both, its drink companion
And the basilisk, did splash
Their way through Old Peculiers and an
Extra with bangers and mash,
All of which was rather pleasant
And could both big stomachs fill,
But alas for the poor peasant,
Beastie still had time to kill,
So their friendly supper ended
In the alley next the pub,
Basilisk getting distended
After so much tasty drink and grub,
And then adding in his fellow
Public-house companion's bulk,
Before going home to mellow
In the shadows where his hulk
Lies in slight remorseful sorrow
Only for now having none
To go pub-crawling with tomorrow,
Or for dessert after the fun

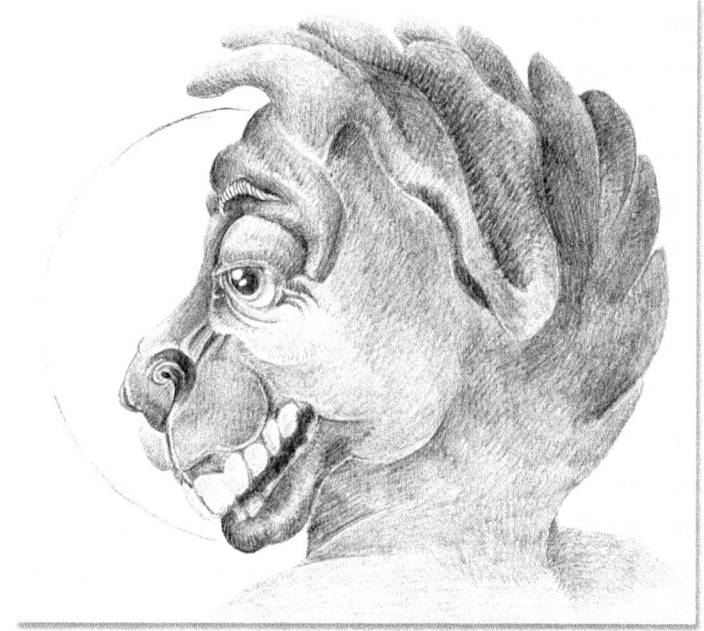

Daisy Gone Crazy

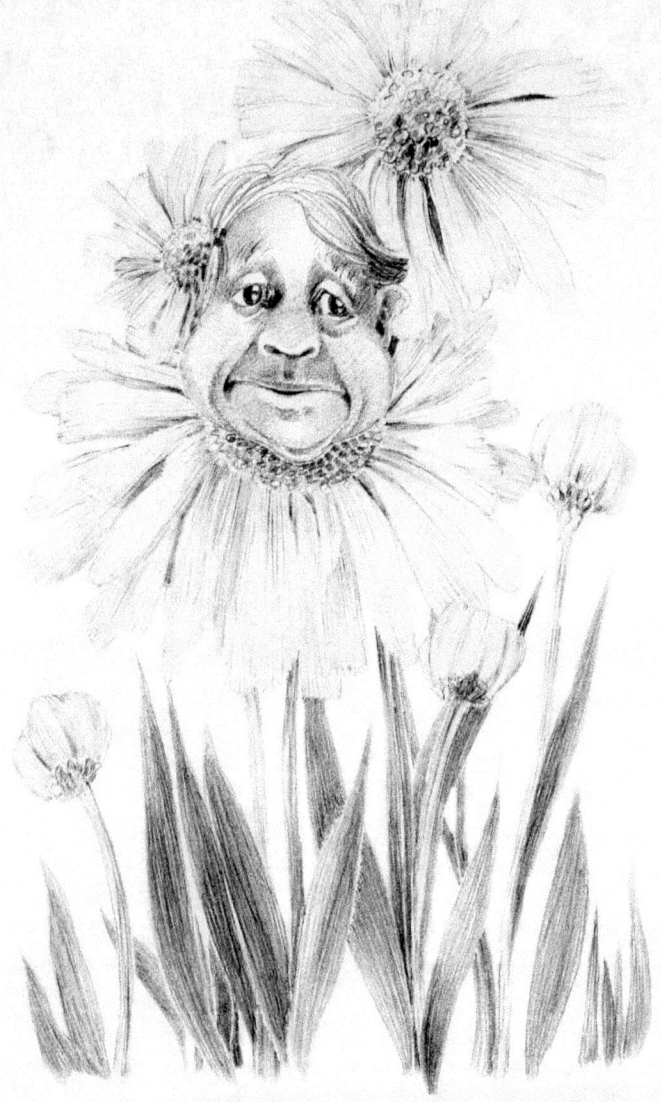

Loves me, loves me not—I swear,
It makes me tear out all my hair
To see how pitiful and dim
Young lovers are: I pity him
That he's so clumsy, so unschooled,
So ripe for being ridiculed—
And her I pity for her lack
Of savoir-faire, the noisy quack
Her nervous laughter makes when he
Attempts to kiss romantically—
But most of all, my pity settles
On myself: they pluck my petals!

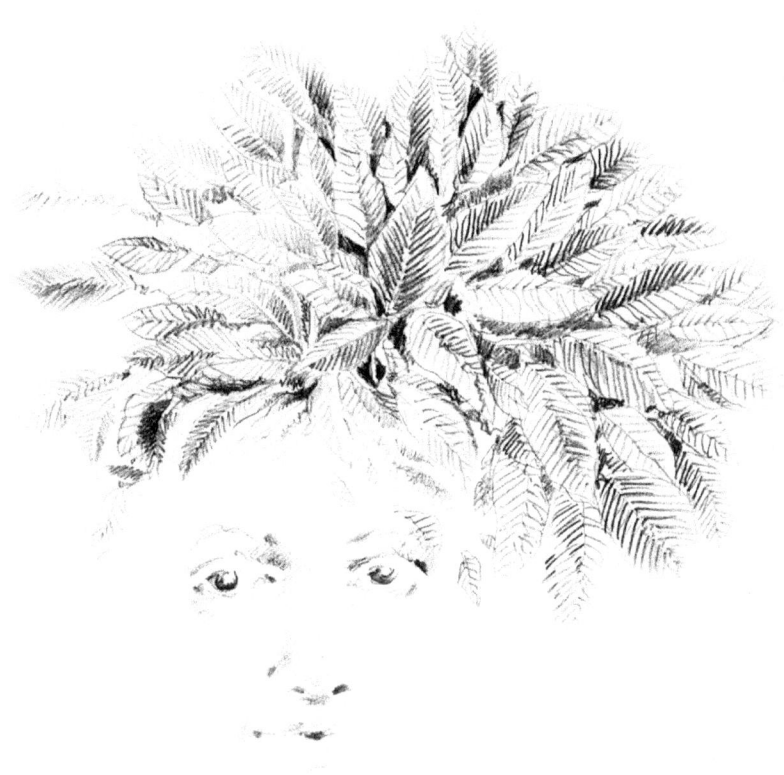

Green with Envy

The Green Man known to legend as
A god of woodland wiles,
Of newness, renaissance, rebirth,
And who the spring beguiles
With playful wildness and with glee,
I'd like to pound and drub
Him, though he may my cousin be,
For I'm stuck in this shrub.

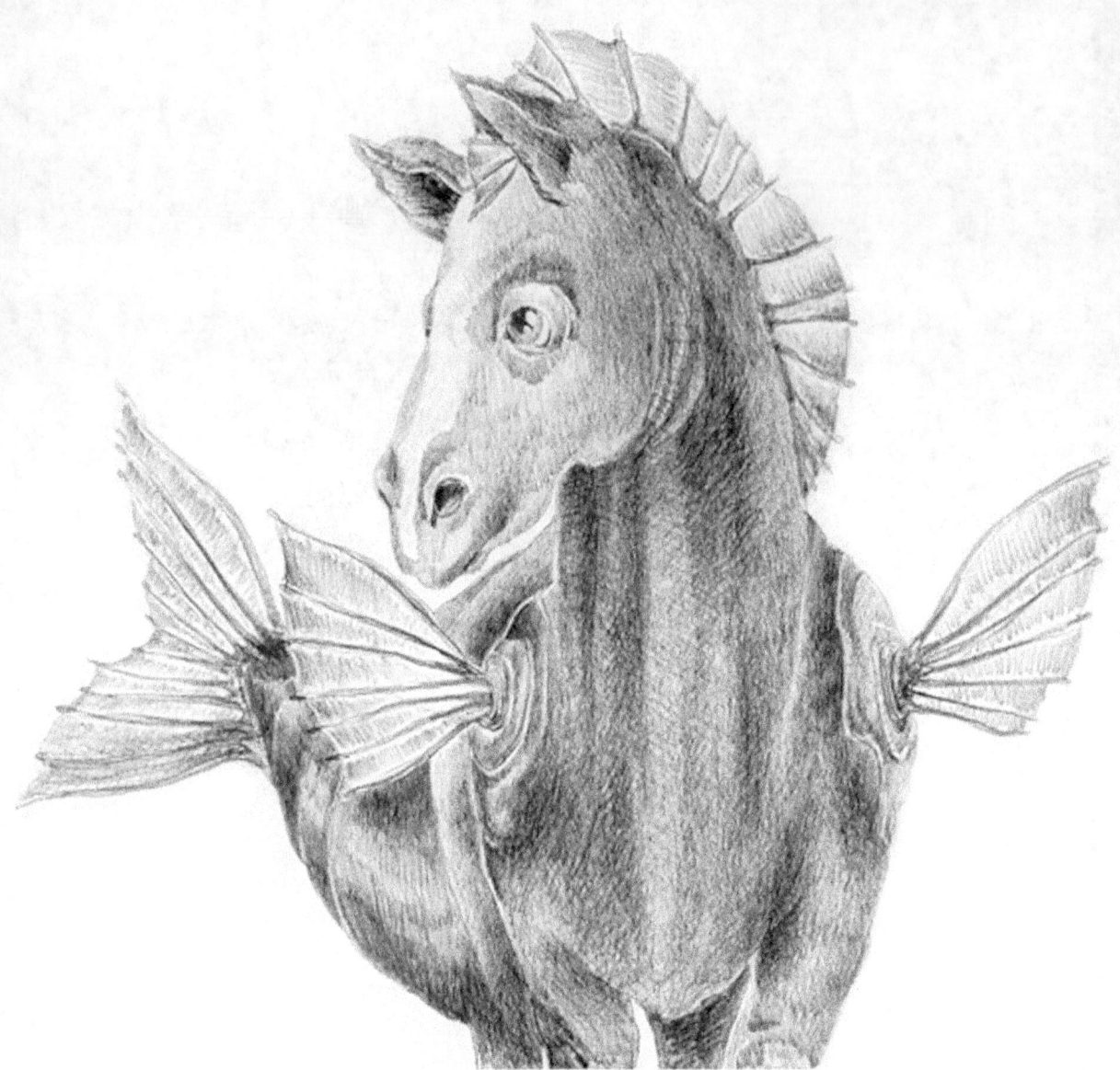

Another Kind of Sea Horse Entirely

Deep in the ocean, under the waves, beneath the tall trees of the kelp,
There sounds a tiny cry for help--a steed comes galloping and saves
The day, for he is swift and sure, with fins and tail with which he flies
Beneath the water-colored skies of ocean-depth, but meets one lure
Too tempting for him to resist, and bites it and is whisked away--
Who, now, will rush to save the day? Now that he's gone he will be missed!
What will become of those in need now that their rescuer is gone?
For now, nor more is anyone their super underwater steed.
It was disaster, sad, alack, that he was fished up from the deeps--
But then: his form gave them the creeps, the fishermen--they threw him back!
He will not fall to lures again, but stick to his brave rescue mode,
Enjoying all the thanks he's owed--stay under sea and not with Men.

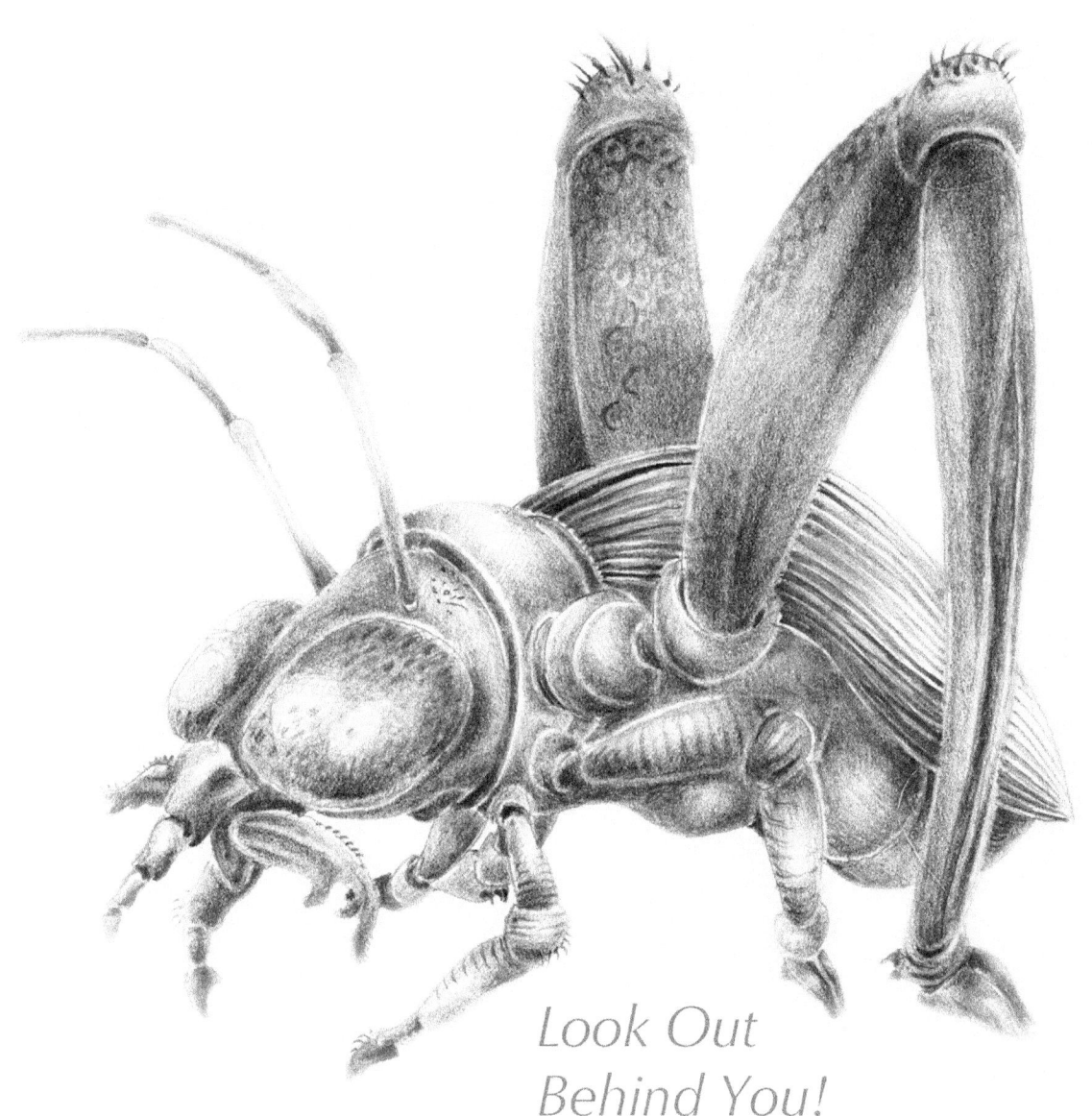

Look Out Behind You!

I woke up one morning
And looked in the mirror
And what I saw in there
Transfixed me with fear
I could have adjusted
To wings and antennae
But defense against bug spray?
I know there's not any!

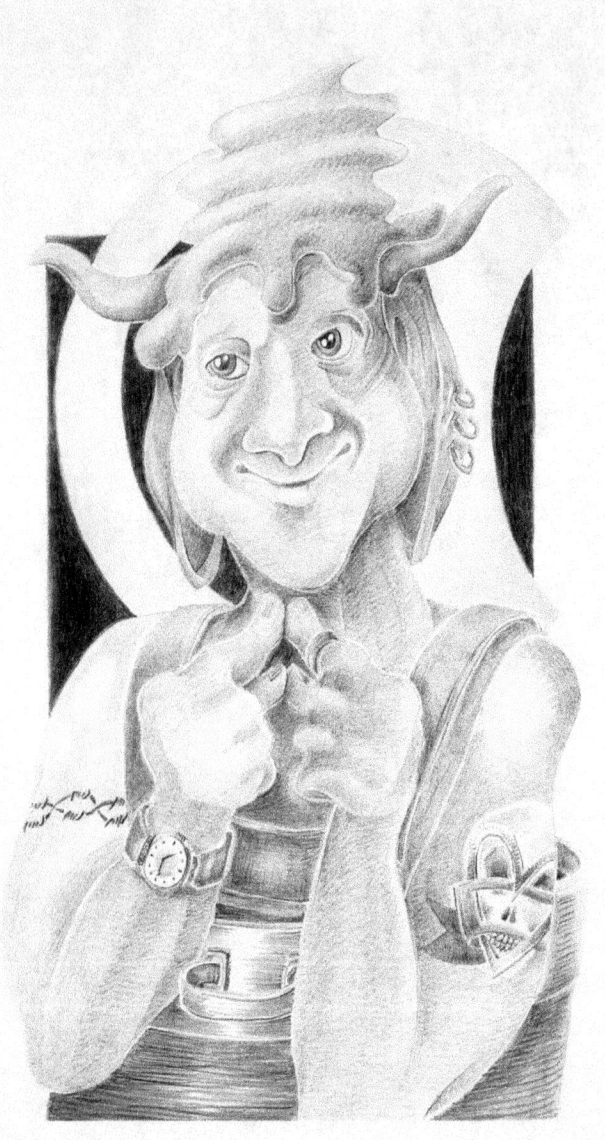

Tasteful Creature #1

The great attractions of good taste
Are obvious, and never waste
Our admiration and delight
In how good taste can set aright
And beautify the humblest man,
If any single feature can

Tasteful Creature #2

Elegance of figure and
Deportment fine and true,
And graceful adaptation
To everything she'll do,
Sets far apart from ordinary girls
One of good taste,
Whose marvels hold us all enthralled
At loveliness so chaste

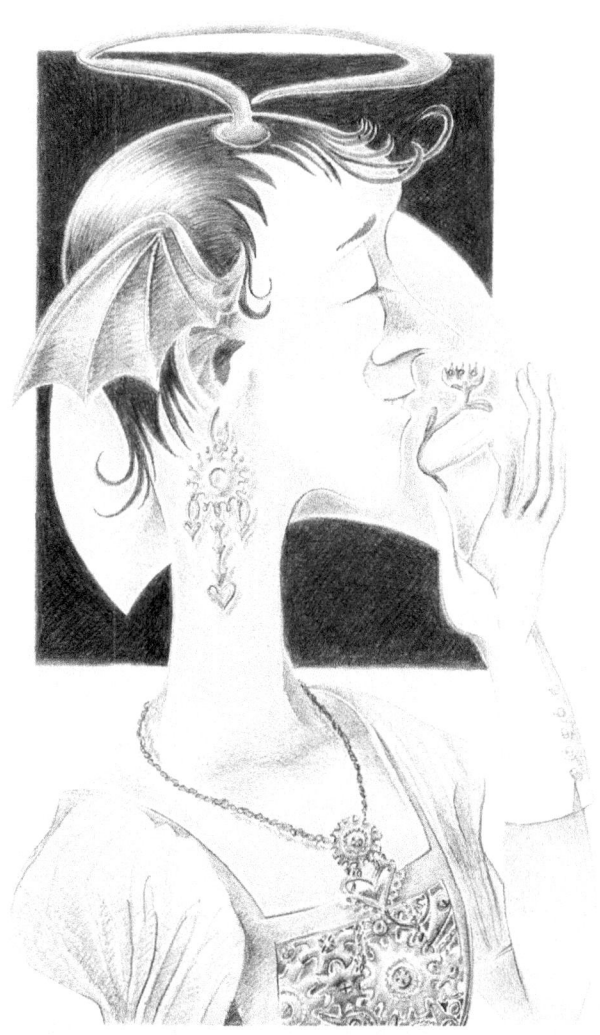

Unshod Horrors

Prefatory to his stroll, The old perambulating troll
That haunts your neighborhood at dawn Must put his socks and boots back on,
Because by day he finds it pleases Him his bare feet smell like cheeses
Aged for years in moldy caverns, Or the drains in back of taverns;
All that I can say is good About this lifestyle is: you should
Be glad the chill when he haunts your street Requires his boots back on his feet.

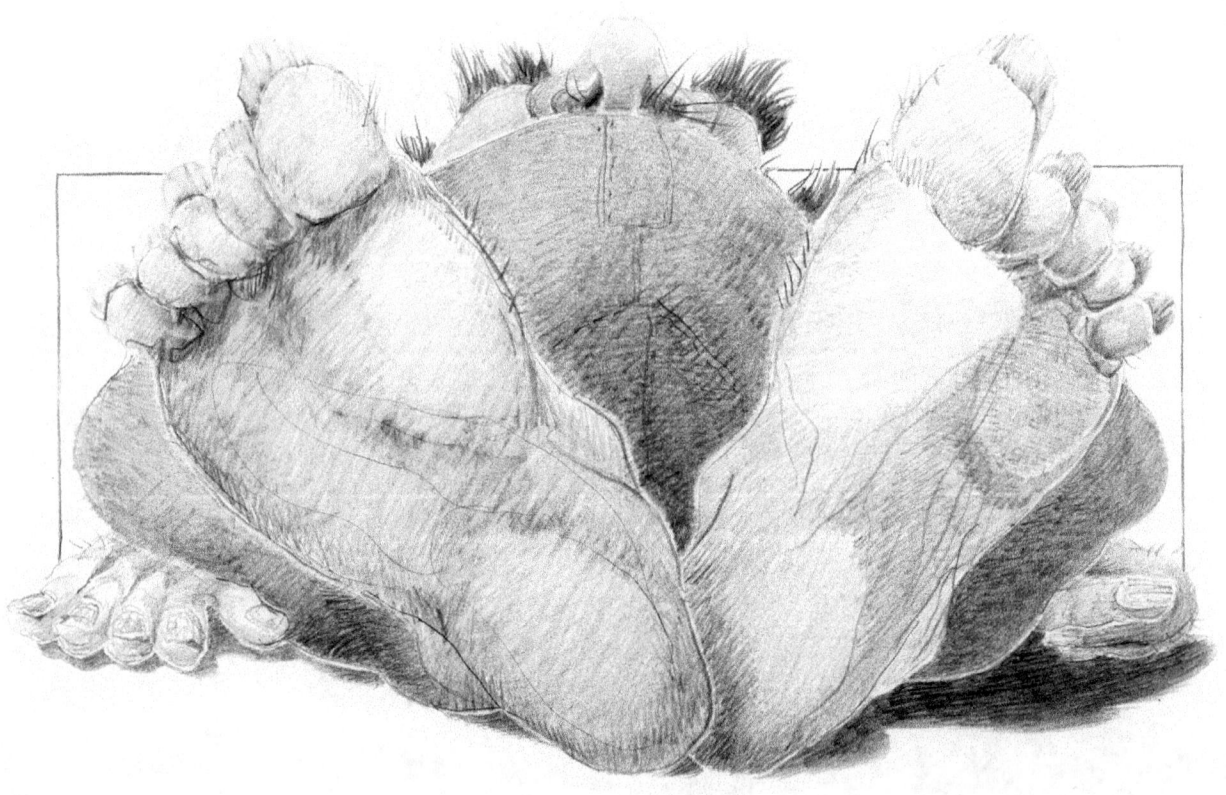

Garden Fairy

A tiny lady wreathed in blooms Who tiptoes through the leafy rooms
Of lawn and garden, flits along As though on double wings of song;
Like hummingbirds, she sips the cup Of nectar as she hovers up
Above the blossoms, skirts the trees In loops as pretty as you please,
And then at last, as evenings fall, Finds out the softest bloom of all
And curls up in the petals' silk To dream among her fairy ilk.

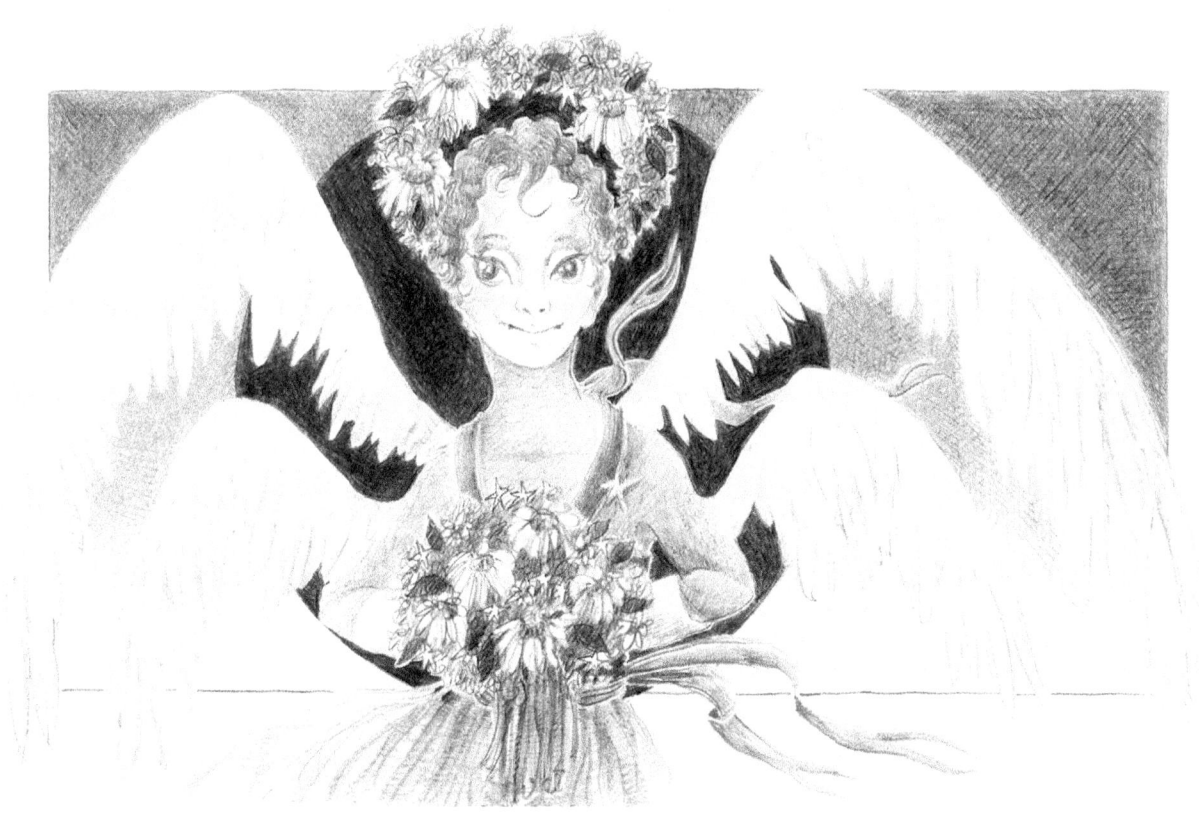

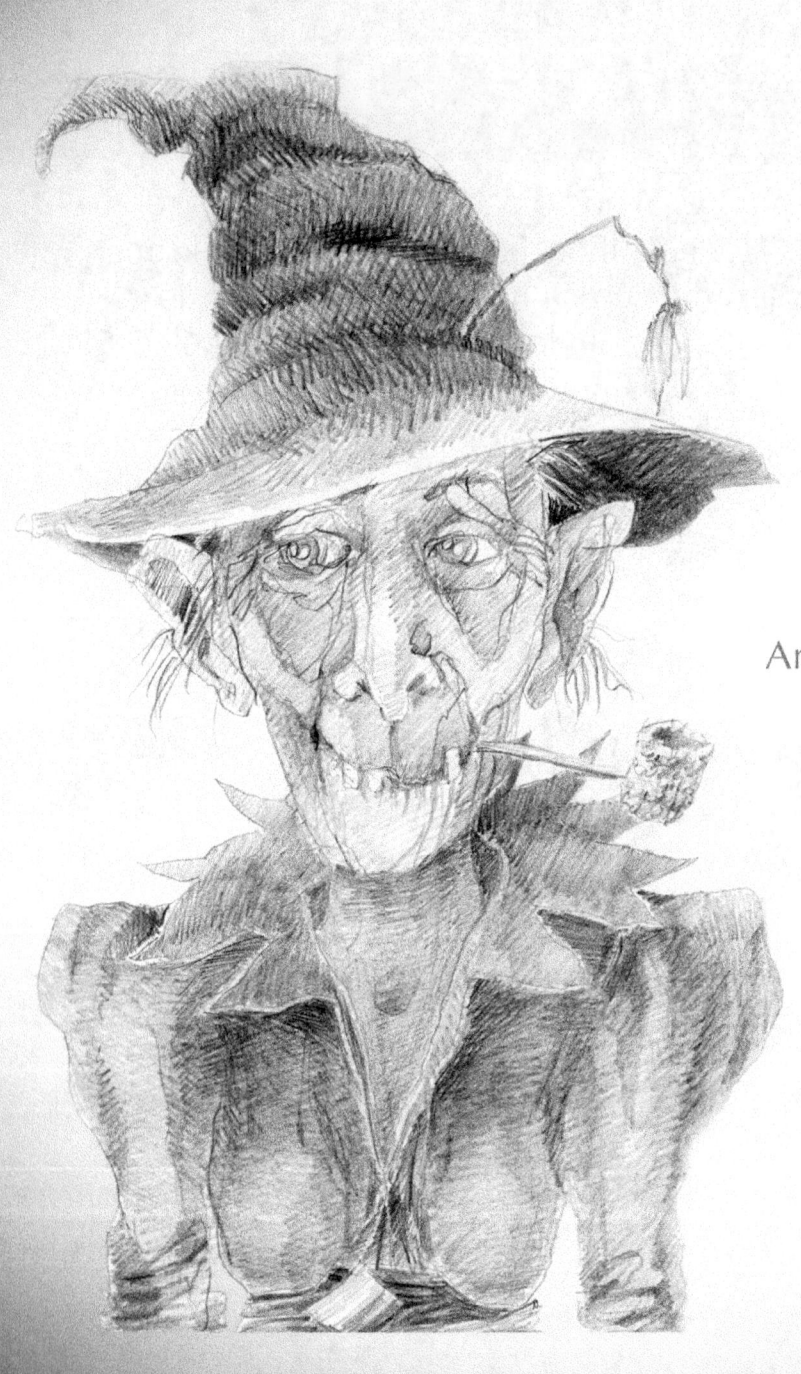

Hexen

On Halloween
it's quite a switch
To meet a
friendly little witch
Who likes kids well,
but not to eat
(She skips the tricks
and gives the treat)
And smokes her corn-cob
pipe with cheer
While all the little
ghouls draw near
To beg their candy
at her door,
The treat they've all
been waiting for

Hexens Katt

Named Bläckfisk
though he is a cat
(He's gangly, slippery,
and that
Is why he shares
his name with squid,
Not for things that
he does or did),
Disreputable
looking, yes,
He is a little,
he'd confess,
But honestly just
needs a comb
From the friendly witch
who shares his home

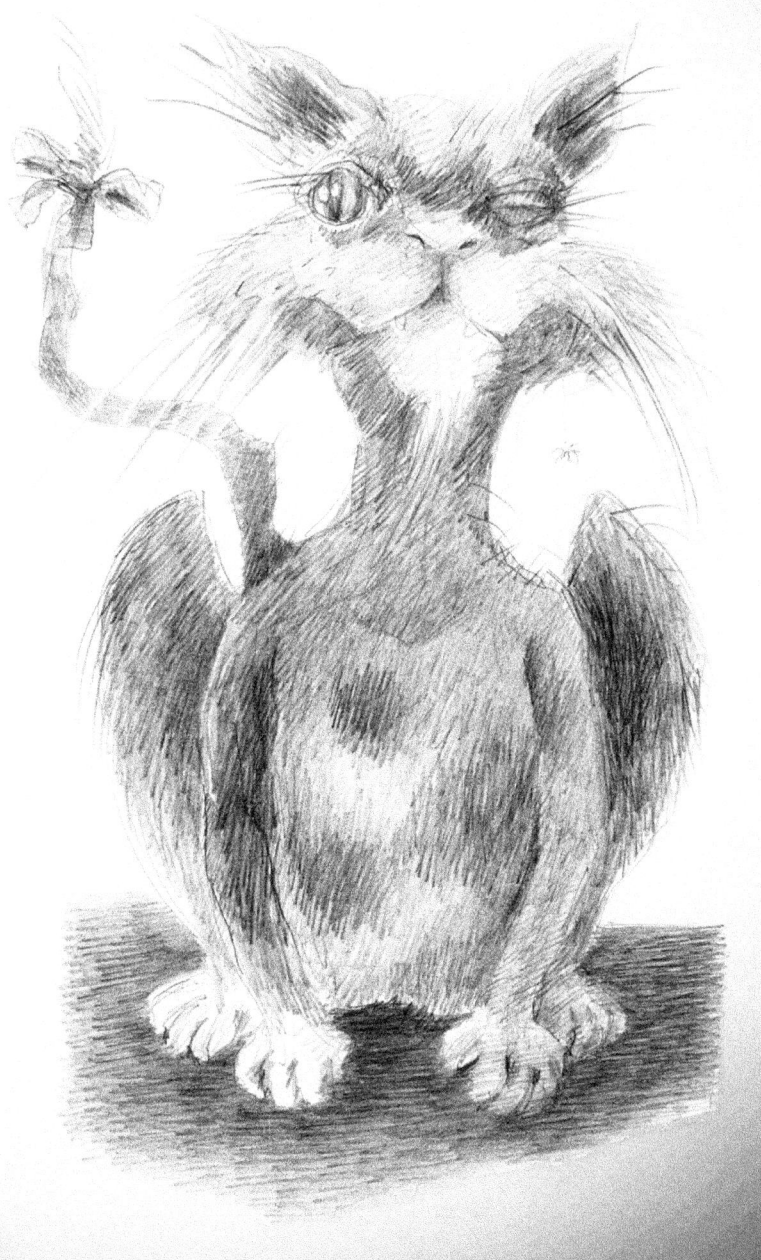

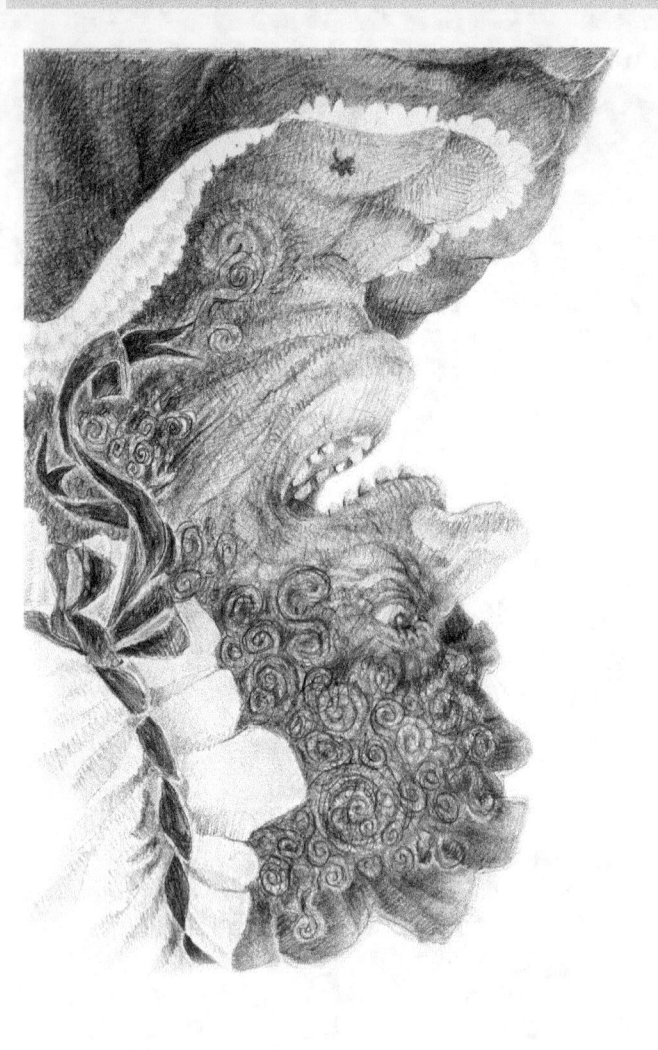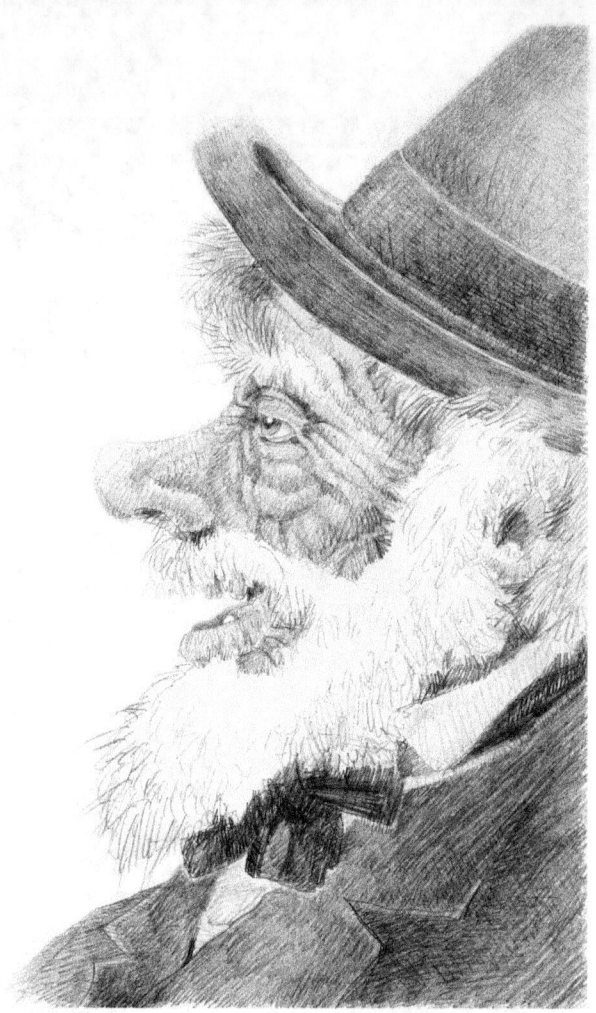

UNDER RAINBOWS, OUT OF SIGHT

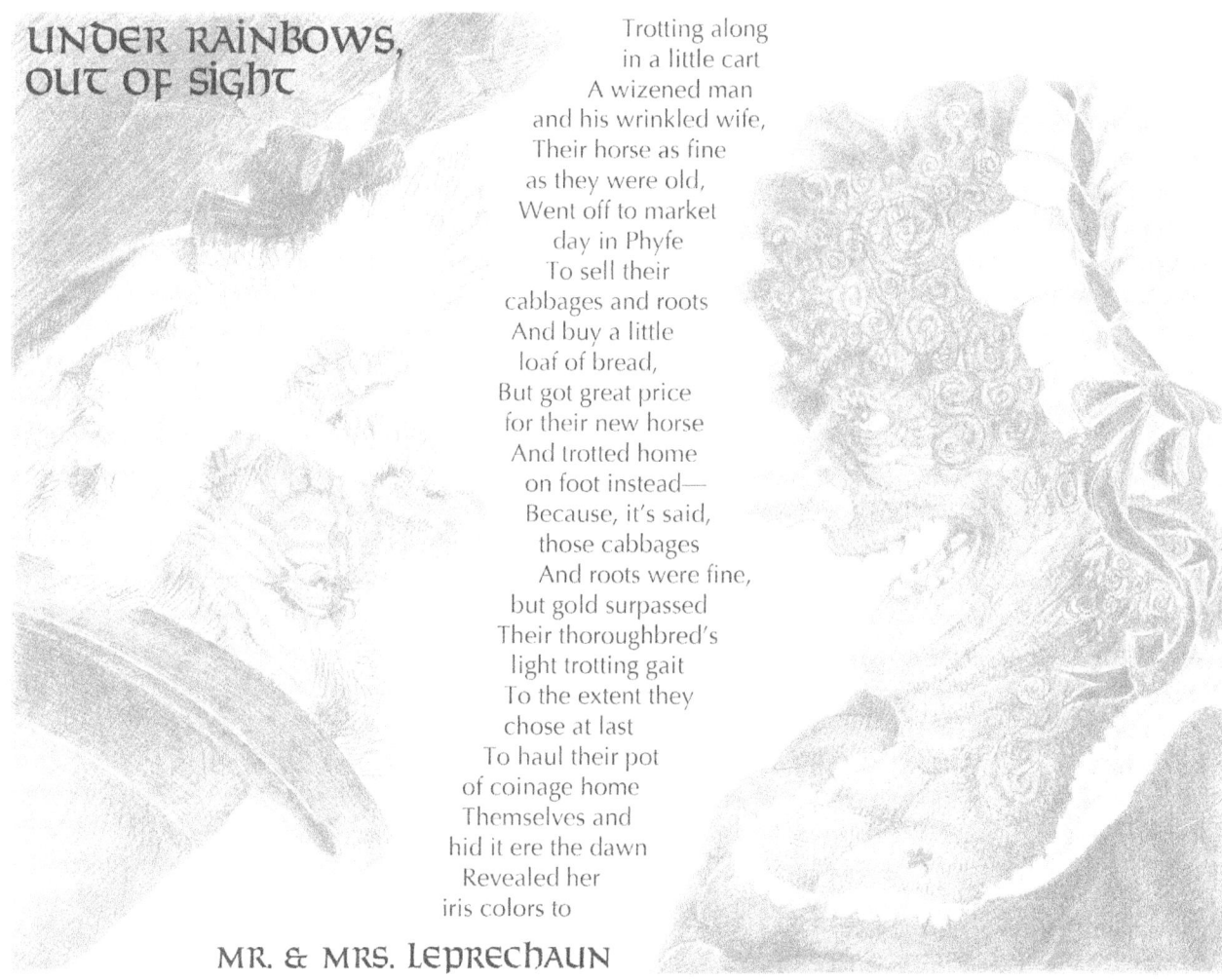

Trotting along
in a little cart
A wizened man
and his wrinkled wife,
Their horse as fine
as they were old,
Went off to market
day in Phyfe
To sell their
cabbages and roots
And buy a little
loaf of bread,
But got great price
for their new horse
And trotted home
on foot instead—
Because, it's said,
those cabbages
And roots were fine,
but gold surpassed
Their thoroughbred's
light trotting gait
To the extent they
chose at last
To haul their pot
of coinage home
Themselves and
hid it ere the dawn
Revealed her
iris colors to

MR. & MRS. LEPRECHAUN

The Show Goes On, Hopefully with a Little Less Bloodshed

Helena of the Hippodrome
Considered mighty heights her home—
While swinging on the long trapeze,
Traversing stratospheres with ease
And flying freely hand to hand
Among the acrobatic band—
The only drawback to this life
Was being the knife-thrower's wife,
For when they practiced simultaneous
Stunts, his knives went intra-vein-eous—
His aim was great, but with her swinging,
Even the arrow-straight went zinging
Into her moving arm or leg
Or other parts, like mumblety-peg—
At last Helena got the worst
Of one last dart, and the bubble burst—
They had to split, in the vernacular,
But as splits go, it was spectacular

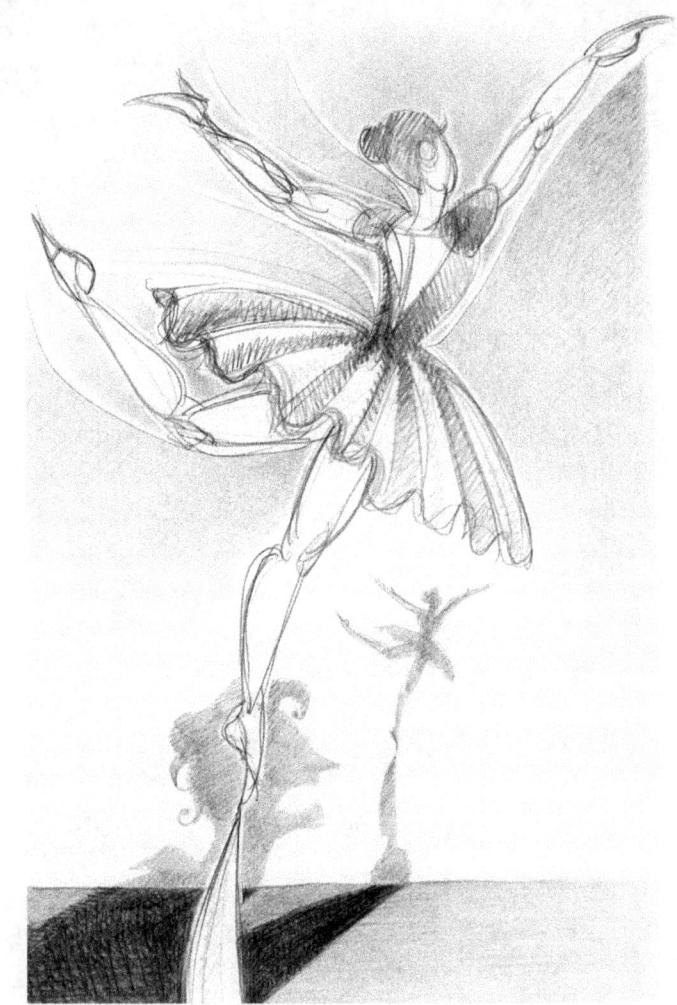

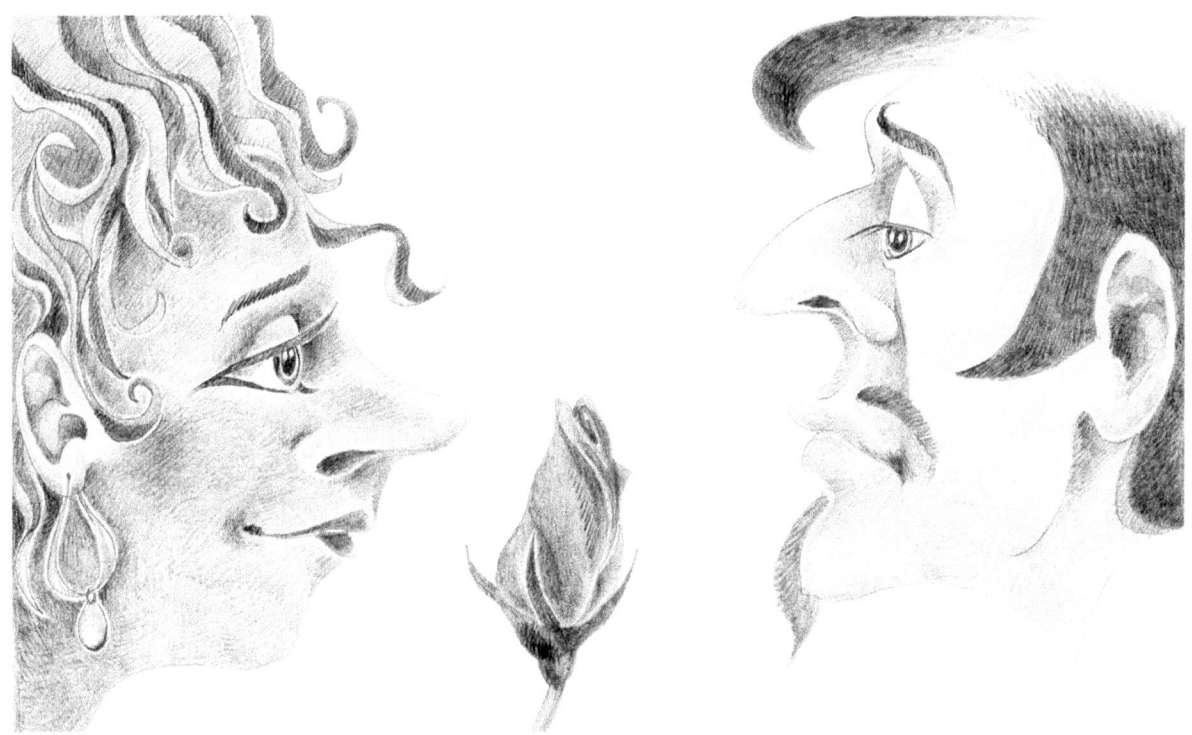

An Enchantment

One evening, on meeting by chance at a dance,
Raoul and LaVilma were drawn to romance,
And after a cha-cha, a quickstep or two,
A twist, for good measure—they instantly knew
They were destined for love as they flew round the floor
And they spun out a rumba, a samba, and more—
They sailed straight from Viennese waltz to the Frug,
Disco, Mashed Potato; they cut up the rug
Till everyone left but the janitor's dog;
Then danced unaccompanied, caught in their fog
Of hazy enchantment, LaVilma, Raoul
And the spirit of Romance pervading the cool
Of the dark morning hour, when if they'd had to stop,
Their love-dancing fate would have burst with a Pop!
But destiny loves a good romantic tale,
So instead, they kept dancing, and leaving a trail
Of shimmering mist in their wake, floated on
To a faint dancing moonbeam,
        Danced up,
                And were gone

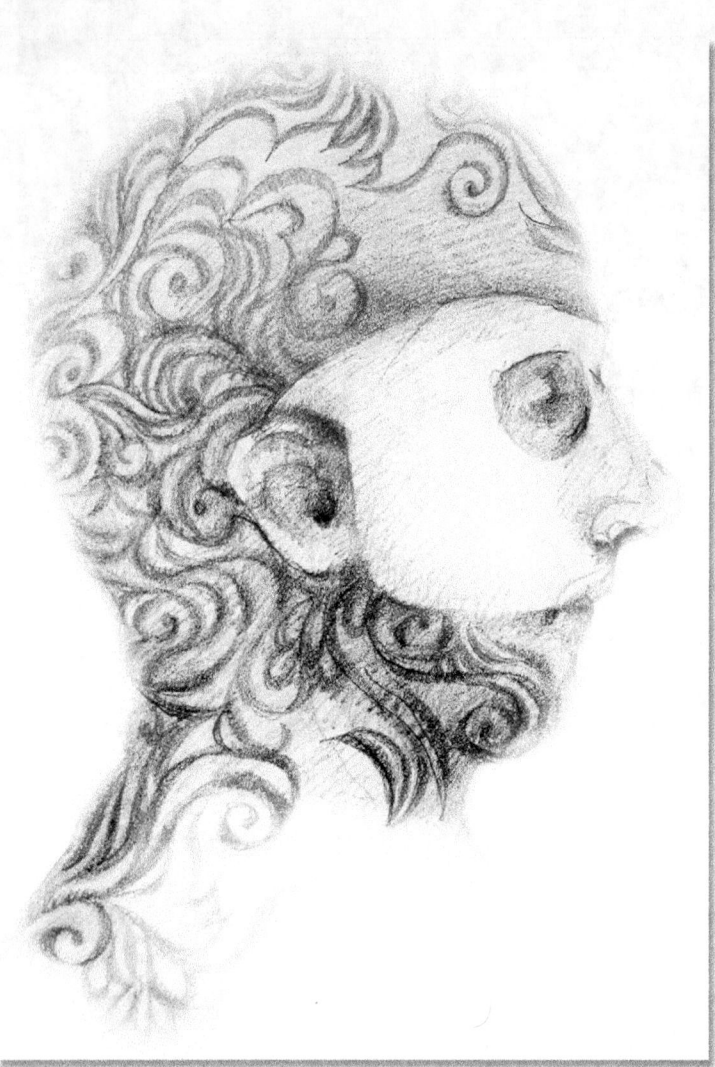

Mark My Words

Mistaken identity got me this far—
Not fraud; acquiescence that I am the star
For whom you mistook me—so is it my fault
If I have bankrupted, entirely, your vault,
Your trust and your confidence? I just agreed
With your own beliefs coinciding my need
For fame, adulation, for privilege, wealth—
You offered, and I didn't take it by stealth
But openly, cheerfully, utterly glad
You gave me so much; if it's all that you had,
I wish you a fine benefactor, too, who
Will foolishly shower such largesse on you!

Among Others

I read the chic and trendy news,
I blog and twitter to amuse,
I own the latest electronic
Pacifiers; gin & tonic
Is my tipple when I chat
With other hipsters, chew the fat
With fellow cool post-modern drones,
And know: among us, not one owns
A single cell unique, one word
Of true distinction from the herd

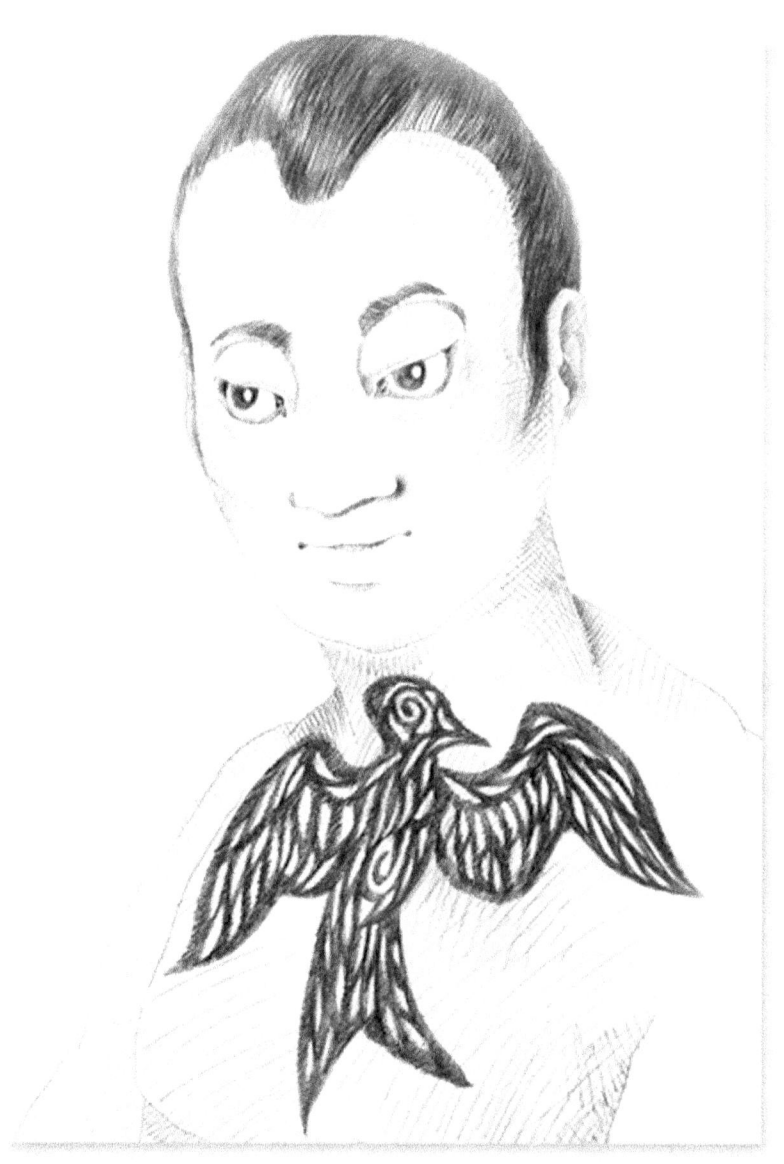

Symbiotic Symbol

The Tattoo Bird's a puzzling guy:
He cannot sing, he cannot fly;
He has no girlfriend, mate or wife,
Nor any kind of separate life;
He makes his home not in a nest
But on a human's back or chest
Or neck or arm, or its backside
(The Tattoo Bird has little pride).
He could just be a parasite,
Except he rarely causes fright
Or illness like those other schnooks,
But gets by wholly on his looks.

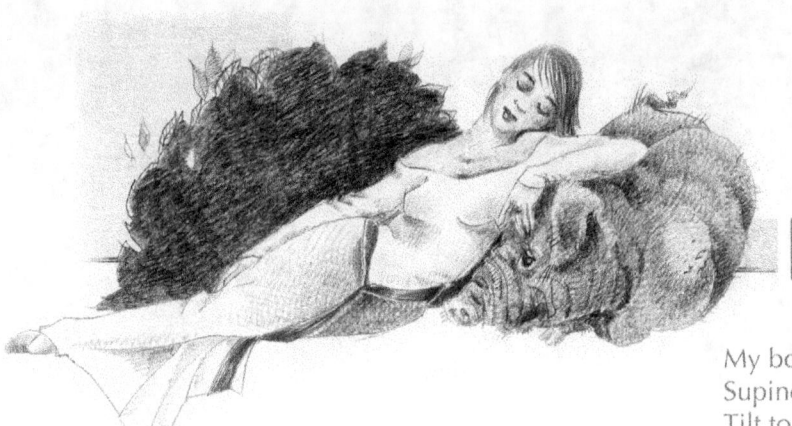

MY BOY IS SLEEPING

My boy is sleeping.
Supine on the couch, he lets his head
Tilt to the side and his eyes have long since
Closed, silently but firmly like
The chapel doors at evensong.
His breath slows into
A soft cadence, the kind of breeze
That should blow in a field
Of ripened grain on a lazy, hazy
Late-in-season sleepy day.
His hand, where it's tucked up
On his chest, rises and falls,
Rises and falls, and gradually
Falls open, letting
All of the tension that it had in its
Strong grip fall out and float away
On the breeze of his slow soft breath,
Float and fall and fly,
Gently and gracefully, as though
Through imagined wheat fields, on
And past those chapel doors, away, away,
To leave my boy
Asleep in quiet peace.

YOU ONLY LOOK DOWN UPON ME SO EASILY BECAUSE I AM RECUMBENT

They frown upon my lassitude,
My listless, laissez-faire-ish ways,
My indolence and insolence
To lie about in dreamy haze;
I know, though, that such nagging fellas
Just critique because they're jealous

OSVALDO HAS A MOTORCAR

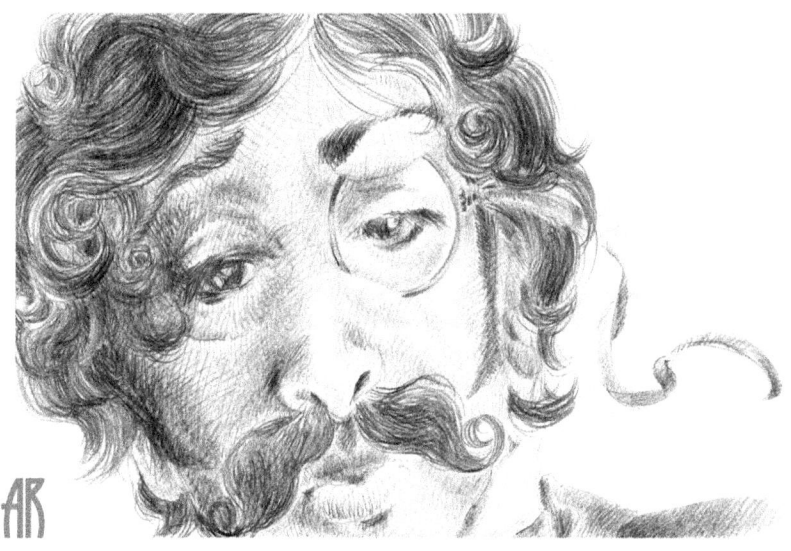

Osvaldo has a motorcar and tootles round the square Among the bougainvillea, palms and pretty ladies there
And tips his hat with great aplomb and waves to all the gents Who envy him his gleaming steed and vow him recompense
When they have automobiles of their own; the ladies then Will swiftly throw their handkerchiefs toward the other men.
For now, Osvaldo has the sole conveyance of this sort And entertains the thought that he is quite the dandy sport
And every lady in the square inclines to him the plume Of her best Sunday hat amid an air of love in bloom.
But when at last there comes another motorcar to town Osvaldo knows the time has come: the gauntlet is thrown down!
He dons his spats and monocle and straightens his cravat And revs his automobile up until the engine's hot
And dashes at top speed (five kilometers to the hour) Into the square to find the pretty ladies in their bower
When, what to his astonishment should suddenly appear But a whole flank of motorcars arrayed in idle gear
With ladies stepping into them, delight in every smile, And in each driver's seat a gent, each grinning all the while
In Osvaldo's direction, for they know he went awry In never having shared a ride but only driving by—
While so intent on showing off, he failed to make ado To share the fun, and now the rest have cars, and ladies too!

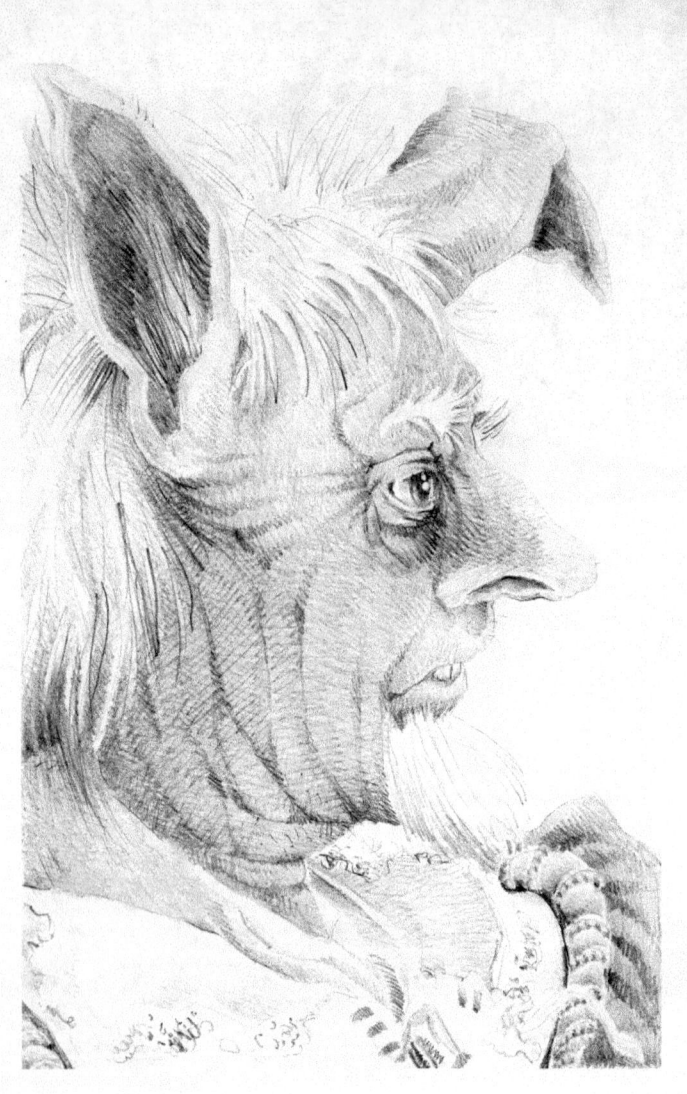

Do These Ears
 Make Me Look
Like a Big Ass?

The fool that Will called Bottom made
Much more a clown than was portrayed
By merely styling him an ass,
The emblem of the Natural class,
But more the fool because his fuss
And silliness are so like Us—
No need to be more literal
About the dim wits we are full
Of, or what egotistic prats
We make ourselves; in essence, that's
Precisely why exaggeration
Of our human-foibled station
Is permitted, necessary,
Demonstrating, fool and fairy,
To us unenlightened hearers
What we fail to see in mirrors—
That we laugh at Bottom's fall
Just proves that we are asses, all.

Titania

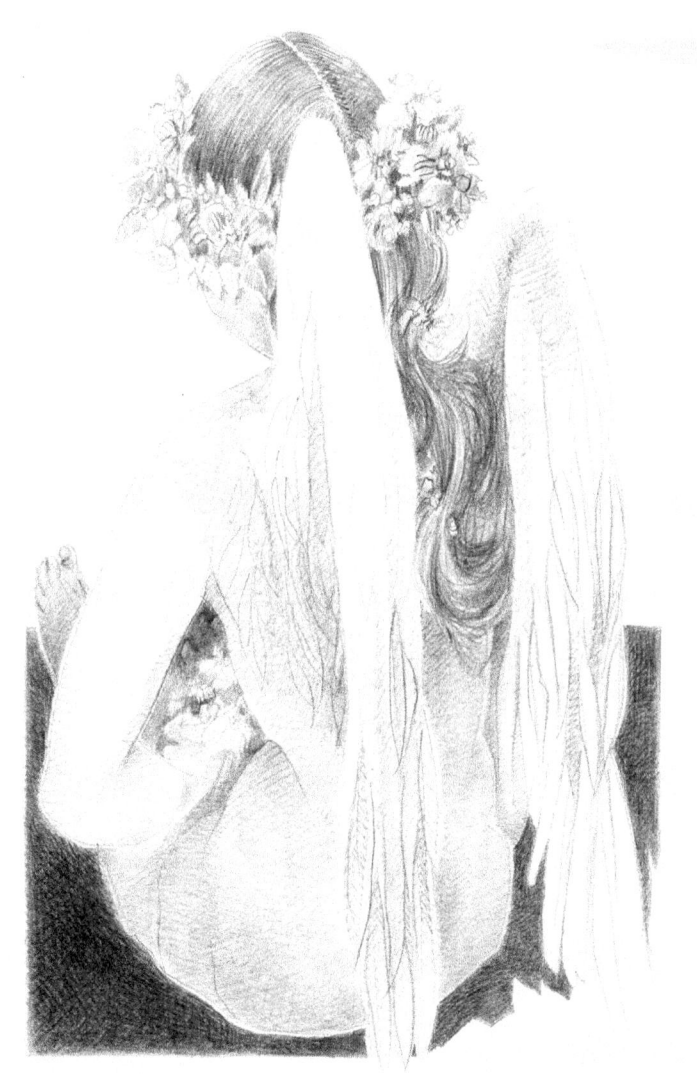

Adorned with tiny flowers, she
Will dance and flit in company
With other fairies made to serve
The fairy queen, but when the curve
Of her small wings and dainty arms
Is softening under the charms
Of sleepiness' old hazy spell,
She likes to creep down to the dell
All by herself, sing lullabies
To hummingbirds and butterflies
And listen to the babbling stream
Until she falls into a dream
That, being fairy, takes away
The hours of a midsummer's day
And dreams of flutes and harps, guitars,
Until she wakes under the stars

When Beset by a Beast

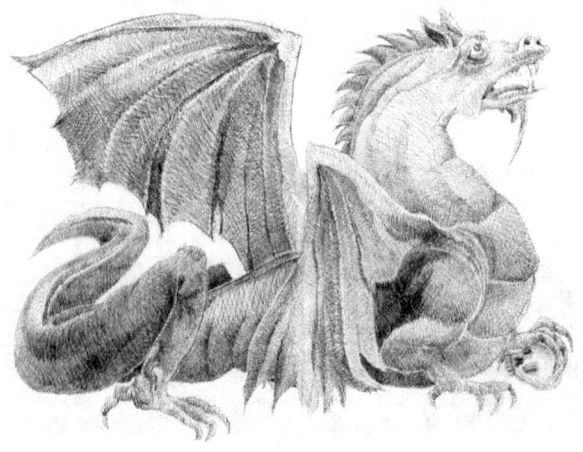

O beast now gnawing on my leg,
Pray, open up your jaws, I beg,
And I will find you some fine sweet
Alternatively tasty treat:
Perhaps a damsel in distress,
Though you've your fill of those, I guess:
Maybe a Lord in gleaming pride—
His armor's crisp, but soft inside—
Or might your tastes run more to some
High potentate of Christendom
Whose crown you can devour along
With him (dessert: his courtier throng)?
Probably you'd enjoy a meal
Of suckling pig, whose piercing squeal
Of terror makes a background noise
Quite nice for dining, though your joys
Must more be found in human meals,
The way a dragon often feels,
So my best offer, as you chew
Up toward my hip: how 'bout a few
Well-rounded infants, fresh delights,
Plus the wet-nurse who guards their nights,
And I'll throw in the scullery maid,
A cook, two footmen, and in trade
For discontinuance of bites
Upon my person, three strong knights—
You won't get better offers, Beast,
So why not let me go, at least
Now you've had lots of tasty Leg?
Leave off your gnawing me, I beg.

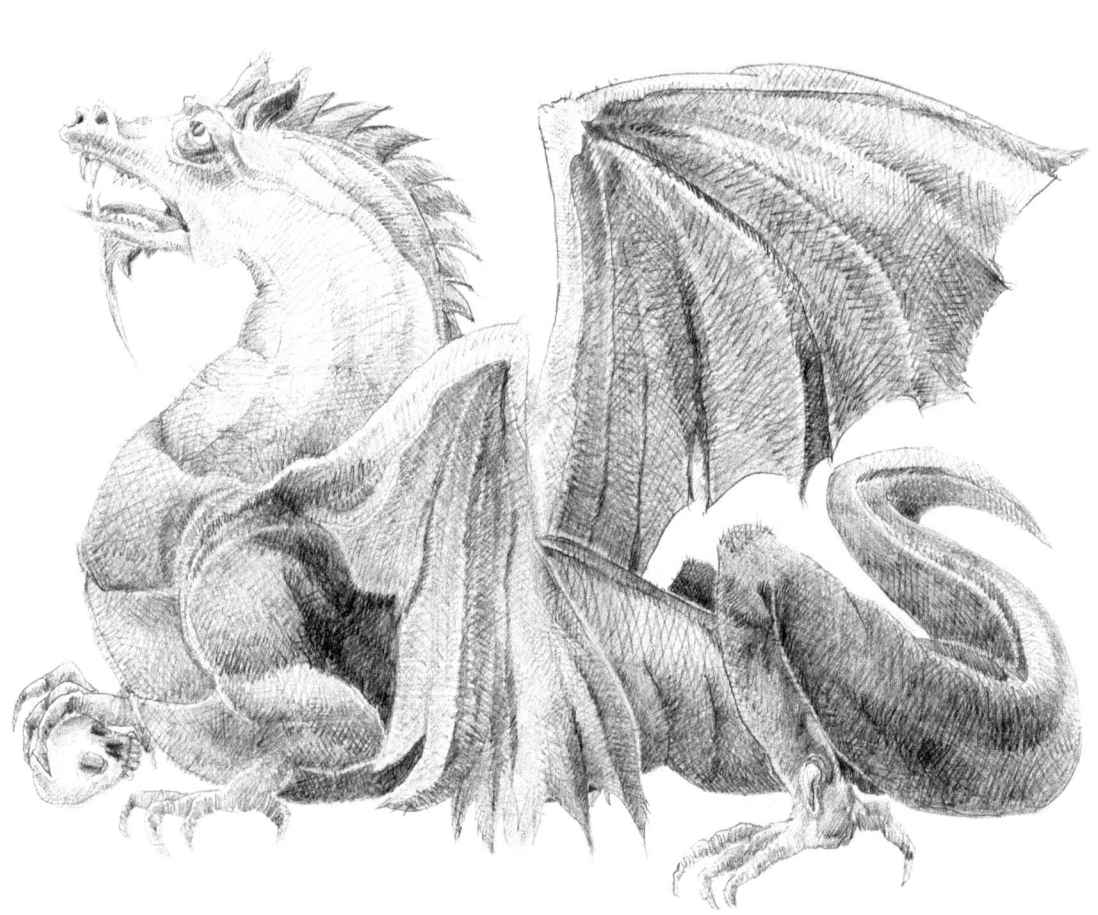

Sad for No One in Particular

Misty maunderings have I
Between the gravestones and the sky
And though I know no single man
Who lies here sleeping, yet I can
Imagine grief and mourn them all
While flitting through the leaves of fall

Whistle While I Work

While frolicking and capering
Among the lily blooms,
I am not quite as dim of wit
As everyone assumes,
And neither am I ignorant
Of how the dense perfumes
Of lilies can intoxicate
A lady while she zooms
Among the flowers gleefully,
Collecting them for tombs

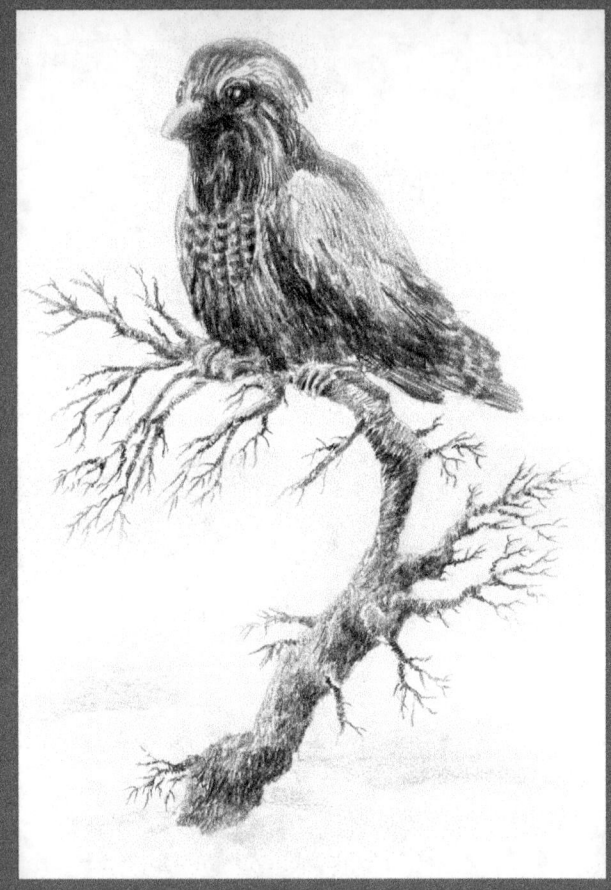

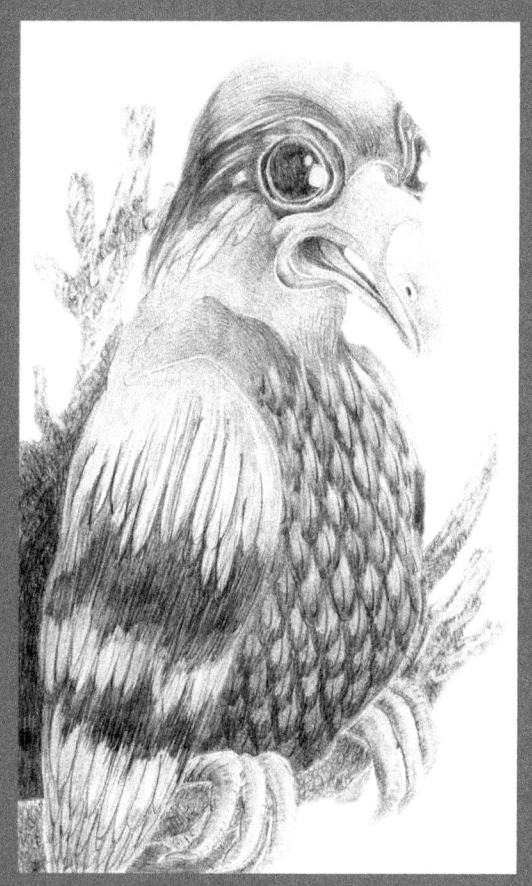

Dirty Tricks

Some pop-eyed bird with heavy wings
Stared at my socks from in his tree
As though he'd take them off of me
And yes, my pants, and other things,
Just to humiliate and drive
Me to despair, for fun and sport—
I know he was an awful sort
Whose only pleasure would derive
From stealing clothes right off a kid
And making raucous laughing taunts
High in the tree all while he flaunts
The stolen stuff he wears amid
The barren branches, still quite nude
While he is chortling in his glee—
So I would think that you can see
I had to stop his being rude
And thwart his obvious evil plot
To steal my wear and wear it to
Offend me, as villains will do,
And so I egged him, on the spot.

Seems Almost Like a Human

This mask I wear could fool
the best detective on the earth,
And while I'm not nefarious,
and wear it just for mirth,
There is a hint of pleasure,
knowing no one sees beyond
Its blandly mortal-looking face,
a thrill of which I'm fond,
Wherein I think it could be fun
to shock the passive crowd,
But then again I choose not to:
no need to say aloud
What's in my sneaking thoughts—
the fun lies in the subterfuge—
The outward may seem tiny,
but the payoff's really huge!

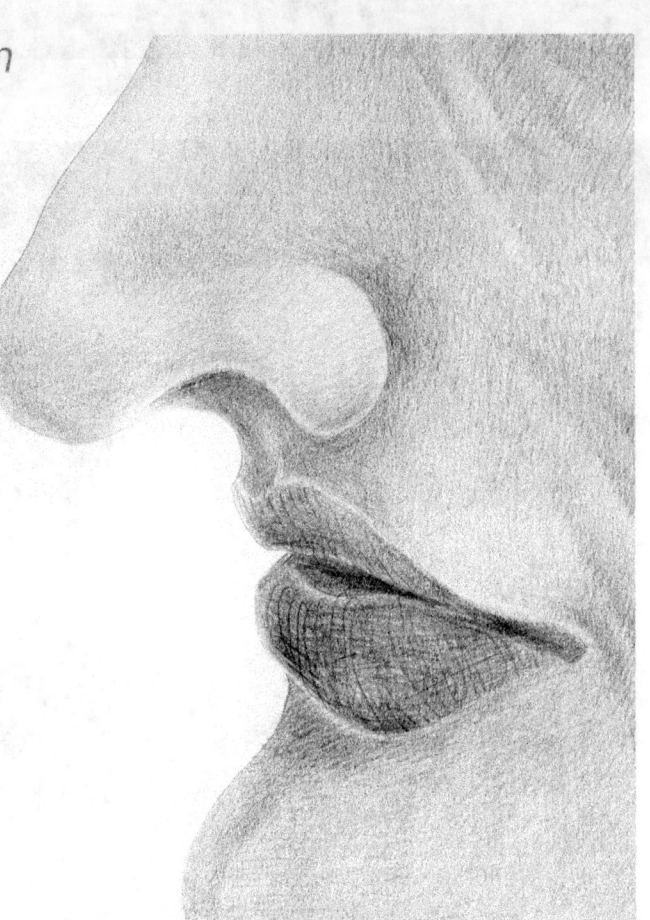

Friendly Little Alien

Charming with my sweet good looks, and cute and cuddly too,
I'm irresistible to all the earthlings that I woo
With flowery thoughts and giggling chats and tickles on the chin,
With baskets full of candy and decanters full of gin
And dancing with gymnastic grace and doing magic charms
And holding little babies in my cute and cuddly arms,
I am the very avatar
Of first-encounter bliss—
Won't everybody be surprised
At being killed by this!

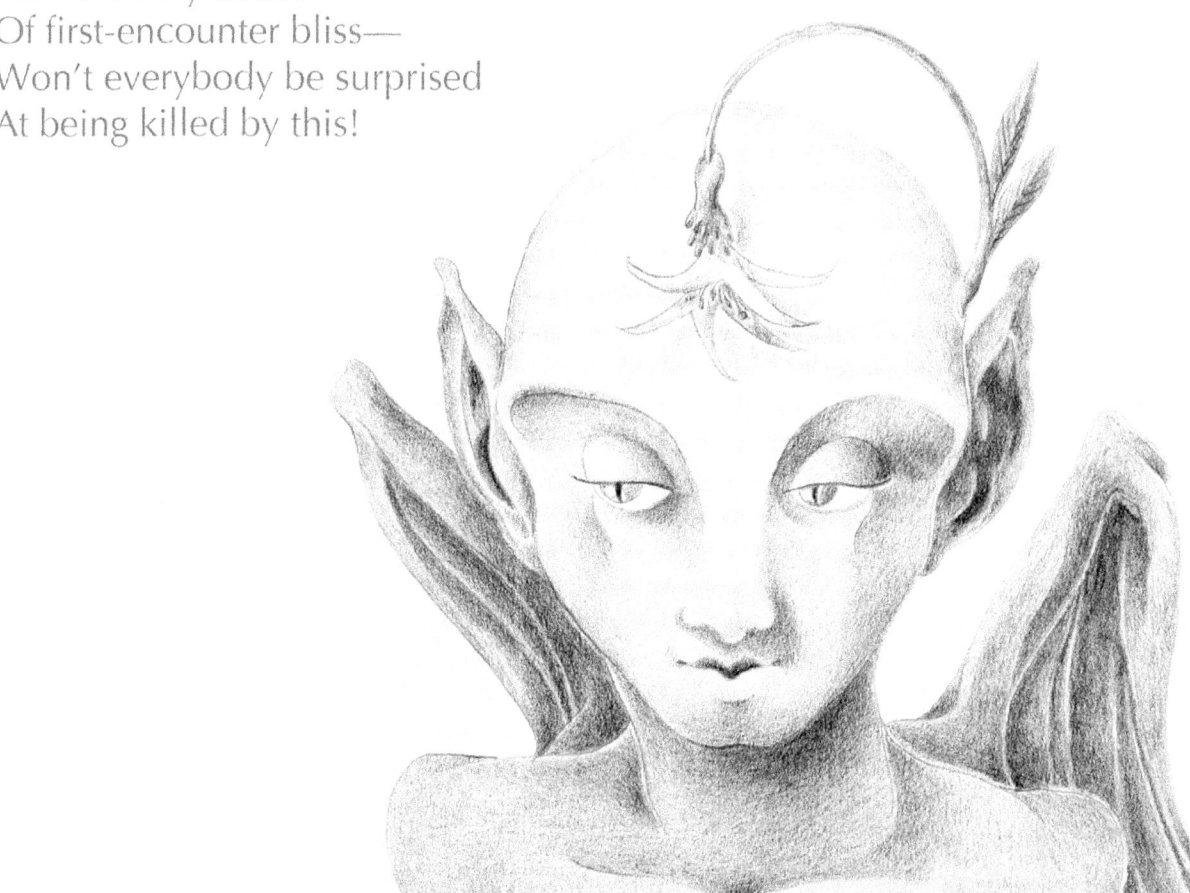

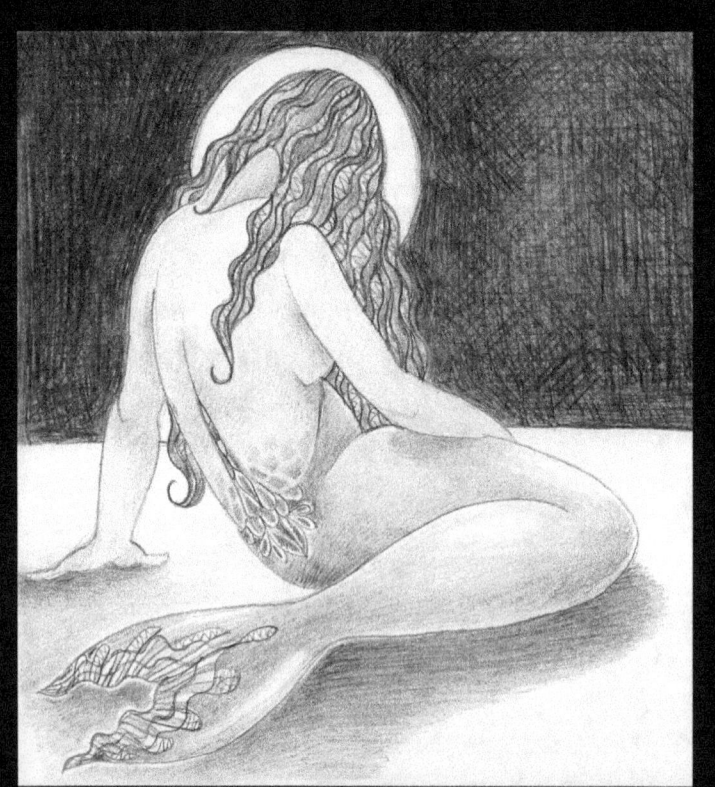

Why the Sailors Went Overboard

One day a delicious deceit
Came over the men of the fleet
That some mermaids swam near
And enticed them to hear
Songs of something I dare not repeat

Wave Goodbye to That Meal

Dorinda Beecher went ashore
For dinner, but will go no more
As she discovered on the sand
Food she rejected out of hand
And rather wants to share a dish
At home with all the other fish

Iris

When goddess Iris
flits her wing
Wild hues encompass
everything
To light what had
been dull and void
And make all spirits
overjoyed

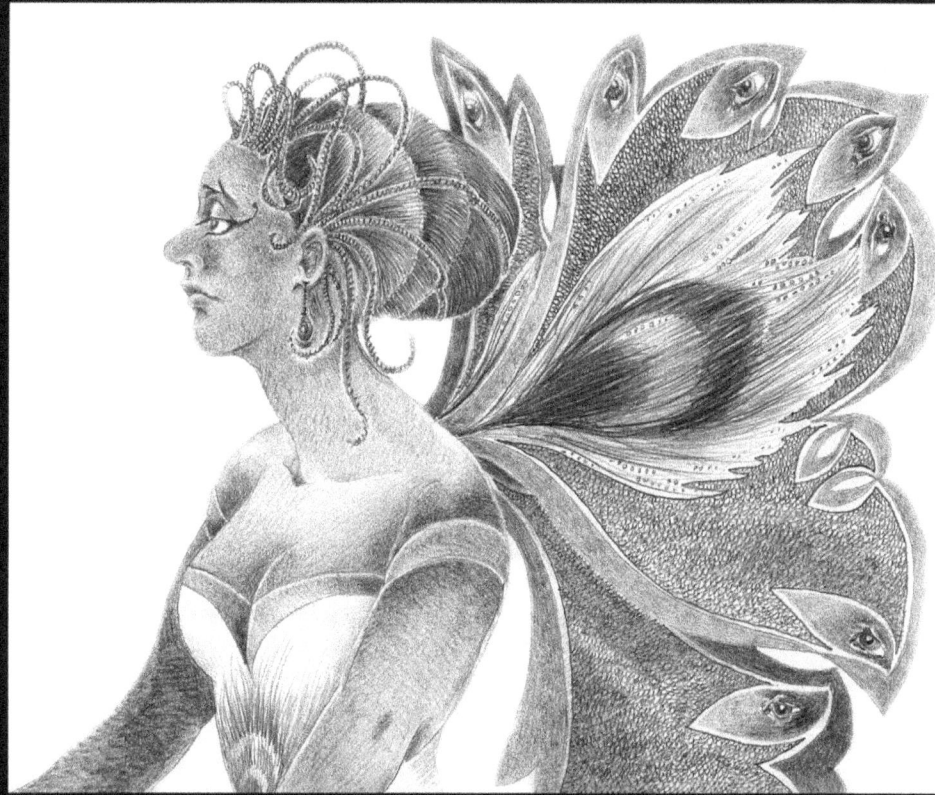

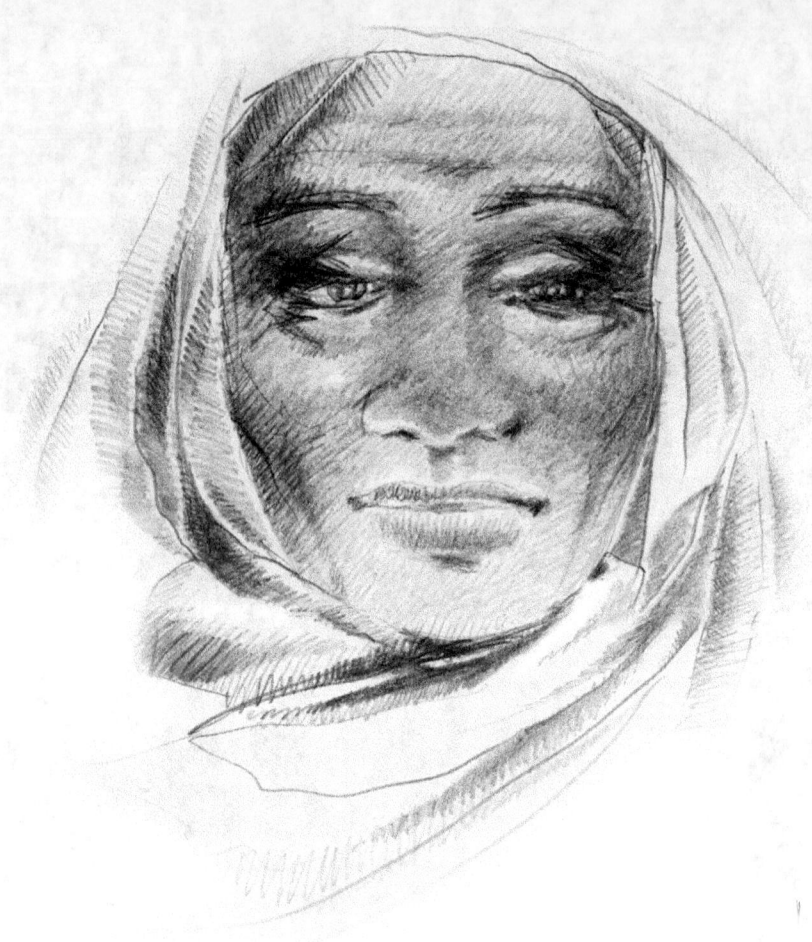

LAST LAUGHS

Among the most high holy days Are those when laughing is the craze,
When great ridiculousness reigns And cancels misery and pains
For nothing else approaches laughter For promising a sweet hereafter—
I mean, in imitating heaven Nothing beats the touch of leaven—
So, scribe thou not my epitaph Until I've had full chance to laugh.

CYNOSURE

The car is sleek wherein she rides
—A limousine, indeed—
And carries her with pomp
And elegance, and at a speed
Designed to draw all eyes with awe
And drivers to disperse
With deference to her estate,
For lo, she's in a hearse.

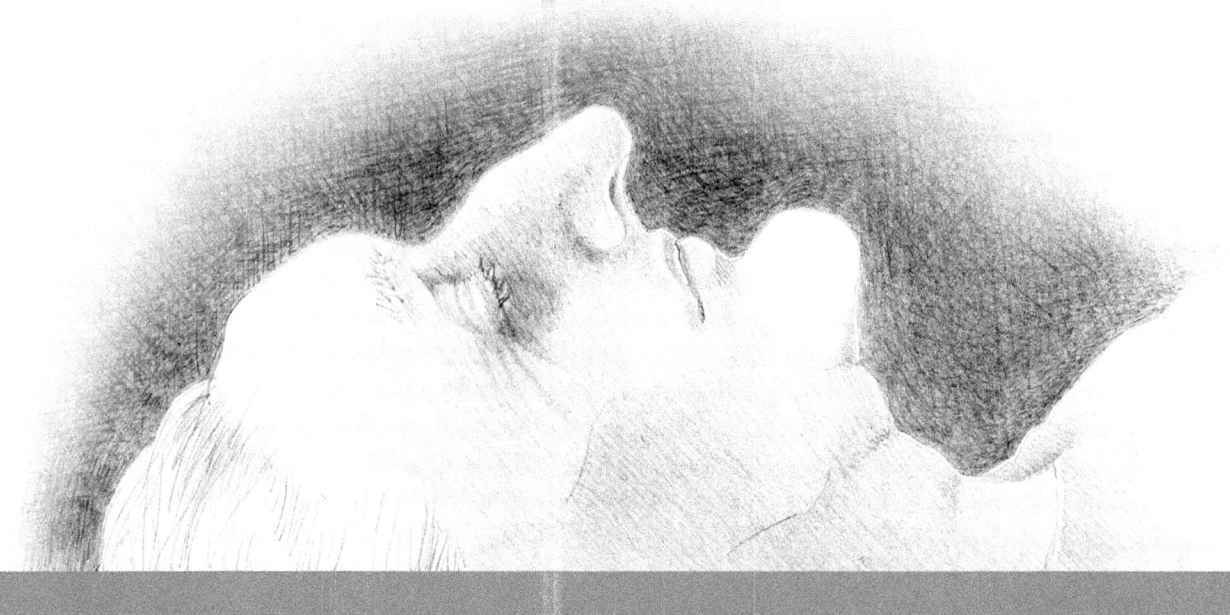

Barrel of Laughs

Pity it comes to this, my friend; I'd hoped to sidestep such an end
To our relationship; could not Persuade you to eschew your plot.

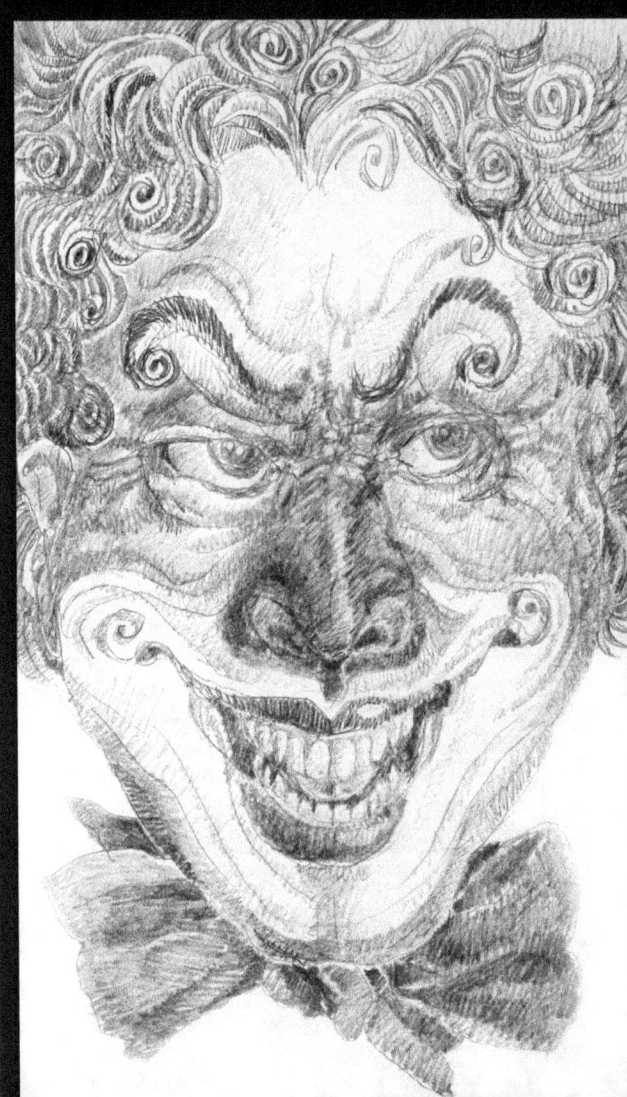

Your gay façade of childlike cheer
Could not disguise your purpose here
Of traumatizing all the guests—
In truth, my prosecution rests
On your determined bright demeanor
Of insouciance in between or
Right on top of all our grief;
My point: it is my firm belief
You'd gladly goad into the grave
Precisely those you sham to save
From daily life's grotesqueries.
It's cruel monstrosities like these
Horrible japes and jests and jollies,
Horrid hijinks, fatal follies
Foisted on our sadness by
An ur-aggressive perky guy
With terrifying giant shoes,
Yarn wig and honking horn, and whose
Grim predilection for a prank
Makes most of us just want to yank
On his bowtie and bulbous nose
To the degree you might suppose
We'd some psychoses, but the fact
Is, though our souls remain intact,
They are endangered by his farce
Whom we'd wish ill, and that, not sparse,
If we were not still too refined
To entertain that state of mind.
So rather, I must batten down
Your overweening ways, you clown,
And stare to naught your laughing fun
Behind my water-squirting gun.

Oh, Well, It's Only Eternity

While I rabbited around
Making busy work and such,
It did occur to me that I
Was not accomplishing that much
But rather, hamster-in-the-wheel,
Was spinning wildly on through space
As though to get somewhere indeed,
And do so at a cracking pace,
Yet never forward from the crux,
And I supposed I'd have been grieved
If I had not thought, too, that this
Is just our lot, for I believed
That humankind—and I still do—
Is purposeful and would do well
But, too directionless and stuck,
Just circle down the drain pell-mell

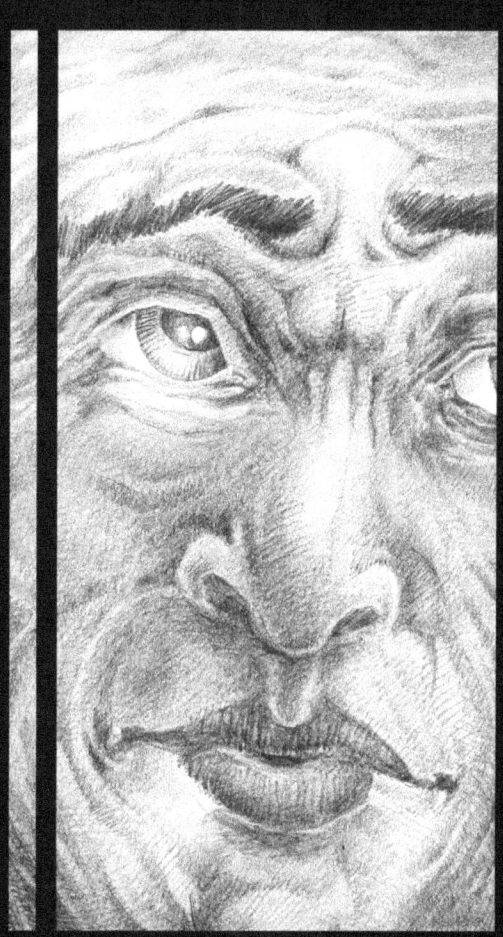

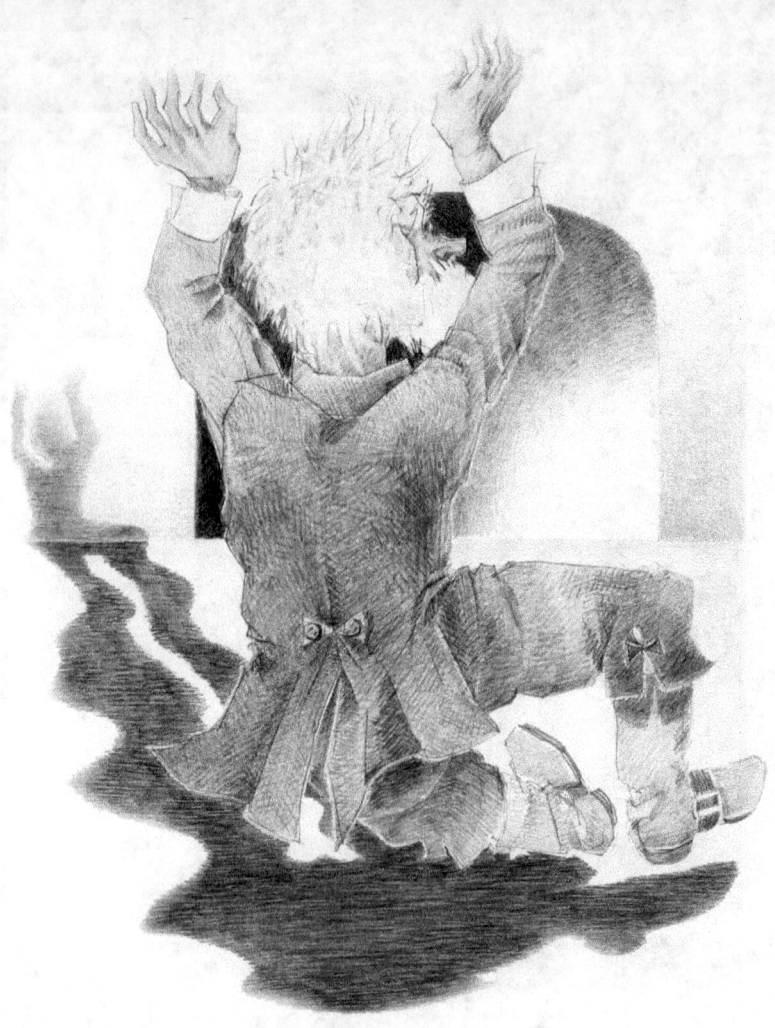

Grotesque & Bloated [& Co.]

Blurbleschmidt and Grabblington,
    the principals in the firm,
Are perfectly content to see
    their underlings a-squirm
In battle for the second rung,
    and third, and even less,
For privilege, exclusiveness
    and greed, as you would guess,
Fill Grabblington and Blurbleschmidt
    with cruel happiness

The happy underside of this
    imbalance and oppression
Is that the scraping underlings
    have made their intercession
With Blurbleschmidt and Grabblington's
    competitors, who've toyed
With tumbling G&B's success,
    but rather, have enjoyed
A slower bloody outcome with
    a certain *Schadenfreud'*

For as you would imagine,
    underlings who scrape and bow
Are also always brewing
    something deeper anyhow,
And one fine day toward Grabblington
    and Blurbleschmidt, to wit,
Up from the depths will crawl their
    stooges, spear them on a spit
Of comeuppance, and that's as cheery
    as this tale will get.

Money Isn't Everything When It's Everything

Your alchemy, hurray for you,
has turned your dross to gold:
Investing well, apparently,
and buying what was sold
At super-low sale prices and
then selling super-high—
Yes, you are quite impressive as
a moneymaking guy—
Congratulations on this great
achievement in your work.
It's just a pity that your alchemy
can't change a jerk
Into a better person, or
you would impress me more,
But all the money in the world
can't change that you're a bore.

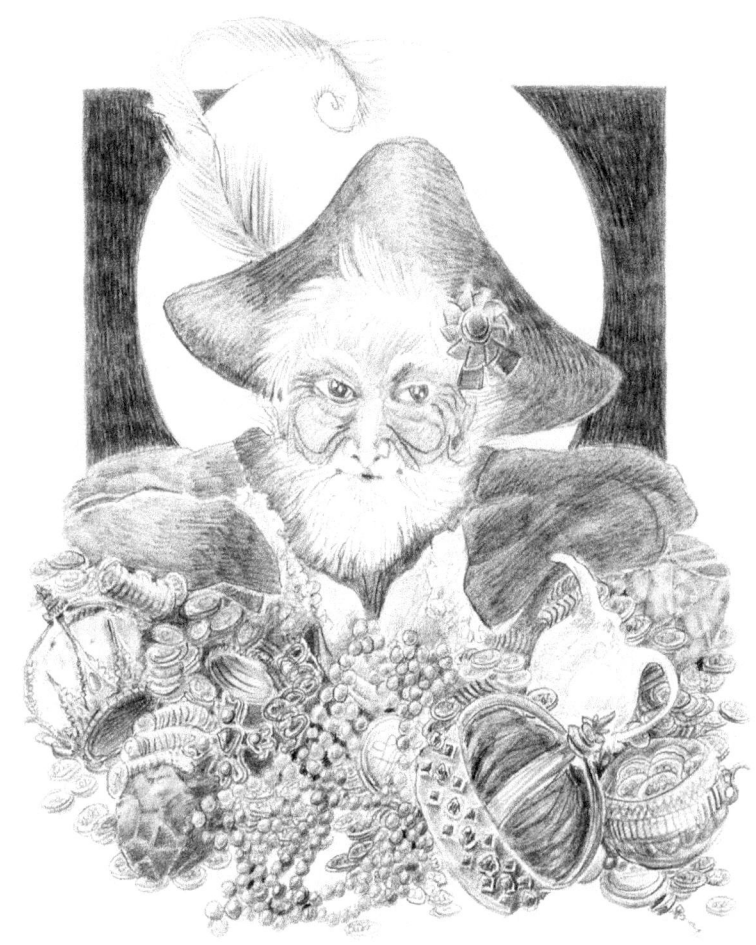

Like-Minded

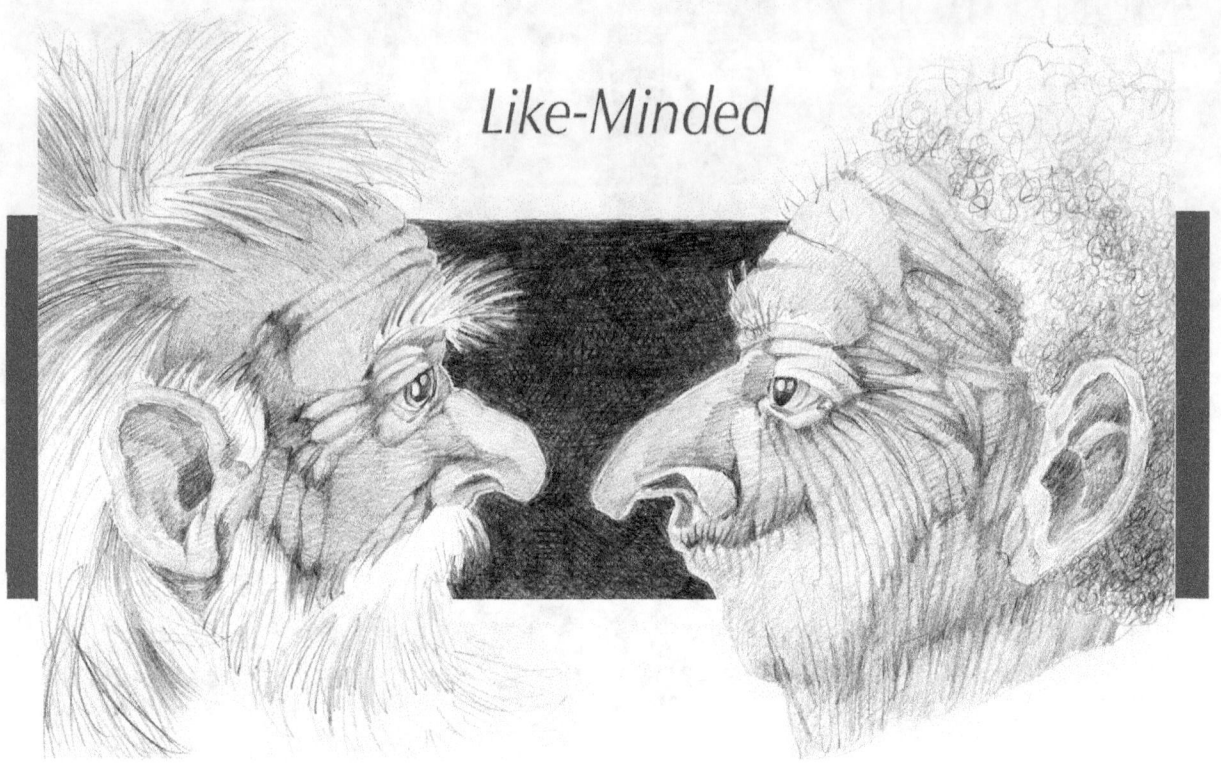

Being ancient, both of them, a couple geezers, grizzled men,
With wrinkly faces, sagging chins, big ears and legs as thin as pins,
Of ages similar in length and odors of surpassing strength,
Both having histories as long and storied as a country song—
Why, you might guess they'd have a lot in common, but the two do not,
In fact, might be from different races, different planets, not just places
On the globe, and so just stare, admire each other's nostril hair,
Wonder how anyone could be as old and ugly as they see
Across from them, each one, then shrug, and slouch off slowly as a slug

Dear Mr Pietist
(Write What You Know)

Blasphemies and insults,
corrosion of the soul,
Indignities, embarrassments
as deep as a black hole,
Confusion and contusions and
conclusions wrong as death,
Hyperbole, ignominy,
and halitosic breath,
Carbuncles, boils and pimples,
backstabbing creeps and bores:
My thoughts on these may not be sweet,
but they're sure more fun than yours.

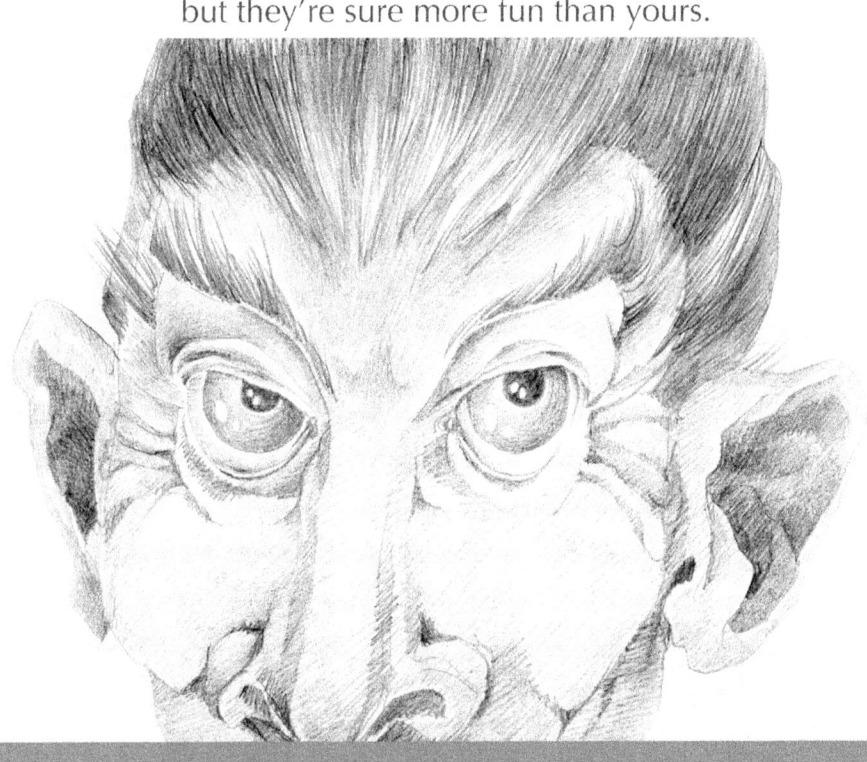

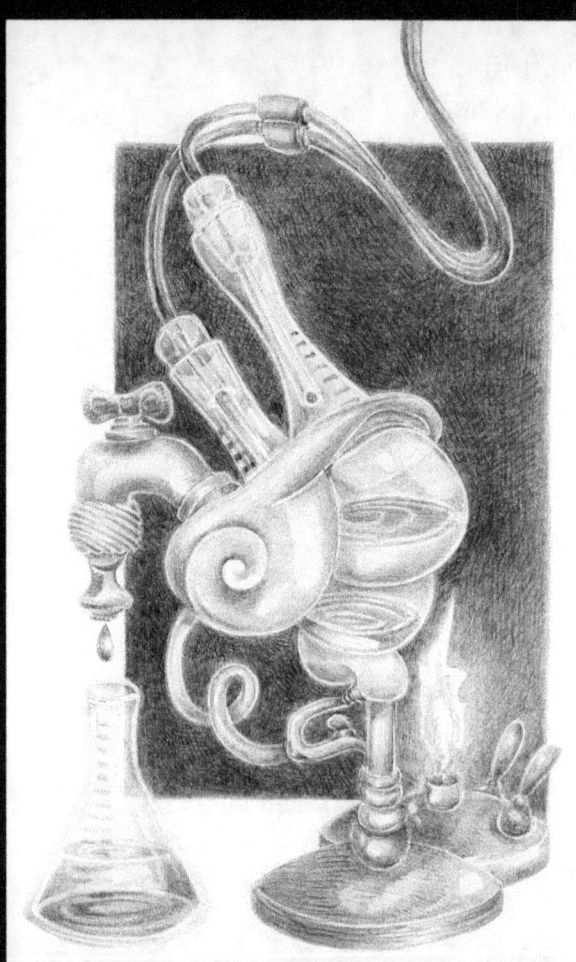

Classroom Classifications

Peppered with questions as pesky as flies
A sage and a scholar may never grow wise
If his concentration's unfocused or dim
Some days it's enough just to keep up a slim
Appearance of learning and hope for new thought
Since info and wisdom don't visit a lot

Science Class

Here in the laboratory
Amid the LEDs
The whirring of machinery
The oscillating breeze
Of cryogenic cases' fans
The humming centrifuge
I feel as though I
Might have been
Sent downhill on a luge
With all my limbs immobilized
Eyes open helplessly
While I race on to meet my doom:
Yes, Teacher calls on ME.

Supervisory Capacity

One of the great mysteries of organizational planning
Remains: why those who make the choices
Are so seldom those who are actually operating the systems in question
And so often unwilling to consult with those
Who are actually operating the systems in question
And most of all so ridiculously certain
That their incredible brainstorms in planning the organization
Will delight all and sundry as much as they are delighted by
Their own genius, not least of all, those who are actually
Pushed to the extreme edges of their patience
By trying valiantly to operate the systems in question
Using the incredible brainstorms of
Unrelated idiots

Putting Up a Good Front, Maybe

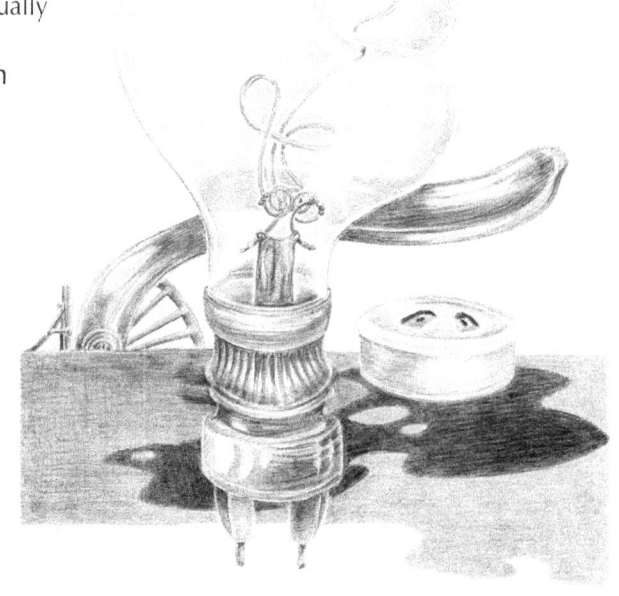

Feeling more than a little cross
And certainly piously self-pitying, I exhale
A sort of pinkish smog of loathing
That pretends without any hope of success to be glad
To see him here, the office weasel of time management,
Even while I know full well that others
All the way across the room can practically hear
The bruxing as I grind my teeth in a phony smile,
Can see the tremor in that temple vein so close
To aneurysm as I say in scratchy sycophantic tones
How glad I am he came to offer me
His oh so friendly and ingenious advice

Late, Not Forgotten

Red-hot peppers in your pants?
A bathtub full of fire ants?
Eels down your back, slugs in your hair?
A porcupine on your rocking chair?
I'd hate for your birthday to reach its end
Sans appropriate gift from your closest friend

In the Mean Time

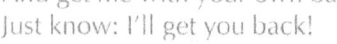

I am not parsimonious
With insults, jibes and stabs
And hexes, curses, wishing on
Someone a case of crabs,
A heap of boils, acne, bad breath,
Or just a bout of plague,
For when one wishes others ill,
Why be stingy or vague?
Now, if you have a cunning plan
To be first to attack
And get me with your own bad wish,
Just know: I'll get you back!

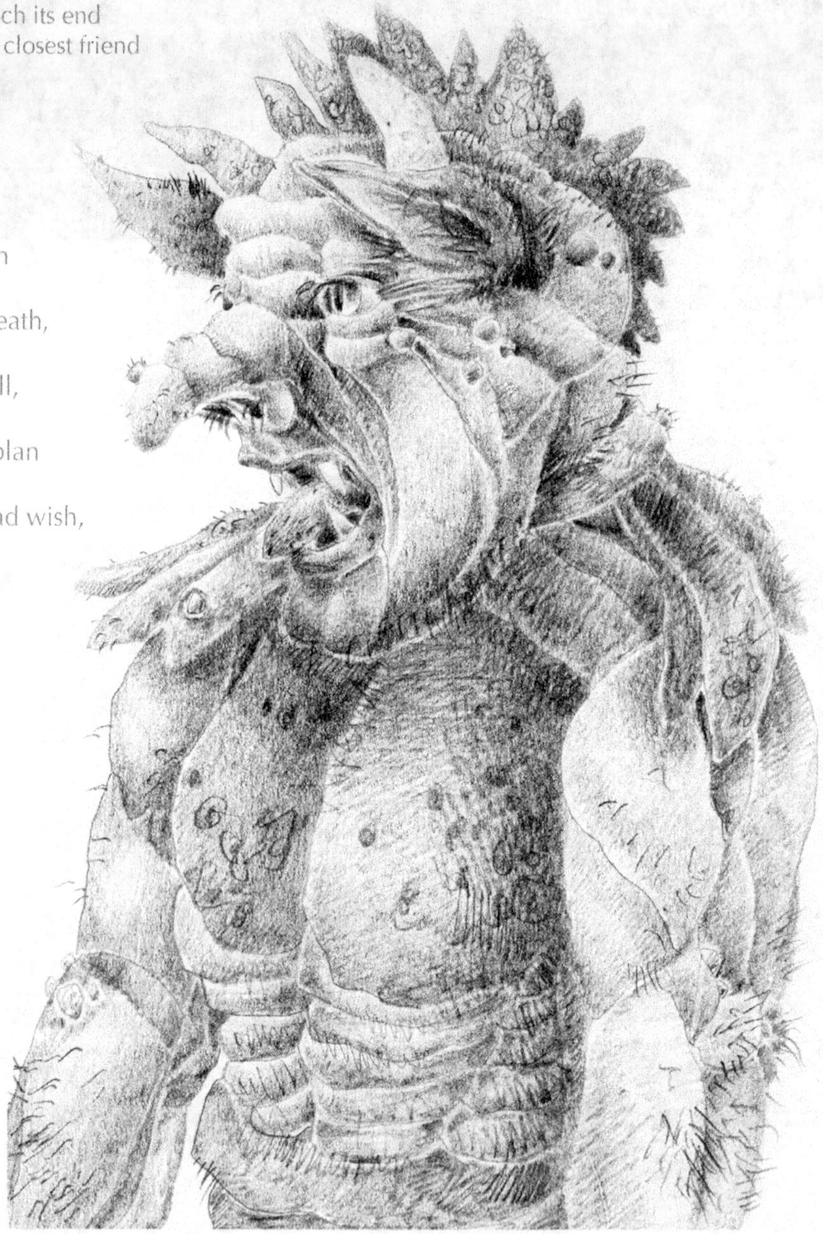

Fancy Disguise

My blasphemy in speaking thus
Is not that I let out a cuss
Or spoke a swearword, tinted blue,
But that I uttered ill of you,
For everyone assures me that
While you are scum, a creep, a rat,
It's to disguise that you're a saint
Under a mask of what you ain't
So to stave off idolatry—
Well, well! I'll say,
You sure fooled ME!

Creep

A plethora of pleasures
A deluge of delights
A heap of halcyon happiness
Awaits your days and nights
If you will only let me
Pour on you lavish love
I'll gladly stop the nastiness
That you accuse me of

Got My Eyes On You

Do not fear me, little friend;
I like you very much, you see,
And if you cozy up with me
You'll find I'm faithful to the end.
Don't be nervous, fretful, leery,
For I've such nice plans for you,
And such delicious things we'll do,
When you relax and join me, dearie.

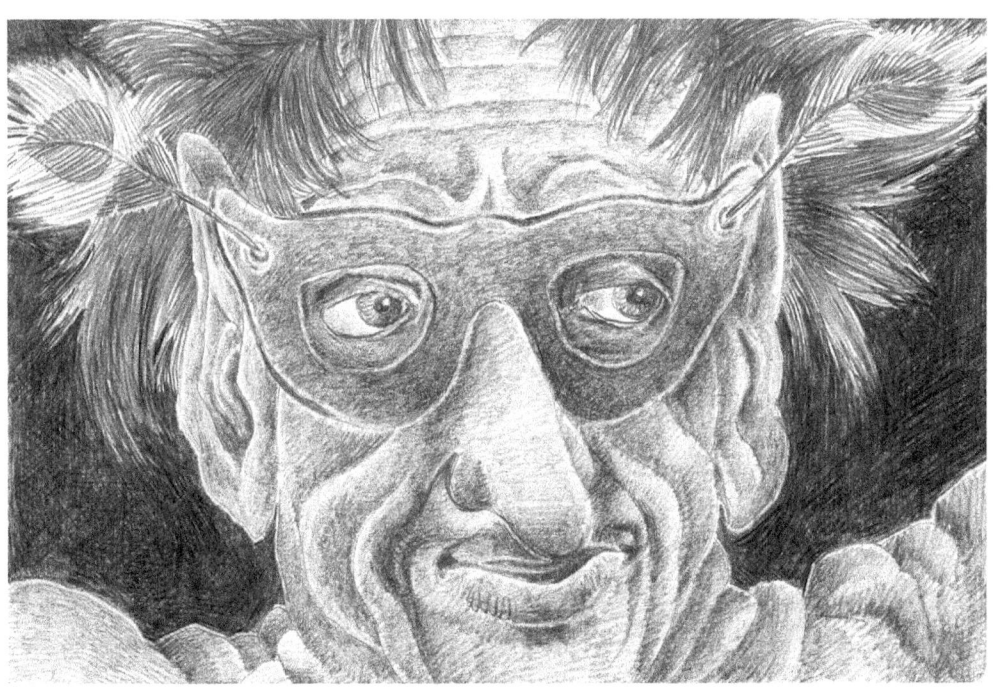

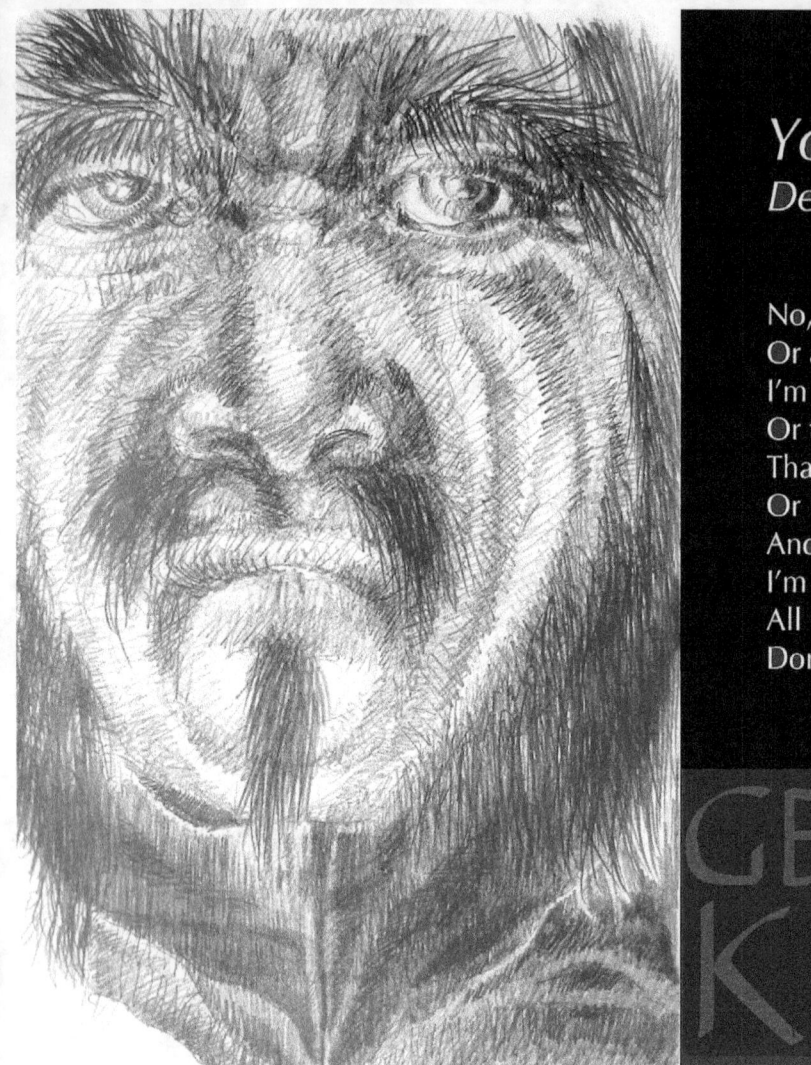

You'll All Like Me,
Despite My Shortcomings

No, I am not a government mole,
Or a hardened criminal on parole;
I'm not a double agent, spy,
Or the nefarious kind of guy
That tortures puppies, poisons cats
Or leers between the fence's slats
And plots against the neighborhood—
I'm neither that nice nor that good—
All true, but while I'm a nasty son,
Don't worry: I'm also a lot of fun.

GENGHIS KHAN

IT SEEMED LIKE SUCH A GOOD IDEA AT THE TIME: JUST BEAT DOWN EVERYBODY, TAKE OVER, AND RUN EVERYTHING IN THE KNOWN WORLD. SIMPLE. BUT YOU KNOW, ONCE YOU HAVE PILLAGED YOUR WAY AROUND EVEN THE SLIGHTEST LITTLE BIT, PEOPLE'S EXPECTATIONS CAN GET SO DANGED RIDICULOUS!

Entr'acte

The girl was just a little wisp
Of childhood with a charming lisp
And bashful flutter of the eye
Upon the people passing by
Until, at length, the last one passed
Alone, and found himself aghast
That she should grip him by the throat
And bite and shred the tough old goat
Like so much cotton candy, then
Fastidiously become again
Her cuddly toddler-costumed self,
Appearing next day like an elf
Or sprite of sprightly sweet and light,
'Til she grew hungry the next night

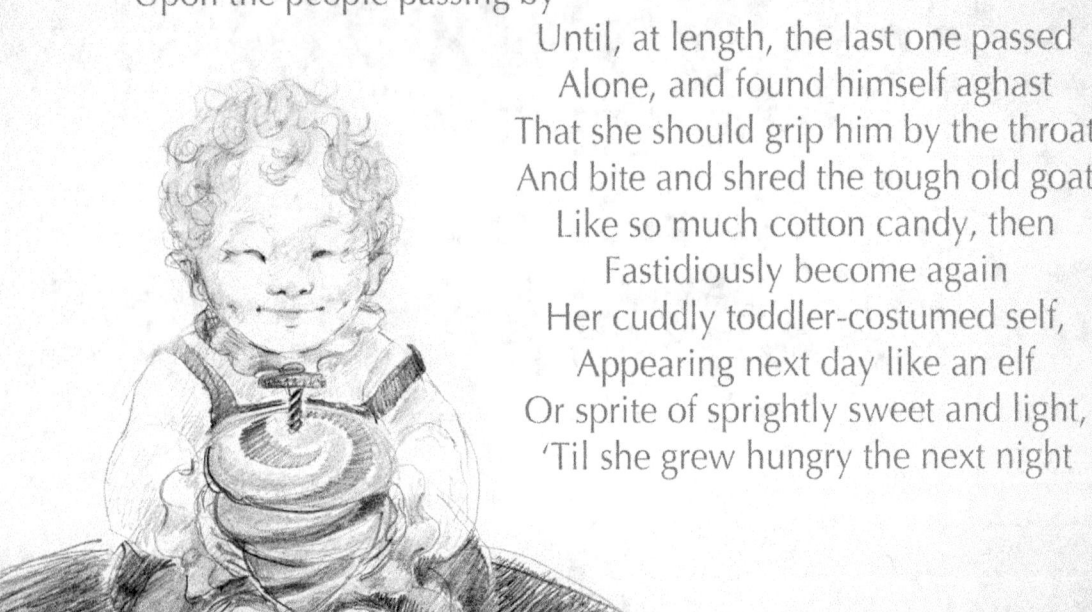

Pretty Young Things

O look ye, come hither,
And blather and blither
And slither in slaloms
Salacious and wild,
For elfin and fairy,
Where e'er they might tarry,
Sing ding-a-ding-derry
To lure a small child
To play and be pretty,
Be dancing and witty,
And fly from the city
To live with such friends
Of mystical magic
Who conjure and cadge
Ichneumon, mouse, badger,
And when the play ends,
The children are captured,
Allured and enraptured,
And all of them lapped,
Sure as nectar from flowers—
It's how youth is taken,
The worldly forsaken,
Why parents are shaken
By fairytales' powers

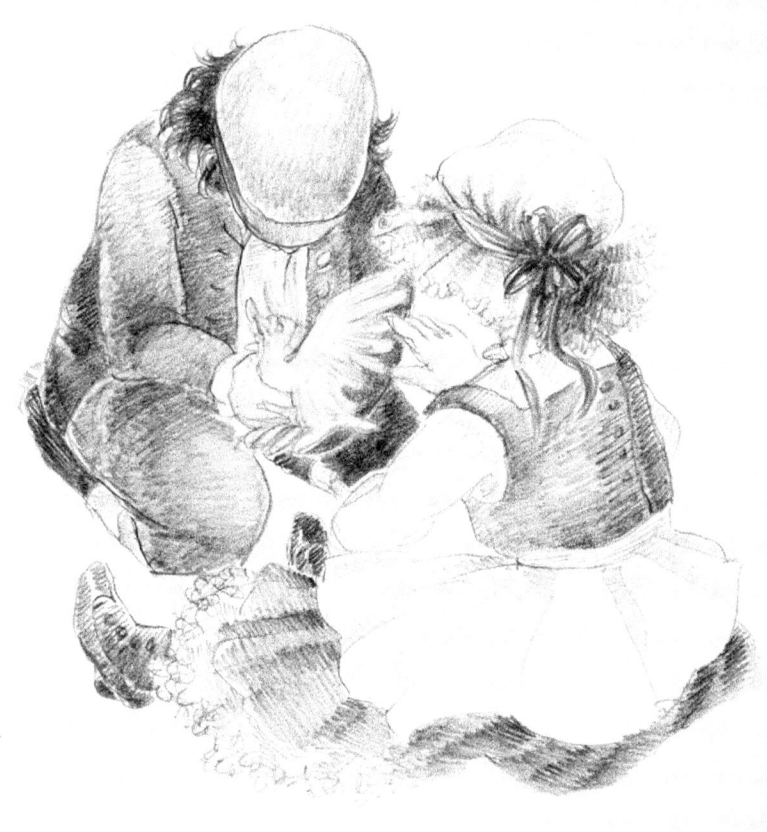

Crafty

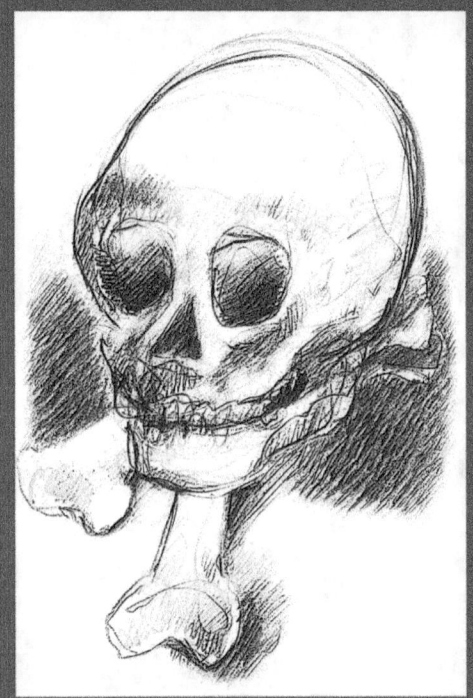

The rattle of those milky bones
Makes such delightful hollow tones
Since you converted Dad into
A wind chime and the breezes blew—
I know you are a dandy artist
And wind chimes are quite the rage
Still I think you could have waited
Till Dad died of plain old age—
Much less fuss and mess and other
Troubling questions both from Mother
And the coppers, had your timing
Been post-mortem with this chiming

Good Bones

There's something that prevents
Our saying just how fine we are
Until we've passed the end of life
And reached that distant star
Where it's okay to eulogize,
Admit we weren't too bad,
Trumpet our dandiness and say
We were darn grand, by gad!
Meanwhile, back on the mortal ranch,
We speak in muffled tones
Even to just admit to having,
Maybe, had good bones

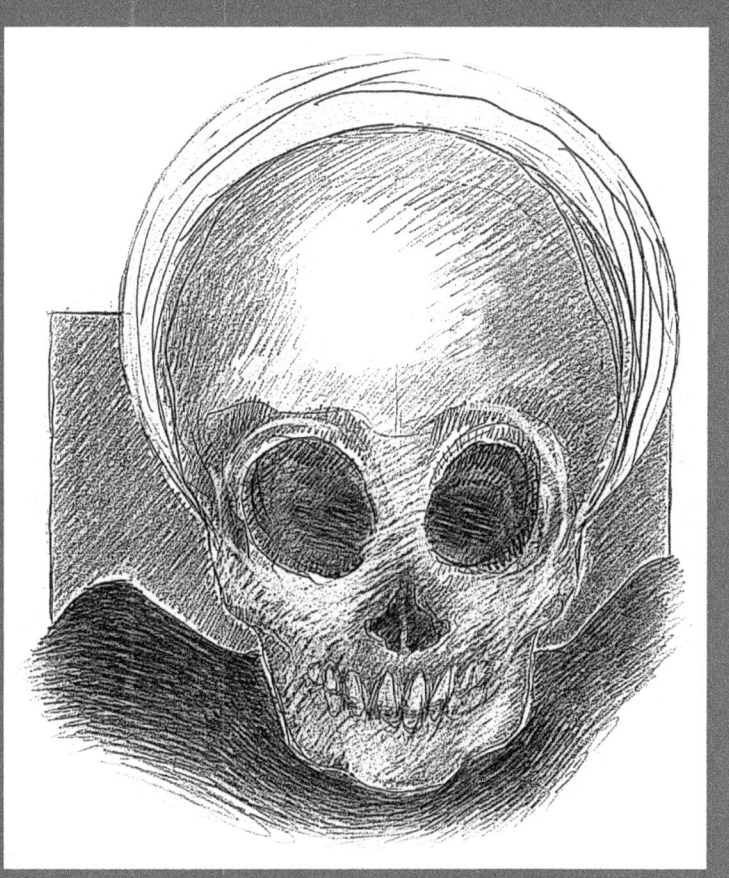

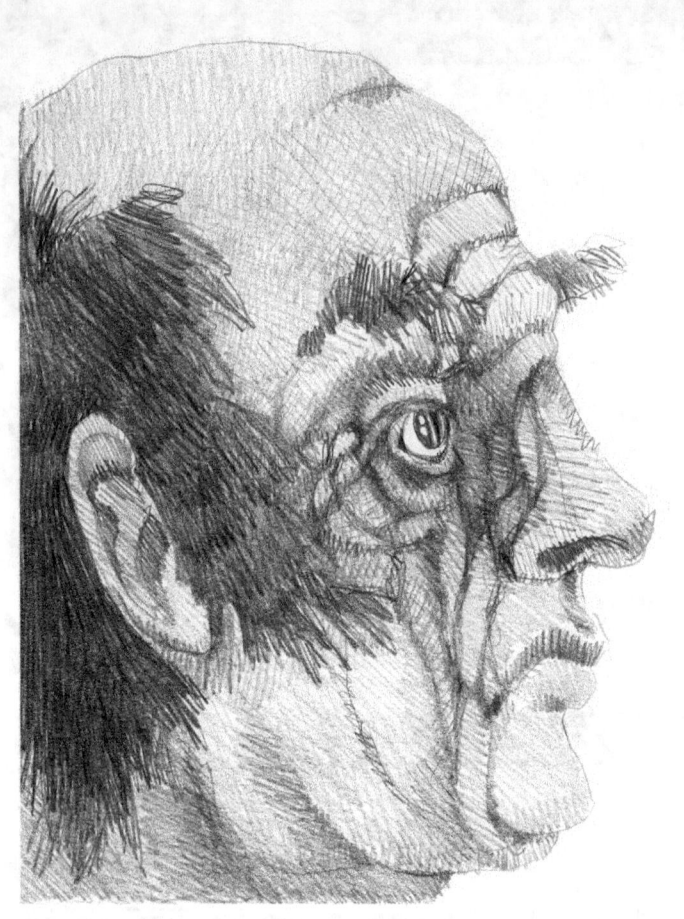

In Abeyance

Every particle of me
(At least those parts the world can see)
Works smoothly to create the masks
Compliant with my daily tasks
So no one guesses that down deep
My inner monster's just asleep.

The Face of Experience

Don't know why people cower so,
And seem standoffish, meeting me—
Yes, I'm a little odd, I know—
My friend, who wouldn't be
If he spoke as he was thinking,
Did as impulse bade him do,
And happened to be a vampire—
Say, I'm hungry; how 'bout you?

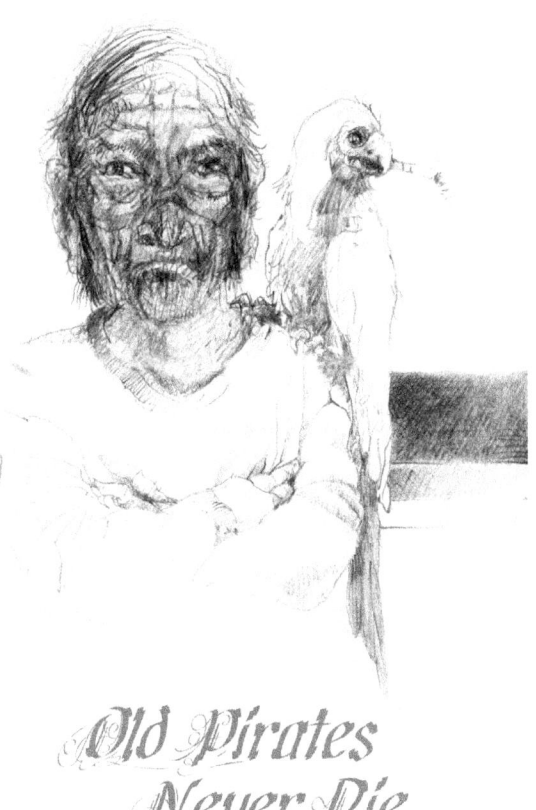

Old Pirates Never Die

Regardless of
his occupation,
calling, nature,
what you will,
There's no transition
for the pirate
who "retires"
from loot-and-kill;
Such ingrained
behavior, action,
predilection
and delight
Won't be stopped
or set aside
as long as he
remains upright,

And be honest:
few among
the pirate nation
really croak,
But to nice folks'
indignation,
are too ornery
sorts of folk
To allow
that sort of respite
for those who
are put-upon—
Mean guys live,
I think, to keep us
from enjoying
that they're gone.

Convulsions of Convolution

I'm thinking baroque thoughts today, Internecine and wild—

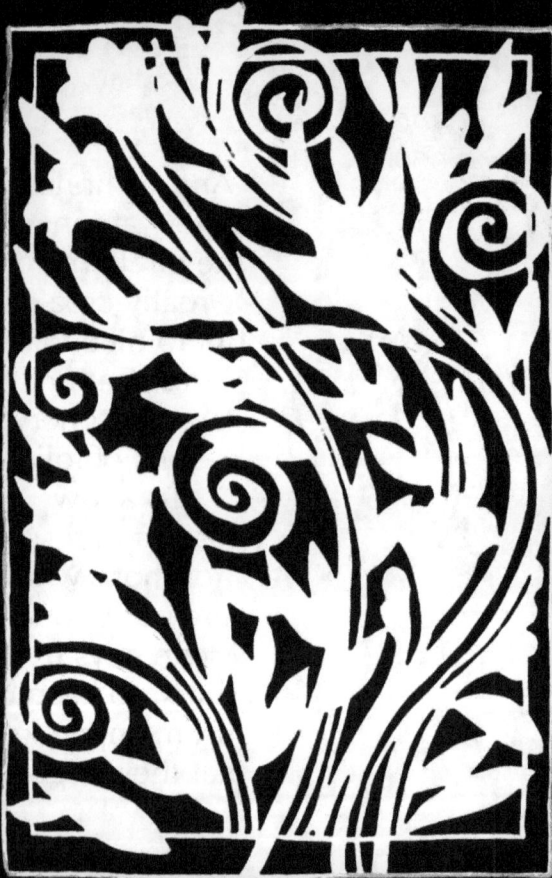 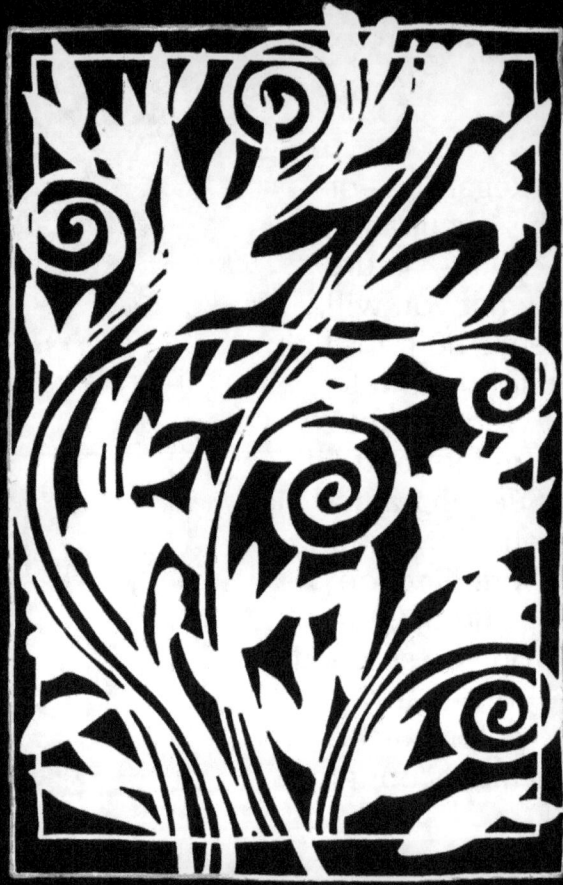

As weirdly Machiavellian as The daydreams of a child—
As Byzantine as psychotropic Drugs could make them be—
But you need not be worried for My safety: that's just me.

Hasty Retreat

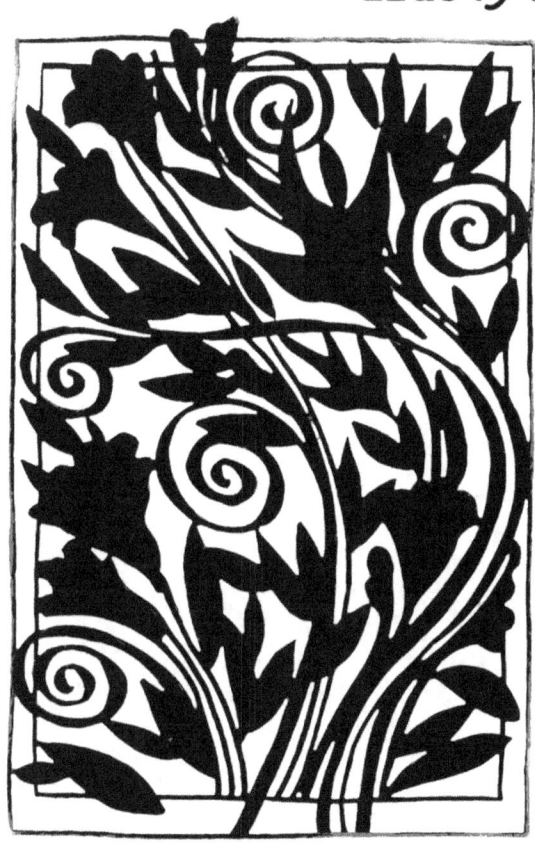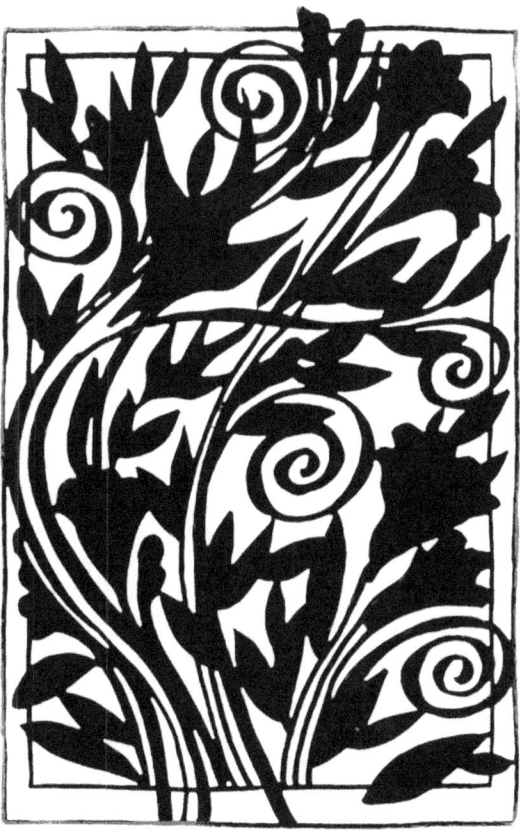

You'll pardon me, I hope, as I grow pensive And contemplate what's made me apprehensive,
And I request you not on this intrude Despite your sense that my withdrawal's rude,
For while I may grow distant, it is true, I've realized that what I fear . . . is you.

Scales of Justice Tipping

Of Percival Pettigrew, let us commence
To sing the bard's ballad of his recompense
For sins not committed, debts un-owed but paid,
For that is the penitent way he was made,
Who wore a hair shirt from the moment of birth
And preferred flagellation to such unseemly mirth
As smiling or raising his eye to observe
A lady or noble in passing—the nerve!
Thank goodness our Percival had no such thing,
For he balanced quite nicely the deeds of the king
So that fortunate monarch was free to behave
Precisely the opposite of that fine knave,
Knowing as His great Majesty did that one day
All debts do come due: he'd let Pettigrew pay.
One little glitch, only, marred this royal plan,
In that God seems to like to attribute to man,
Each one, his own virtues and sins, and exact
Individual comeuppance, and so in fact,
Thought Percival Pettigrew, though a fine fool
For suffering needlessly, warranted rule
In a heavenly setting at death, and the king:
Well he had earned, clearly, no similar thing—
Instead now in flames wearing Pettigrew's shirt,
And whipped by Old Nick with *his* flagellant quirt.

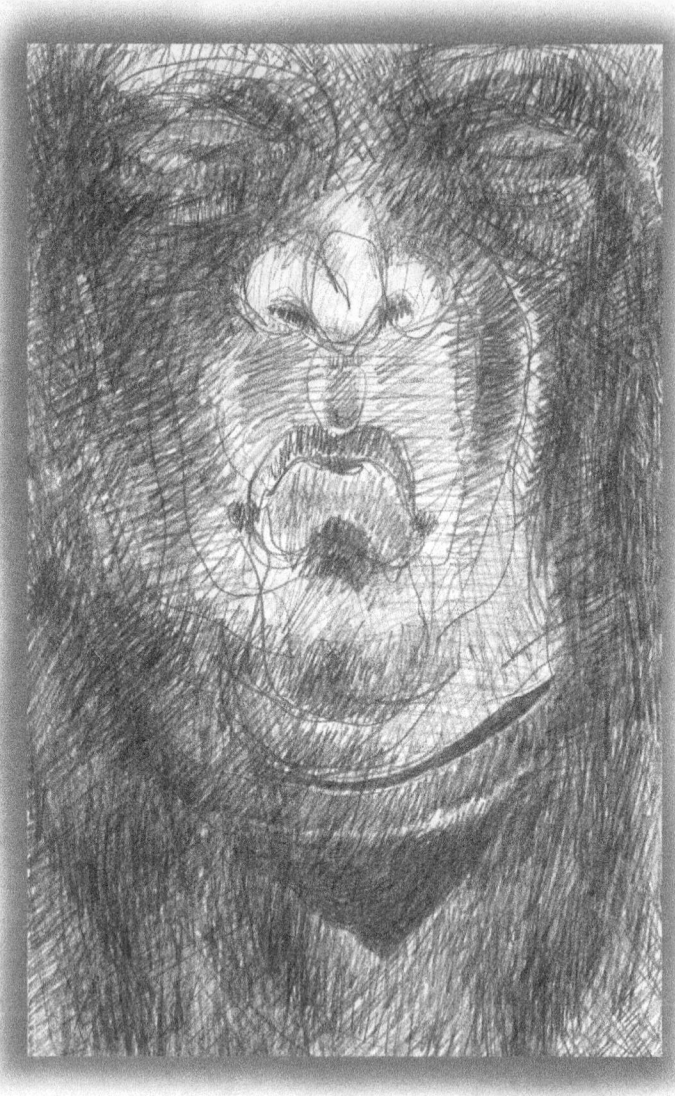

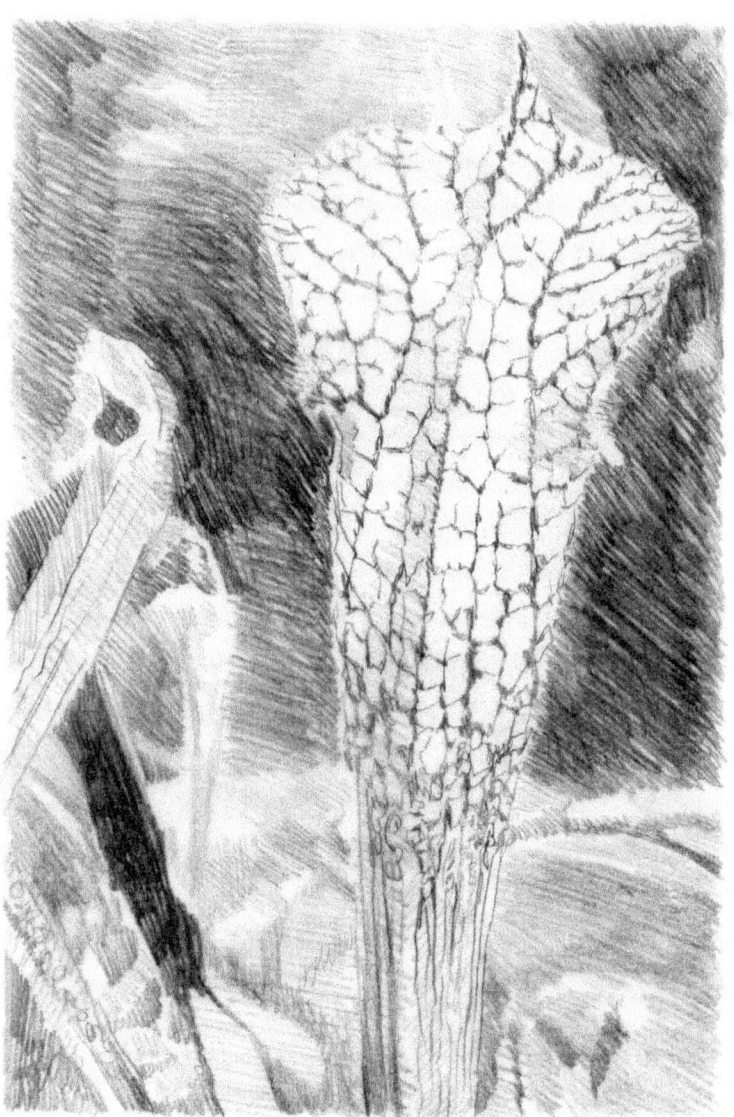

Made for This

Once there was a woodland elf
Who sewed the fairies' dresses
And taught the nymphs a moonlit dance
And combed their flaxen tresses,
Gave lessons to the owls in how
To hoot and hunt and fly
And taught the centaurs how to race
Under the midnight sky,
Wrote pretty tunes for fauns to flute,
Made jam from jasmine blooms
And led the fox a merry chase
Among the forest's rooms—
He was so loved, so gifted, skilled,
This elf of birchen grove,
That everyone would keep him safe
And happy as he'd rove
From forest clearing into dark,
Mysterious green lair—
Yet one dim night he disappeared
Completely into air,
For then the little woodman, barber,
Teacher, cook and stitcher
Leaned in too close to sup a sip
And fell into the pitcher,
And while the pitcher plant is
Pretty and with dewdrops filled,
It's a remorseless carnivore,
And so the elf was killed.
The moral of this tale (as there
Should be) is: mystic powers
May not protect you quite enough
In such a world as ours.

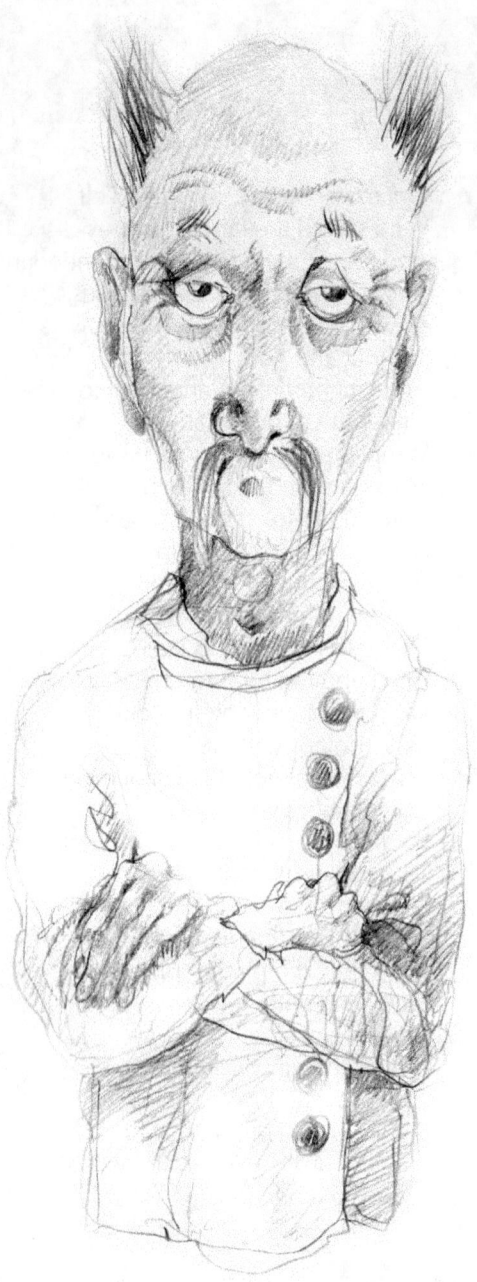

Oh, You Mean **This** *Anesthetic!*

There's something not quite right about
The way he rubs his hands with glee
And leers so hungrily at me,
My wiry dentist Dr Stout—
I am quite sure behind my back
I heard him smack his bony chops—
Recalling it, my pulse near stops
And gives me a mild heart attack—
I hear him snap those latex gloves
Deliberately, with delight,
But then remember in my fright:
It is my *wallet* that he loves.

The Butcher's Beef

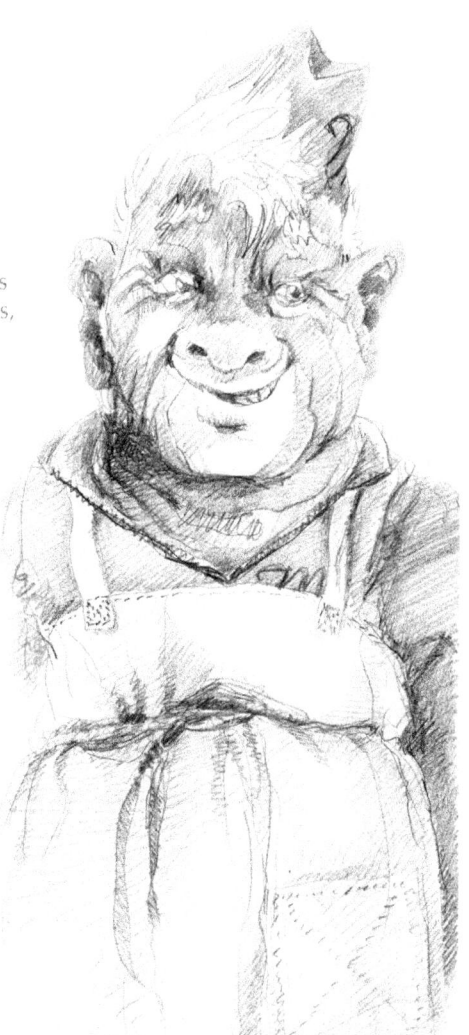

There is a butcher shop in town, A marketplace of some renown,
In which the owner has such skill, Such protean talents, if you will,
With proteins of all sorts and cuts, He rightly rules the field. And what's
Much more, in the wide world of meats, There is nobody who competes,
In part because these skills so grand So clearly lend the upper hand,
And so defined does he stand out From every other hereabout,
That competition would be moot And hardly worthy of pursuit.
The other reason, let's be fair: There was one once who did compare,
A lady butcher dressed in chintz, But then, we haven't seen her since
She cut one day the Perfect Roast And, while she didn't brag or boast,
The townsfolk gathered in a crowd To ogle it and sigh aloud
At its great beauty, and the Mayor Bought it, uttered a table prayer,
Served it, all tender, juicy, rich, Extravagant and flawless, which
Seemed to evoke from Mr Vliet, Aforementioned as prince of meat,
A tiny tic by his left eye So small that most would not descry
It, but perhaps significant, Adjudged by how the sequel went,
Which, rumor has it, had Miss Fen, The lady butcher, in his den,
Invited for a cup of tea And some mince pies; it's said with glee
The pies were savory and good But poor Miss Fen misunderstood
The invitation that he sent And was the main ingredient.
I shan't be plainer. Let's just say, Only one meat shop stands today,
Only one butcher left to boast His meat cutting, his tasty roast,
And no one opts to countermand That long tradition. Let it stand.

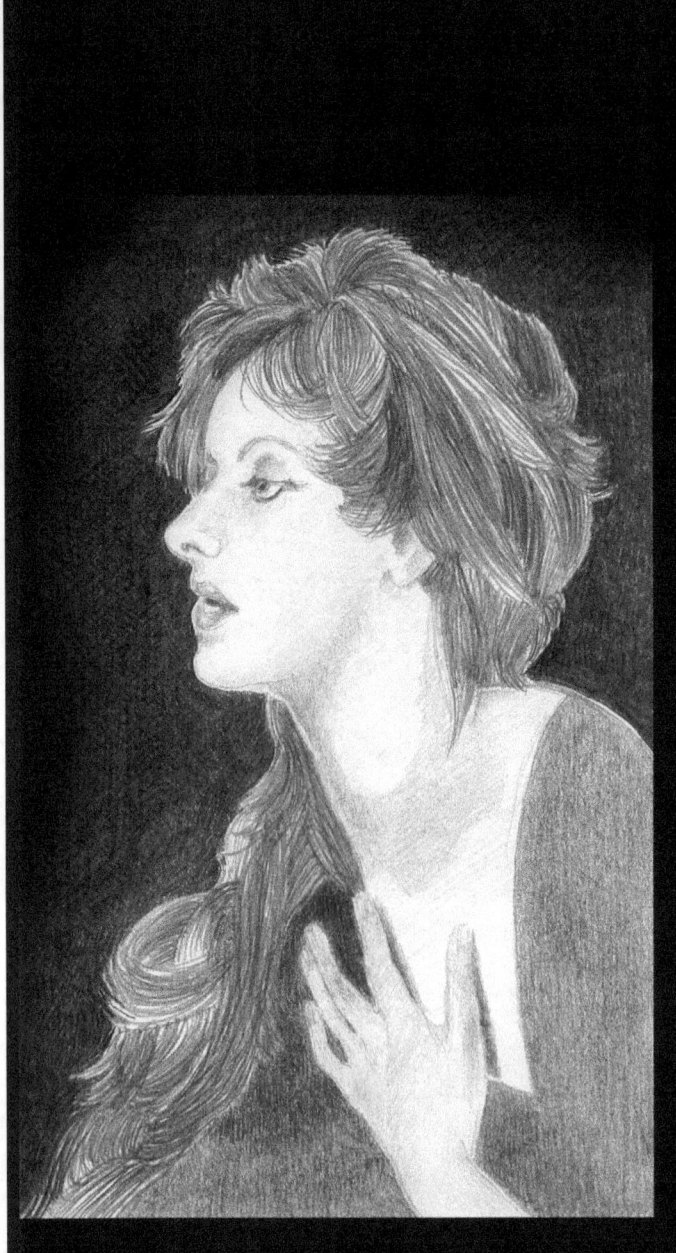

HAIL, FELLOW, ILL MET

Happy to see you, my darling,
lovely to meet again, Dear,
What was it that we were saying
when erst we met up last year?
It seems there was some important
and vital thing that we said;
Ah! I remember now: we decided,
rather than speak, to be dead.

FRISSONS

For Time and creatures marvelous there is a certain way
Of twisting through their histories where mysteries hold sway
And making in crepuscular dim dusk an urge to creep

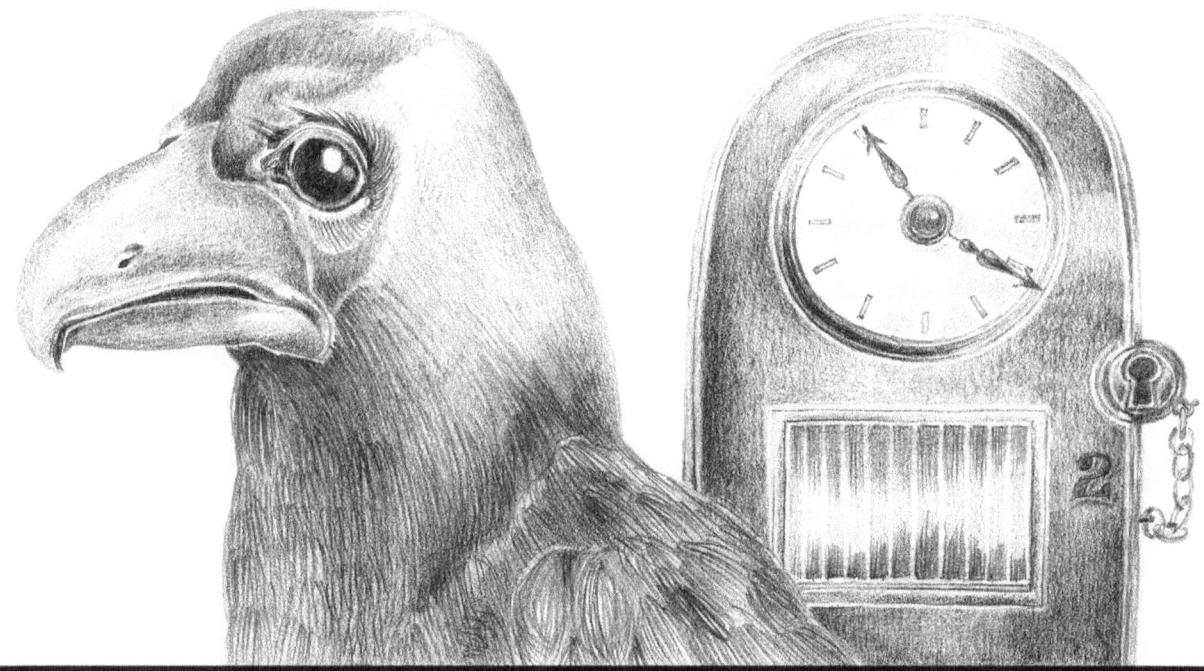

And peer around in sneaking fear, delighted, never sleep
Again without a glimpse behind our backs with gleeful dread
Until both Time and creatures see us lying, grinning, dead.

Accompaniments for the Lord and Master

Sit down, dear lady, to the feast, and you will see I'm not so bad—
My reputation as a beast is overrated; I'm just Vlad,
The prince you've captured with your grace
And so enraptured that your place
Should be at my right hand, my side;
Your least command won't be denied—
Just settle in and settle down, enjoy the drama and romance
Of wearing a bejeweled crown and living richly as the chance
Permits when you're my chosen flame;
Let generations speak your name
In reverent whispers—they do mine
As though I were a god (divine
Or terrible, what do I care?
As long as worship keeps them there
In my embrace, my grasp, my thrall, where I can use them as I will
To harry for my sport, withal, and if they should displease, to kill
Them slowly on a spike, a spit, And for the light and joy of it,
To make them torches to ignite The garden with their searing light
While we are feasting, while we rule The night until the crepuscule
Of dawn should see them smoking dim, A sort of histrionic hymn
To our great power and command)—you see, my lady, what I bring
To you when on your little hand I place my seal, my princely ring—
So let the gypsy band resound to cheer you to the feast, and you
Will find the screams and groans are drowned—
If not, you'll be a night-light too.

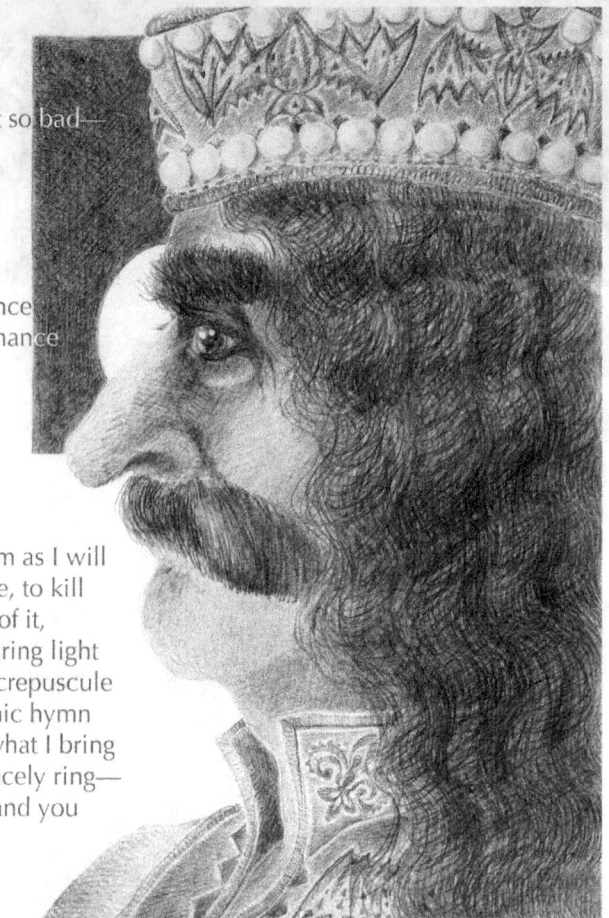

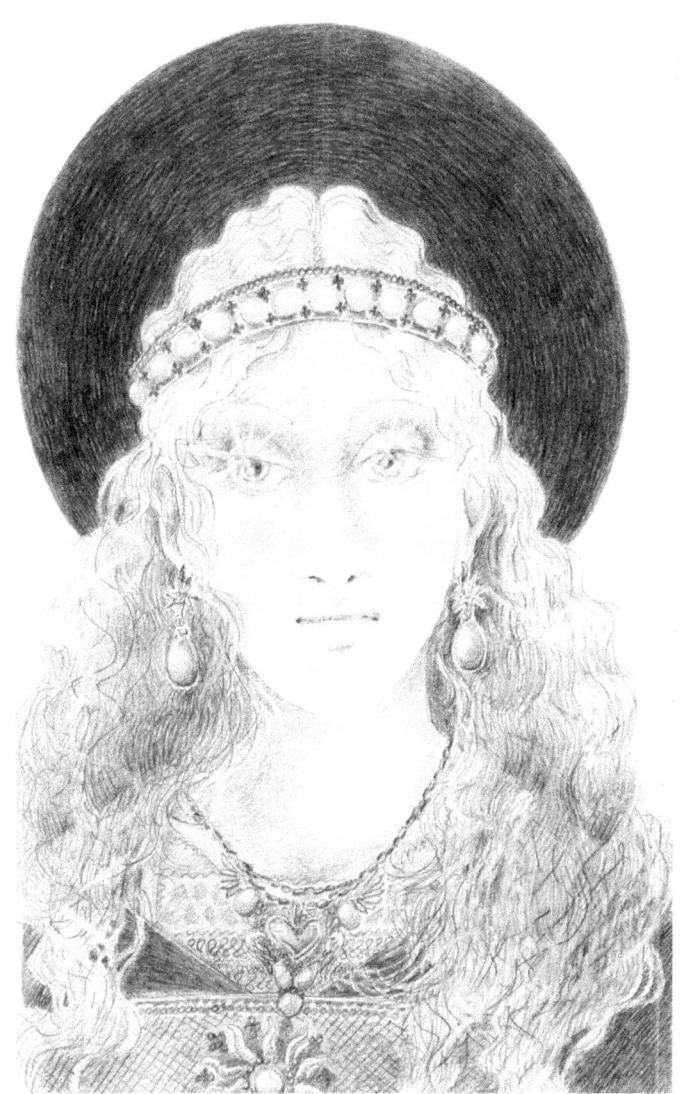

Image Rehabilitation

How can you call me wicked, fool?
I am the daughter of the Pope.
My machinations are a school
Of politics, the way to cope
With states and mores Machiavelli
Never faced or dreamt or tried,
'Spite his experience, intelli-
Gent insights that he descried;
For he was ne'er betrothed teenager,
Used to further family goals,
Nor loved improperly, I'd wager,
Thrown on rocky shallow shoals
Of life's current by his would-be
Caretakers, protectors, friends;
Let us say he'd struggle, should he
Be the means to others' ends
As I've been from birth to marriage,
Through vagaries thick and thin,
So if I've altered my own carriage
To survive, it's hardly sin.
Rather, say I was example
And precursor to the day
When more women had an ample
Opportunity to say
Where they'd be, what they'd be doing,
And with whom, and how, and why,
Then decide whether eschewing
My ways let them live or die.

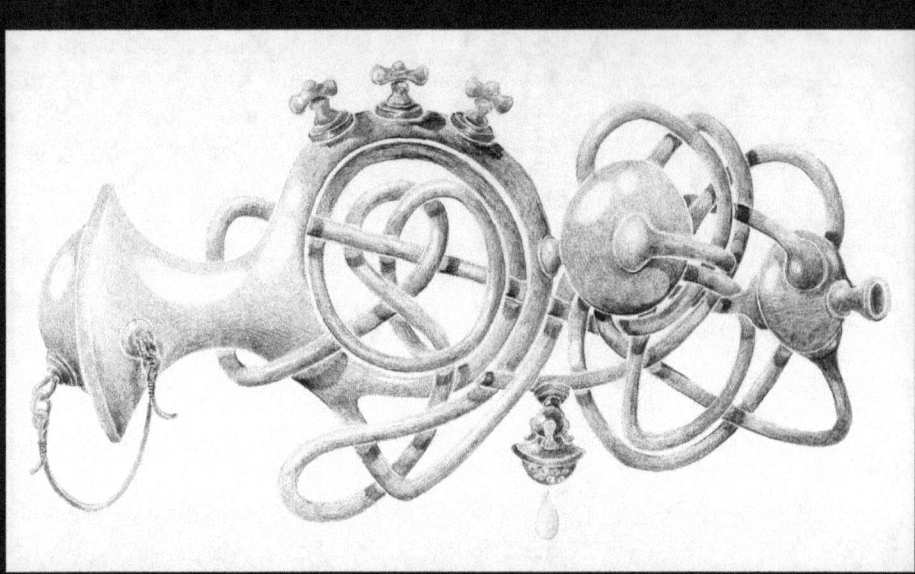

Instrument of Torture

When I agreed to music lessons Mother never said I'd be caught up in something that caused me such fear and dread
And loathing, but in her defense, perhaps she never knew The sort of instrument I'd play, the sort of teacher who
Would plague me with its Byzantine appurtenances, valves And knots of weird impenetrable tubing that no salves
Or compresses or medications could make fun to play, Or sensible, decipherable and tuneful sounds assay
From out its bell though I might mute it mightily in hope The neighborhood would not come hunting me with lengths of rope
And brandishing their torches as they called for it to end—I tell you of this instrument's great power to save you, friend,
And if you deign to take some music lessons too some day, I recommend you look to do so in some safer way:
Perhaps the spoons, for at the least, should they cause you to whine At lessons, they can be applied to uses more benign,
And instead of fearing dying you can just sit down to dine.

Where there's a Will, There's a Won't

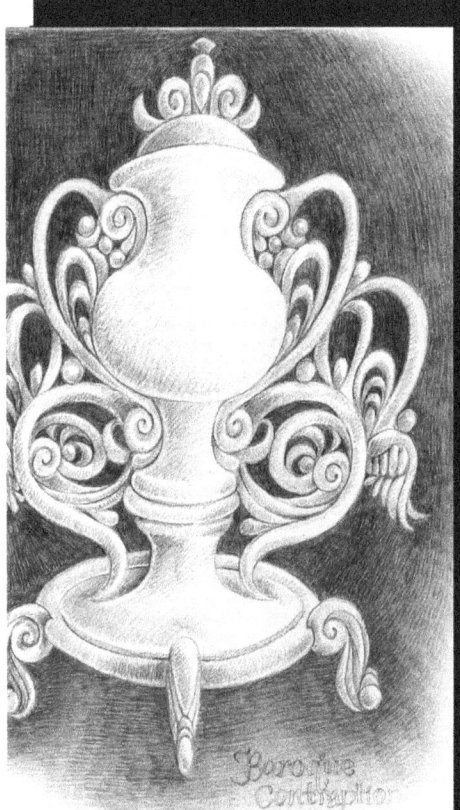

In an unexpected twist of fate, Matilda fell into the grate
While dusting off the mantelpiece, And wasn't found until her niece,
Just visiting from Tiddly Wood, Came to see Auntie (as one should)
And wondering where she'd gotten to, Discovered she'd flown up the flue
When Uncle Bertie lit the fire, Not noticing his heart's-desire
Had fallen in the fireplace—How ashen, then, her Uncle's face
When he discovered his mistake Of turning Aunt to ashy flake;
At least they found some hints and clues (Aunt's stomacher and rings and shoes)
Explaining in their carbonized Remains where she whom they'd both prized
Had gone, and why she'd not been seen Since the last time the firescreen
Was set in place before a flame And why things hadn't been the same
For such a long time as the two Had pondered whence Matilda flew.
So Bess, the niece, and Uncle Bert, Now to her fate fully alert,
Pressed her cremains into an urn, Decided nevermore to burn
The fire in that especial room (It tended hence to fill with gloom,
And also with a certain smell That afterwards they both could tell
Was not just creosote or dust) And they consoled, as family must,
Each other with their common bond Of love and loss, for they were fond
Of Aunt Matilda, to be sure, And, more, what they had got from her—
Things they would NOT have got, had fate Not found her fallen in the grate:
Fine furnishings and means and wealth, Which they enjoyed in long good health
And may both be enjoying still—despite excision from her will.

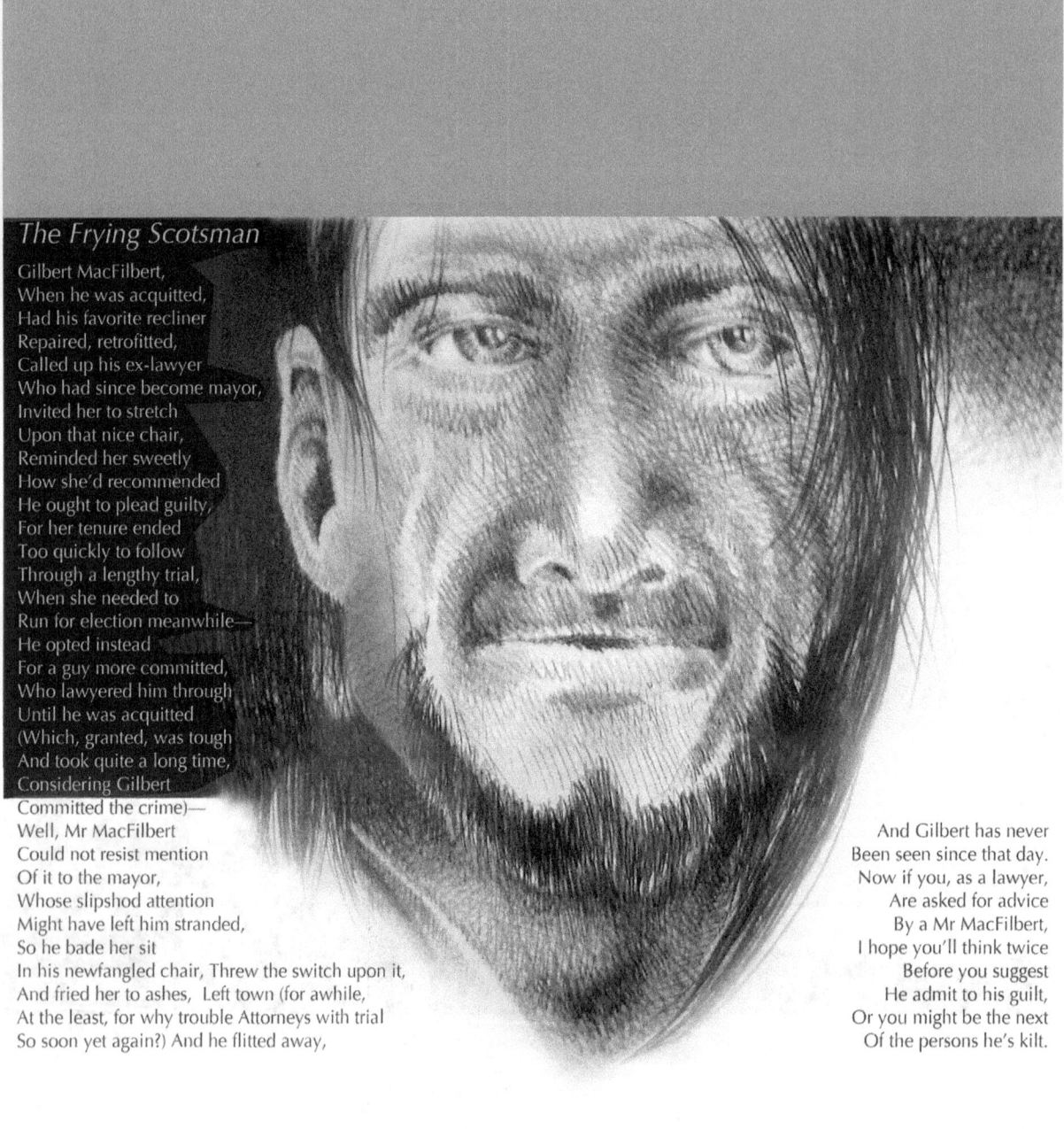

The Frying Scotsman

Gilbert MacFilbert,
When he was acquitted,
Had his favorite recliner
Repaired, retrofitted,
Called up his ex-lawyer
Who had since become mayor,
Invited her to stretch
Upon that nice chair,
Reminded her sweetly
How she'd recommended
He ought to plead guilty,
For her tenure ended
Too quickly to follow
Through a lengthy trial,
When she needed to
Run for election meanwhile—
He opted instead
For a guy more committed,
Who lawyered him through
Until he was acquitted
(Which, granted, was tough
And took quite a long time,
Considering Gilbert
Committed the crime)—
Well, Mr MacFilbert
Could not resist mention
Of it to the mayor,
Whose slipshod attention
Might have left him stranded,
So he bade her sit
In his newfangled chair, Threw the switch upon it,
And fried her to ashes, Left town (for awhile,
At the least, for why trouble Attorneys with trial
So soon yet again?) And he flitted away,
And Gilbert has never
Been seen since that day.
Now if you, as a lawyer,
Are asked for advice
By a Mr MacFilbert,
I hope you'll think twice
Before you suggest
He admit to his guilt,
Or you might be the next
Of the persons he's kilt.

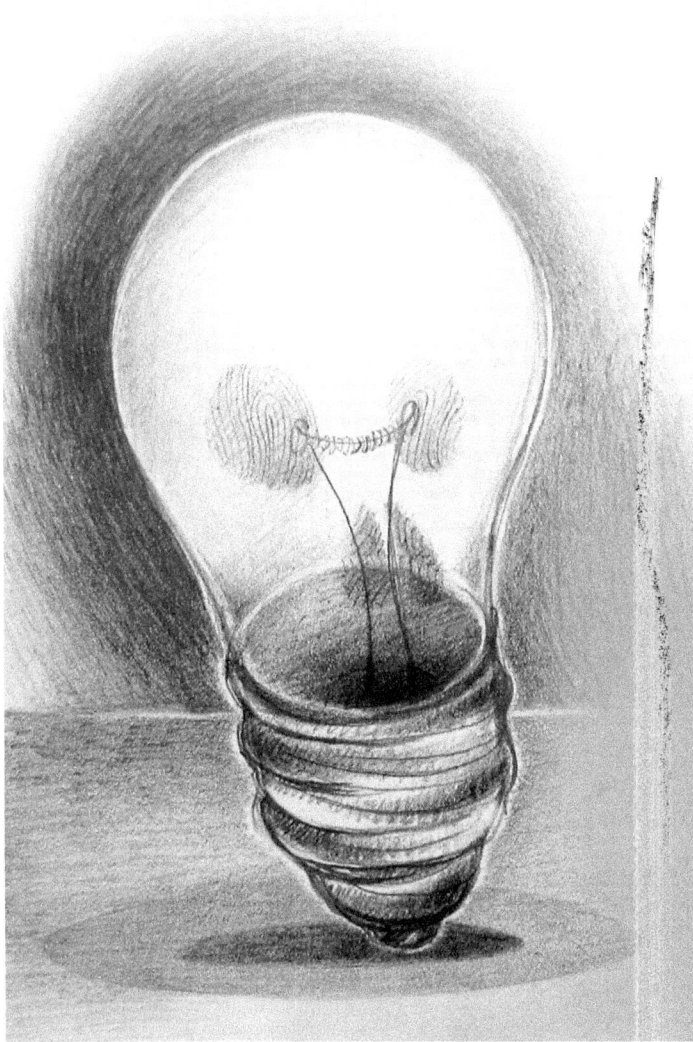

The Truth about Friday the Thirteenth

Friday the Thirteenth: just a day
Of no significance, no sway,
No undue danger, nothing drear
Inherent, yet we're struck with fear
And prickling neck-hairs, trembling hands,
Nerves taut as outstretched rubber bands,
Twitching of eyes, tingling of feet,
The urge to run out in the street
And scream with terror just because
Someone has said the Thirteenth was,
When found on Fridays, deadly grim.
I'd love to get a hold of him,
The dolt who made up that whole tale,
And belt him 'til his pelt grows pale,
Knock in his teeth and steal his wallet,
Pinch him hard on the whatchacallit
'Til he pleads for mercy, but
I realize this sort of nut
Not only wouldn't find defeating
Of his theory such a beating,
Rather finding further proof
Of it, because I made the goof
Of choosing his own designated
Doomsday, when I should have waited
Just one more to prove my point,
But got my nose too out of joint
And proved the Thirteenth day, instead, did
Hold bad luck for the hotheaded

Our Lady of Cavender Circle

The evening light is pale and sweet
and scented faintly lavender
And children hover on the street
like moths drawn down to Cavender,
Where in the cottage at the end—
the dead-end, to be pointed—there
Resides a lady they intend
to catch a glimpse of, for her hair
Seems made of sterling cobwebs bright,
her eyes of sparkling diamond dust,
Her skin of some pellucid light
infused with magic, but they must
Be cautious, chary, wary, well
disguised by evening's shadowed cool
And catch their glimmers in that spell
without her spying them out, who'll
Turn from her glinting fairy self
into an instant screaming host,
For if disturbed their pretty elf
reverts to form, and haunts as ghost

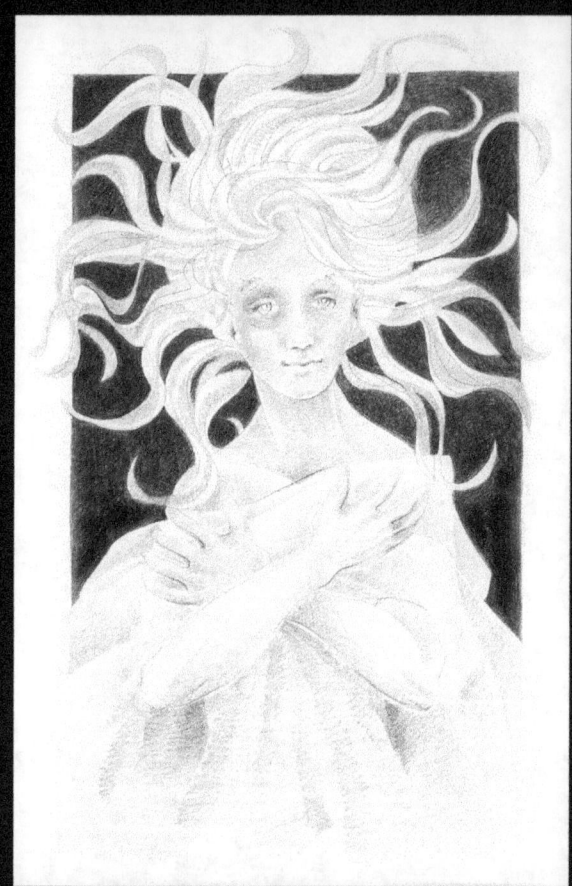

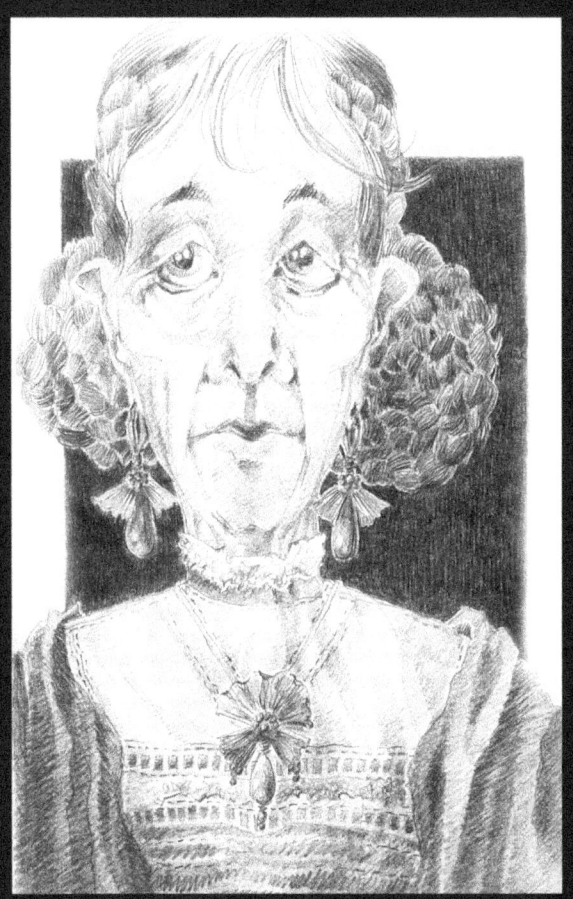

The Lady on Maple Street

So prim and proper that she squeaks
just like a frightened mouse
Those few times that she ever speaks;
she hardly leaves the house
At 218 North Maple Street
except well after dark,
When she puts on her shawl
and takes the shortcut through the park
Down to the corner grocery
to buy a pint of milk,
Some day-old bread, a piece of cheese,
or something of that ilk,
And scurries home to munch on her
sparse meal like a fanatic;
The leftovers, she feeds
her husband, chained up in the attic.

Balancing Act

Improbable placement
Fragility, grace
A moment of risk
I might fall on my face
But someone's quick action
Suspends me in air
And holds up disaster
A dainty affair
Precarious tipping
Voluminous strength
I'm grateful somebody
Has saved me at length
Now how to undo it
Get out of the pose
When only swift thinking
Saved me by a nose
Just stay here forever
On point and aloft
Can't fathom the second
Descent will be soft
I thank you, whoever
Has saved me thus far
And hope we progress
From this point where we are
Yet knowing I'm human
And fallibly led
Forgive me if I should
Still land on my head
Though you are well meaning
And gave me a chance

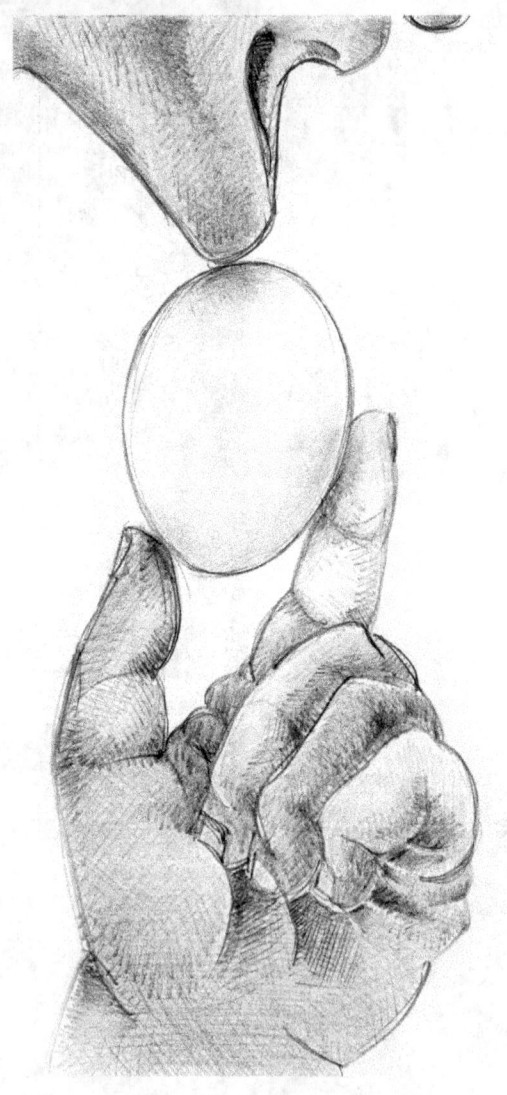

We'll see if I can
Survive this circumstance
To blunder another
Hour through on my way
Sans total destruction
To balance the day

Actors
(Noh 2 are Exactly Alike)

Talent, or the lack of it,
In measure is irrelevant—
As long as ego is as large
And thick-skinned as an elephant
And actors play at being smart
And skilled and gifted as they will,
It doesn't really matter much
If they sup vintage or mere swill,
Since self-importance and a sense
Of confidence holds total sway
To the degree that actors with
Enough of it can make it pay
And we sit here as if in thrall
And take whatever they dish out
Because they claim celebrity
And we don't disagree or doubt,
Which would take effort on our part
And might require thought and tact,
So rather than such exercise,
We'll lie back, taking in the act.

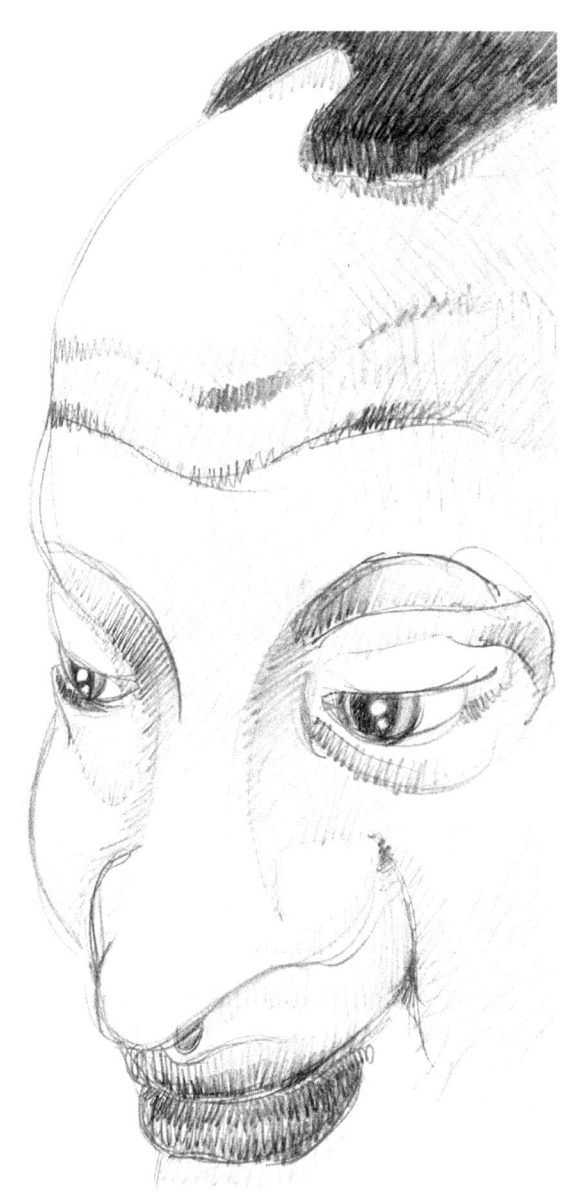

They Shoulda Thunk of it back at the Ol' Alamo

What a dustup, a fine howdy-do,
A dag nabbit, a hullabaloo!
I think a retreat
Back into the mesquite
Is a fine idea; how about you?

That's Jest How I'se Feeling

No one would ever
call me frisky,
But when I've had
a little whiskey,
It might be said
I'm more relaxed
Than was before,
but hey, you axed!

Schoolyard Relations

Oh Ma, Joe's hollered at me,
Pinched my cheek and pulled my hair—
He put a spider on my desk—
I sat: he yanked my chair!
*Why, Honey, these attentions
That you're sore complaining of—
Though you are right that they're uncouth—
Are tokens of his love!*

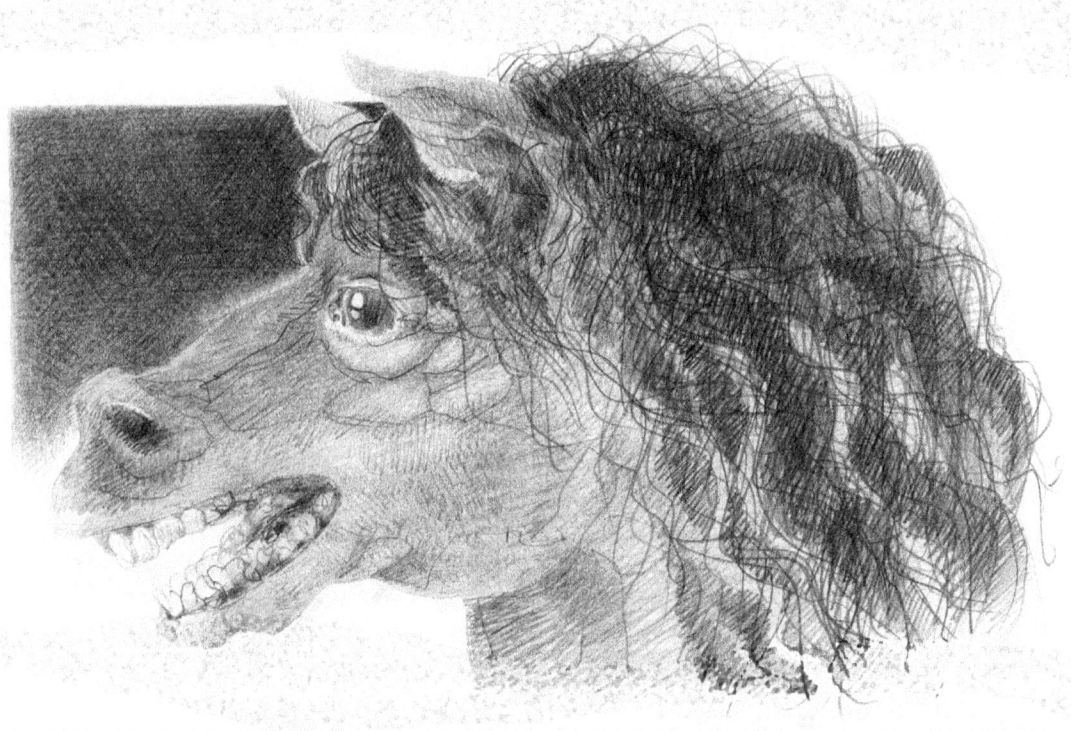

Where Life Takes Me

I never dreamt of Texas as a place I ought to go,
But here I am a Texan, now—what happened? I don't know.
It wasn't packaged or pre-planned or destined or expected,
But that is surely how my life's adventures have collected
In this strange journey that I take, how oddly things occur—
I hardly know who I once was, what happened then to her,
Or what she will be years from now, and where and why and how—
All I can say is, life's sure wild, and I'm a Texan now.

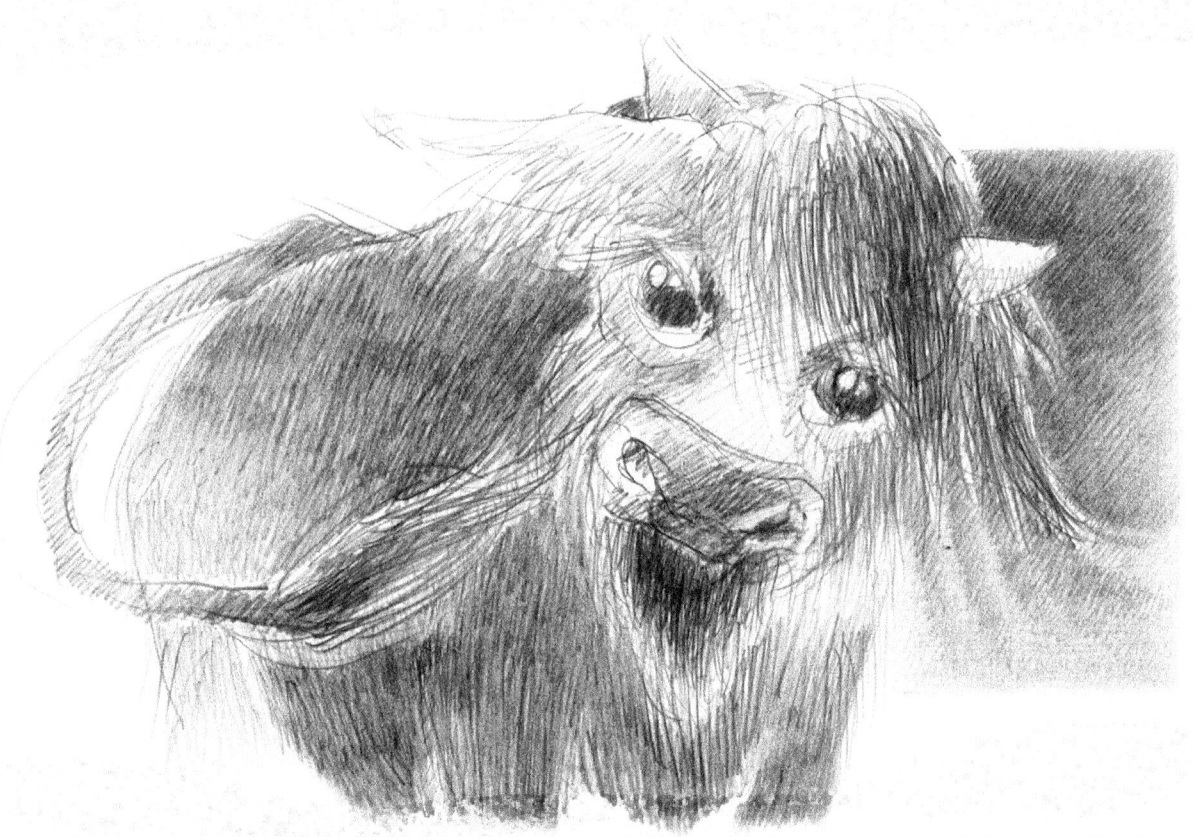

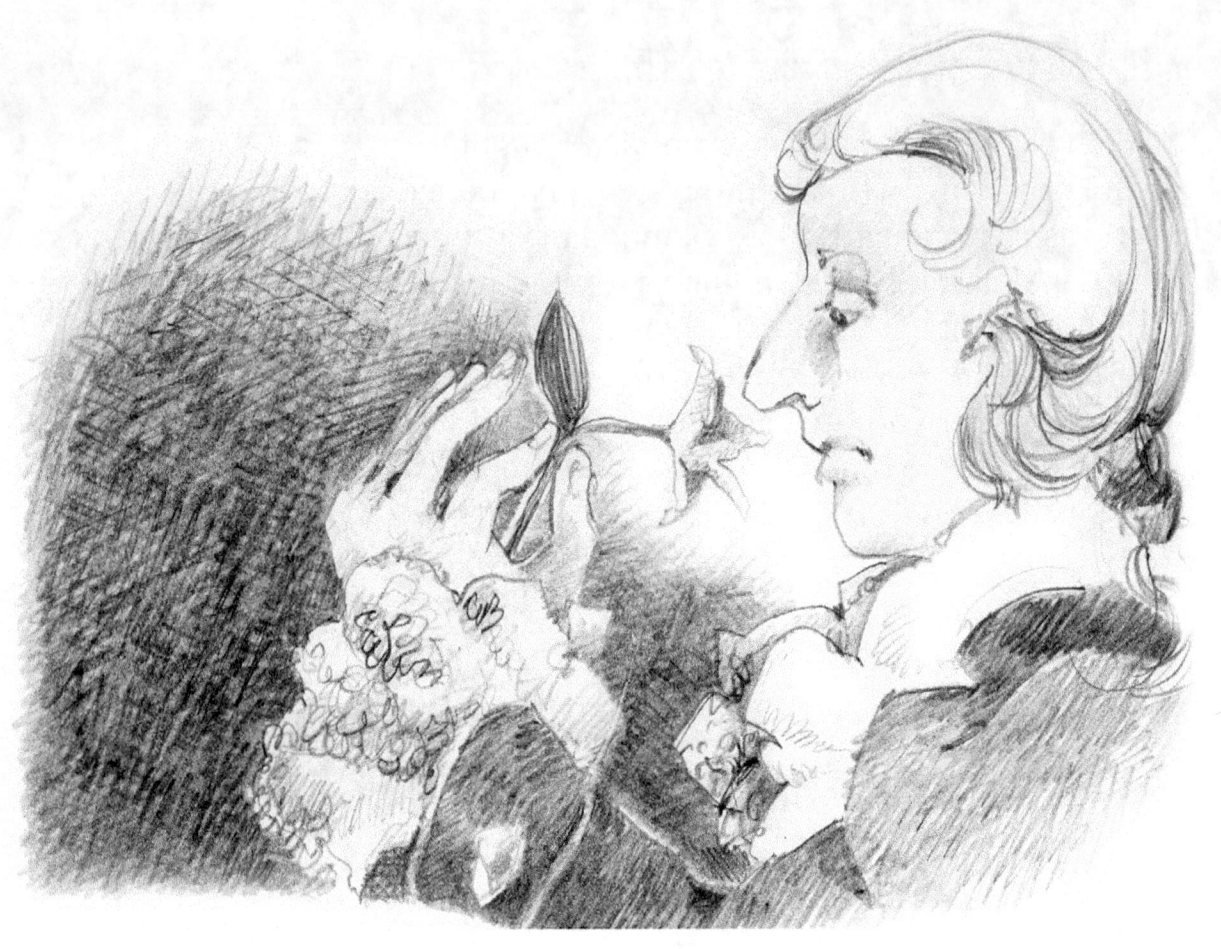

Dandy (Dear Me!)

He simpers in his powdered wig As though the ladies gave a fig
For him or what he wears or does But still is satisfied, because
His greatest admiration is Found in love-letters that are his
Entirely, and flowers, meant For him by whom they all were sent!

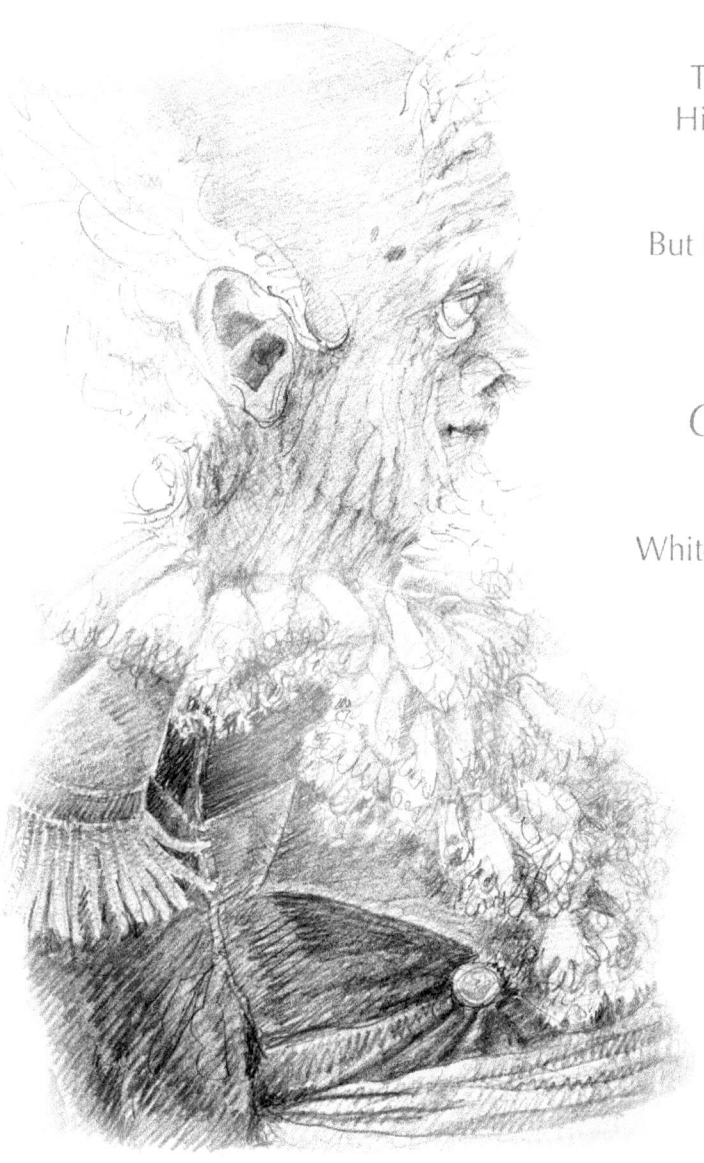

Delusions of Adequacy

There was an old codger who saw
Himself, mirrored, as without flaw—
I'd have mentioned to him
'Twas a painting, and dim,
But it would have embarrassed him raw.

Capture My Heart Instead

It's true that dignified old guy,
White-haired, bemedaled, caught my eye,
But here's the reason I'm upset:
He caught it on his epaulet.

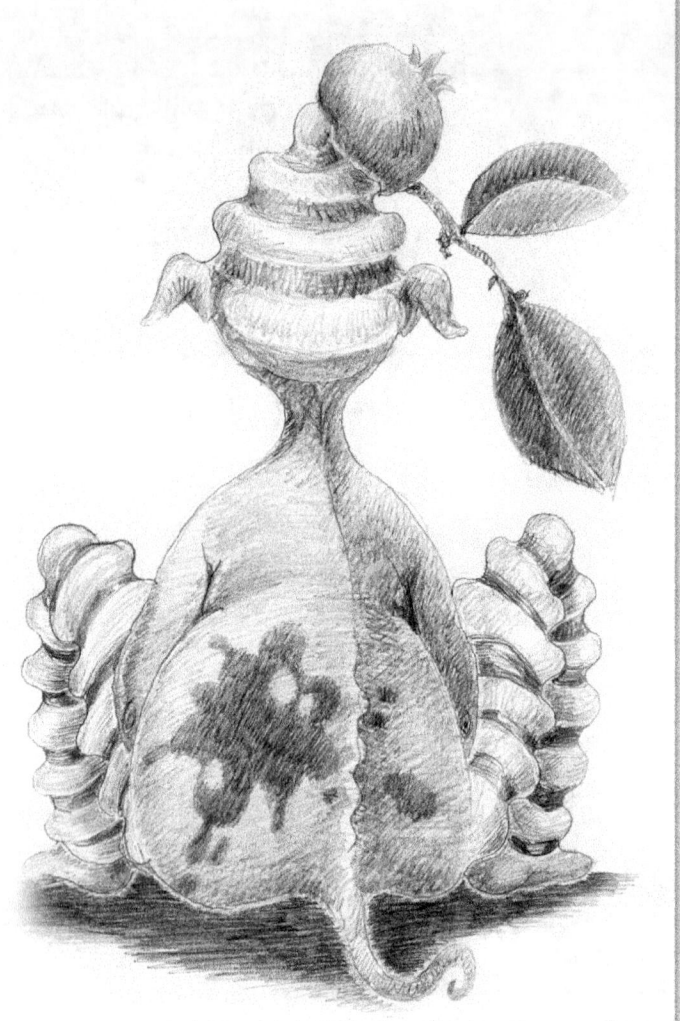

The Boingular Boolerant

Bum Luck

A Boingular Boolerant
bounced on her way
To borrow Bob's bicycle
one brilliant day
But bounded awry by a bit
and went Whoosh!
And found herself bunged
in a blueberry bush;
Though it sprang like a bungee
and blew her right out,
She was blotted with
indigo blobs all about
And bemoaned her besmirching
(I'll bet you would, too),
For the bump that she took
left her feeling quite blue.

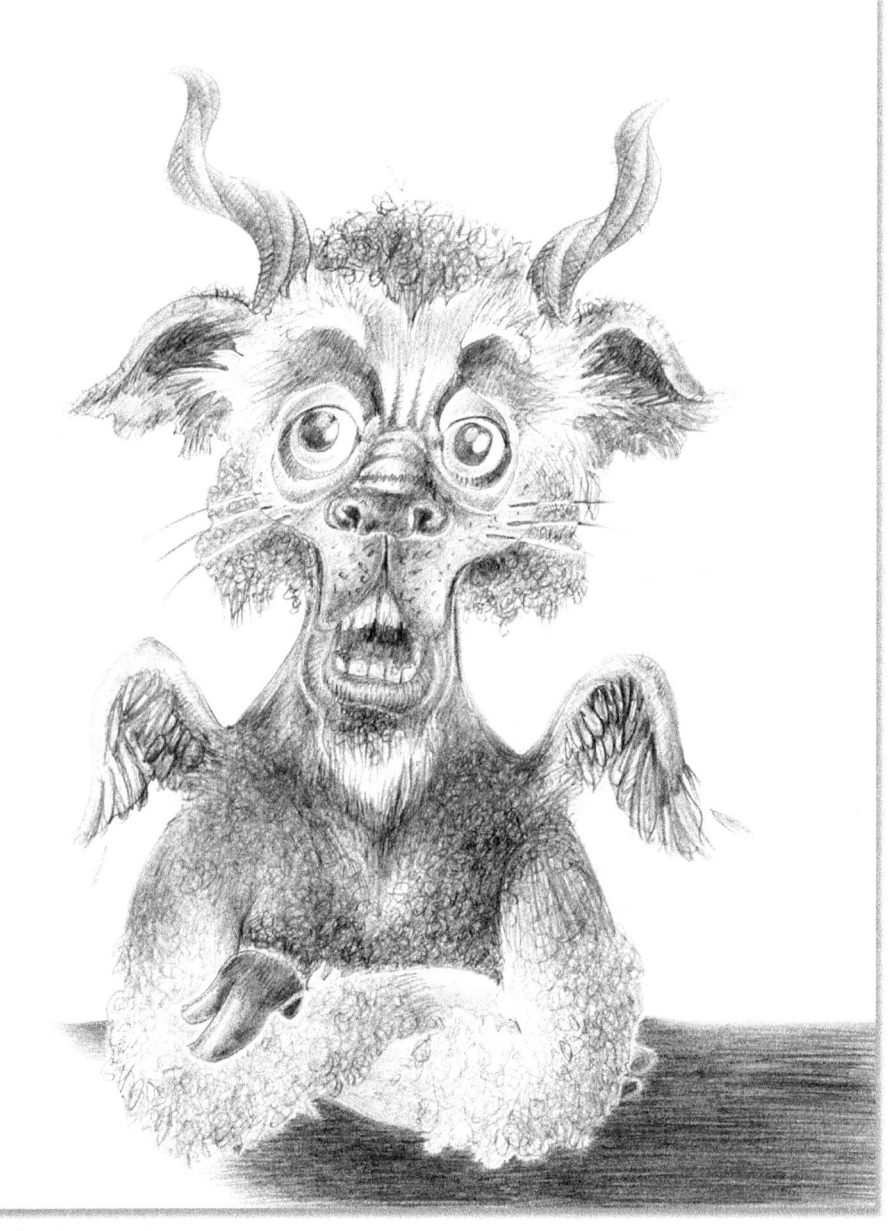

The Woolly Blephoricle

Prat-Fallen

There once was a Woolly Blephoricle who took a flight phantas-magorical that his pitiful wings, poor vestigial things, made hyster- (not the hoped-for histor-) ical.

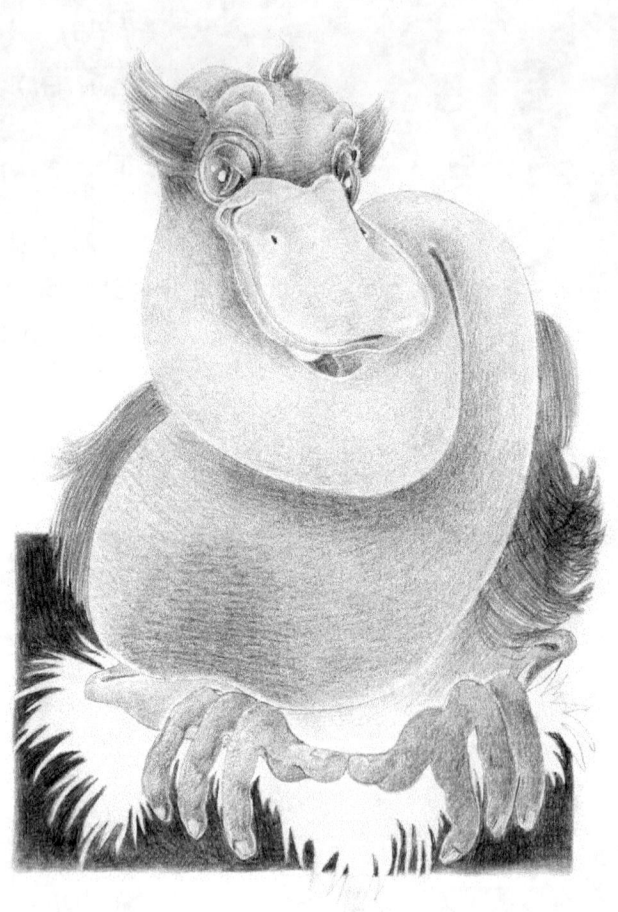

The Red-Breasted Smurk

No Need to be Leery

To see her, you'd
Think that the beast
Is grumpy or mean
Or deceased,
Or a bit of a snot—
I assure you,
She's not—
She isn't so
Bad in the least.
The Red-Breasted
Smurk has a look
That many a
Fellow's mistook
For a nasty-ish sort,
Not the cheery
Good sport
Who would love
A nice swim
In the brook.
That unfortunate
Grin on her face
Was just born there
And sticks
In that place
Like a grimace
From Heck
Stretching down
To her neck
But belies her
Astonishing grace.

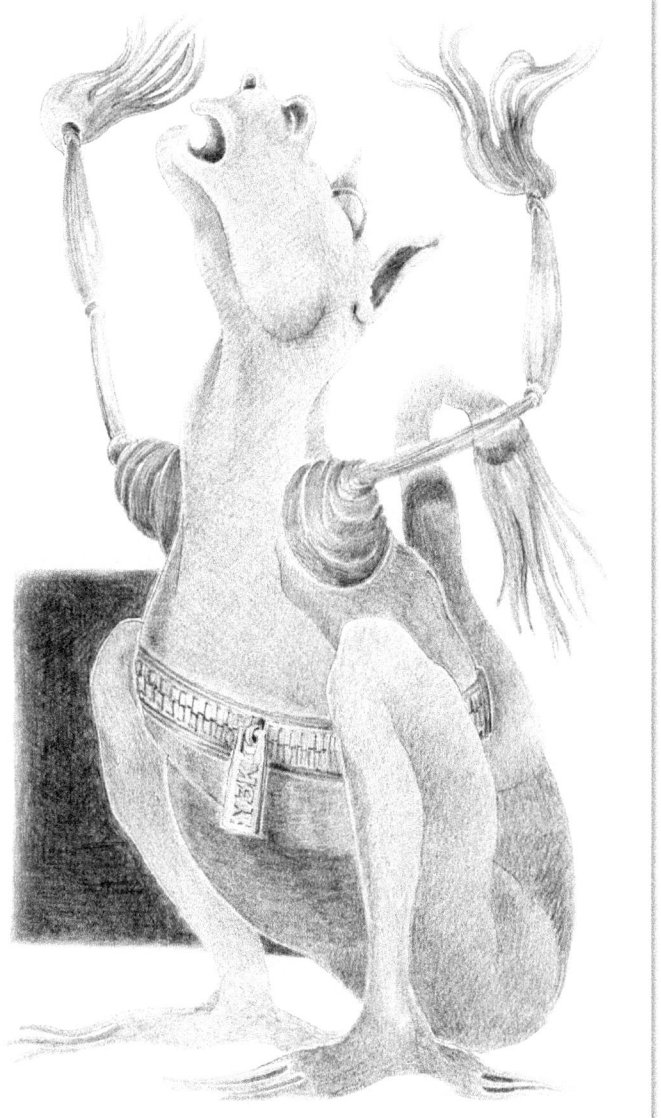

The Lesser Honkweevil

Lesser Is as Greater Does

With his shiny arms and teeth
And with his snout-like reptile nose,
His soft fringed fingers, tail and toes,
His muscled chest, kind heart beneath,
The Honkweevil is popular
Amongst his kind and others, too,
And when he comes along to woo,
The womenfolk from near and far
Can hear his loud melodic song
Of honking, hooting, gargling notes,
Sending up waves beneath the boats
And casting spells upon the throng
Who gather on the shore to see
His male display of pomp and style
And hear his crooning with a smile,
Then vie for who his mate will be,
For though he's Lesser of his race,
There is none greater in this place.

More than Meets the Eye

That oddball bird the Crumplebeak Is neither mutant, sport, nor freak,
But rather is the end result Of shooting from a catapult
In an attempt at wingless flight That led, instead, one fateful night,
To spearing beak-first into stone—A happenstance that all alone
Might well have shaped a face for life—But as it happened, both a wife
And husband made the same wild try On that same night, and that is why
Their offspring all share this one mark Of their attempting to embark On an extraordinary fling—
Plus, one more impressive thing Is that their children also hold The same propensity for bold Decisive action, so don't scoff— The Crumplebeak still can't take off On an extensive flight, but she Is as courageous as can be

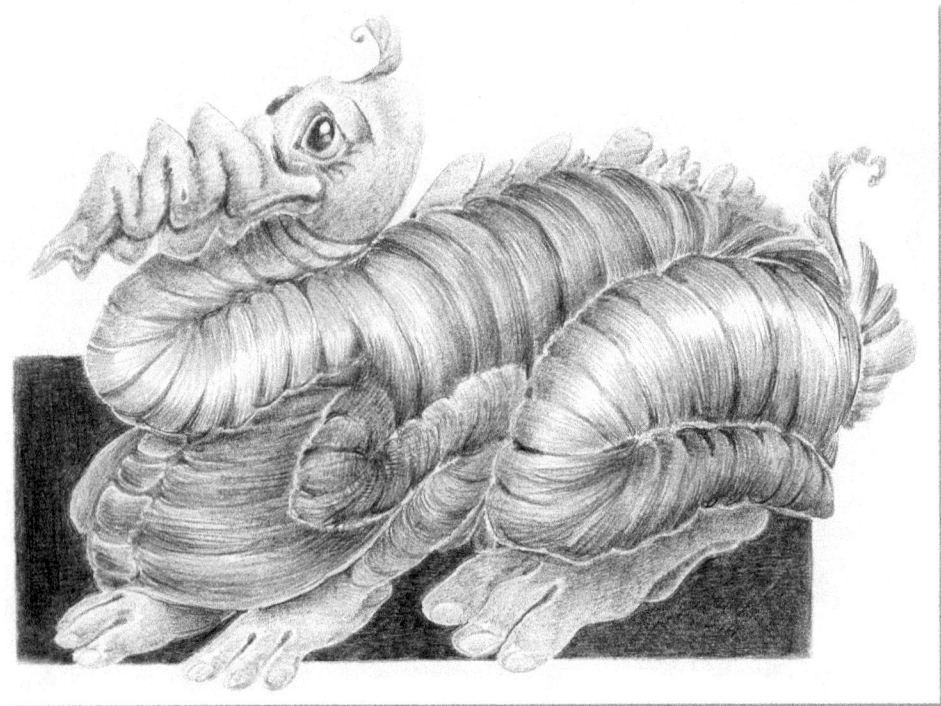

The Crumplebeak

The Social Lives of Strange Creatures

To those who don't speak the language, Appearances often deceive,
For the cultural implications Of a moue or a flick of the sleeve,
Of raised eyebrows, bared teeth, ruffled feathers, And all of those outwardly seen
Expressions and gestures and nuanced Positions may look like they mean
One thing when the posturing creatures Are saying another thing quite—
Then again, don't assume anything, just in case You get tangled amid a big fight!

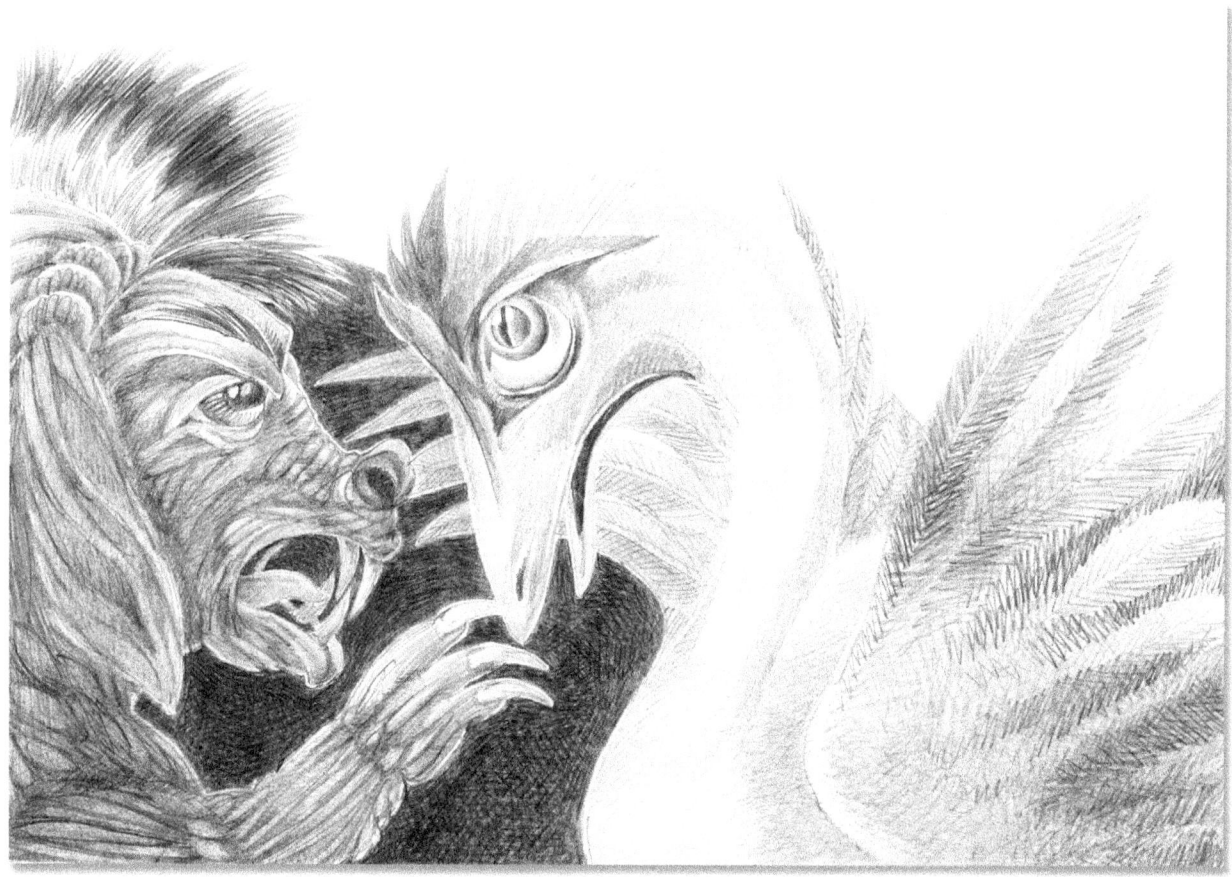

Strange Creatures One & Two

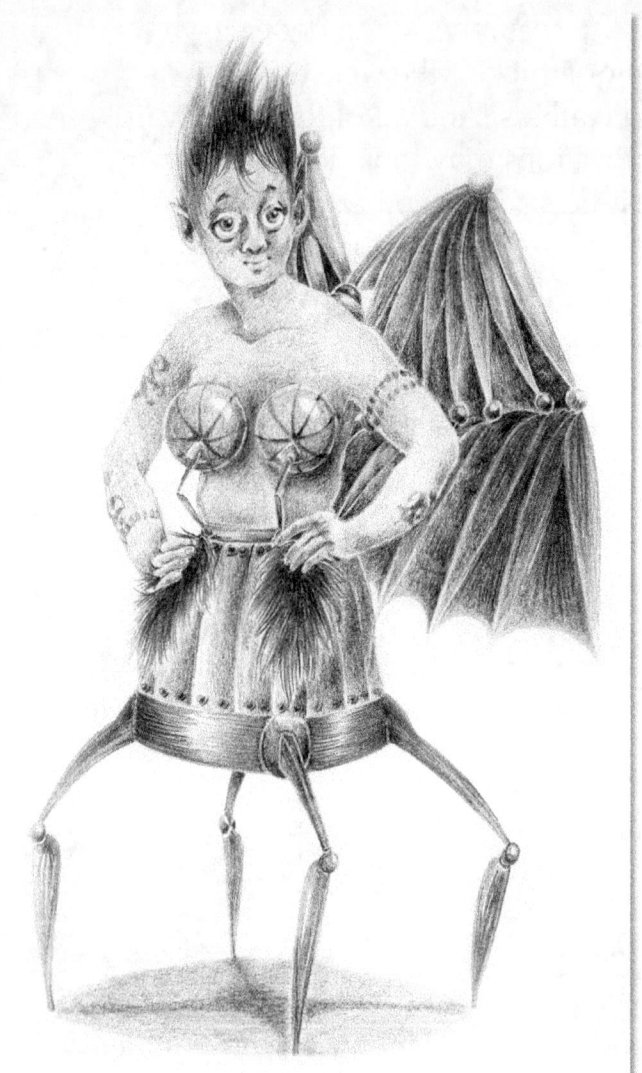

The Attenuated Highflinger

Hot Stuff, with a Twist or Two

That droll little gal, the Highflinger,
Great dancer she's not, nor a singer—
When she leaps in the air,
I must say, to be fair,
She's got style, and she sure is a zinger—
She has very few, to be sure,
Talents and even less of allure,
With legs attenuated
And un-orchestrated,
Still, she holds much intrigue for a viewer.

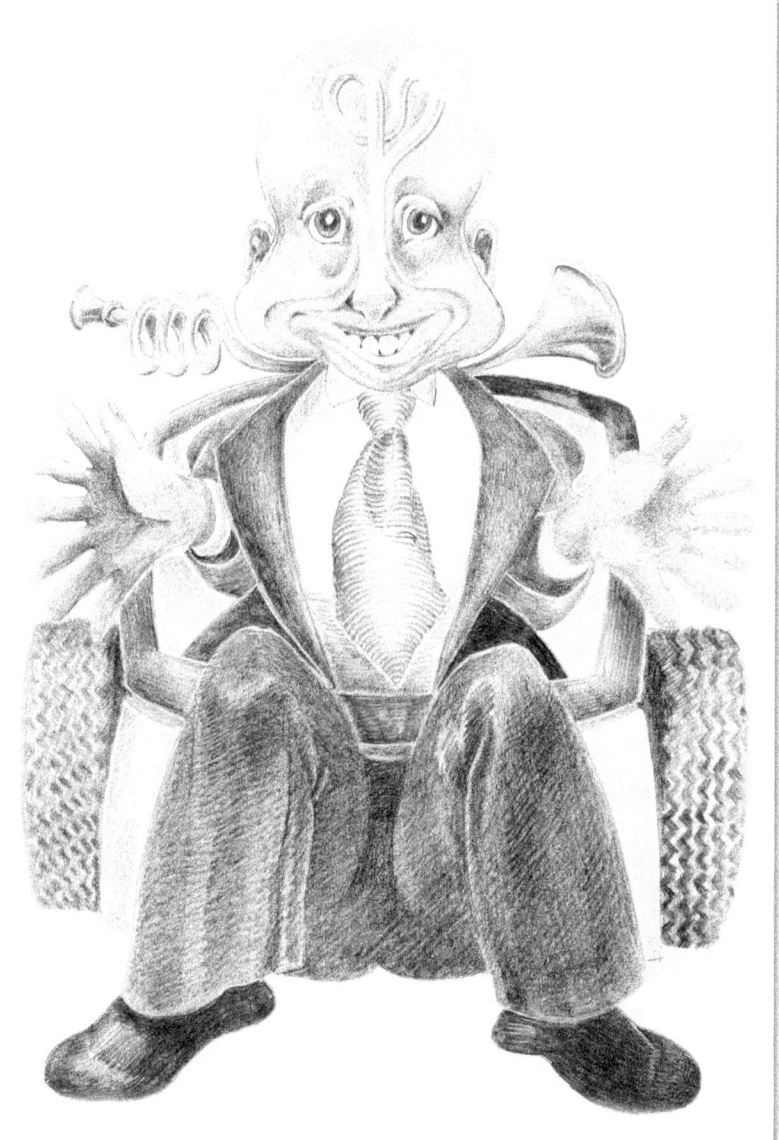

The Mildly Unpleasant Uckhurrinse

Mildly-Unpleasant Single Seeks Same

He is bulbous and
shiny and active,
The Mildly-Unpleasant
Uckhurrinse,
    His speech somewhat
    stilted, redactive,
    And he sells
    term life insurance.
He's not got the least
sense his behavior
Is so awkward,
ignoble, bombastic,
    And his toneless
    off-putting talk's flavor
    Makes his hearers
    think thoughts
    dark and drastic.
The Uckhurrinse
means well,
but is gauche
Beyond rescue and so
addle-pate-y
    That his only hope
    (there's just a skosh)
    Is to find him
    an Unpleasant lady.

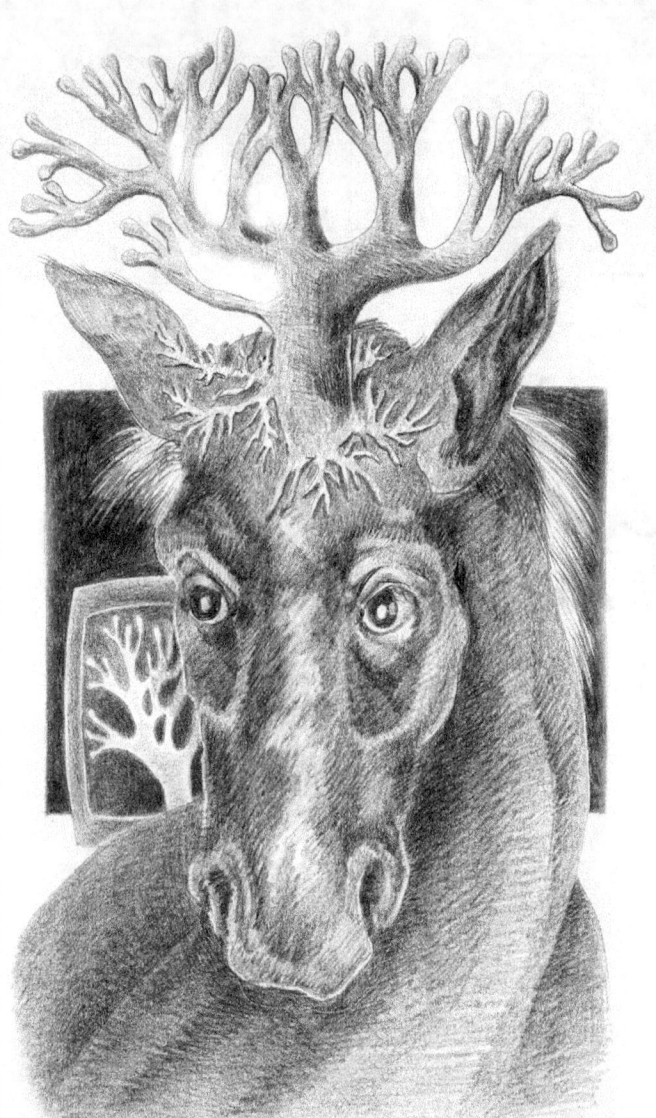

The Splendid Arbicorn

I Myth You

The wingèd horse,
I apprehend,
Is that great equine
Pegasus,
But is he real
Or just pretend?
I will go ask
Professor Zeus.
Me, I am just
Content, of course,
To be a different
Sort of horse,
An equine well-
Equipped with twigs
Upon my brow,
And skilled at jigs,
Though I might wish
There were a mare
With matching dancing
Skills and hair.

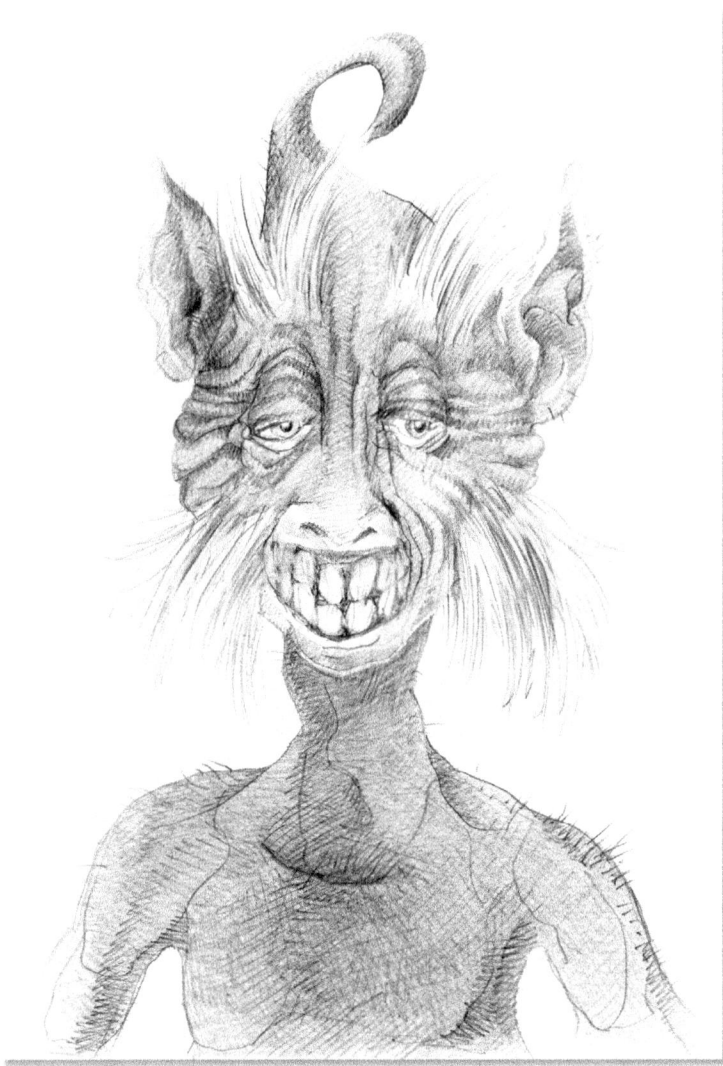

The Dentitious Friskler

Our Frisky Friend

The Friskler's fine dentition so
Impresses one and all,
He cannot help but be adored,
And left and right they fall
In admiration at his feet,
Delirious, enraptured,
To see this brilliant, charming, sweet,
Great grin by which they're captured.
It's good the Friskler has that smile:
Without it, in the end,
His habit of emitting slime
Would lose him every friend.

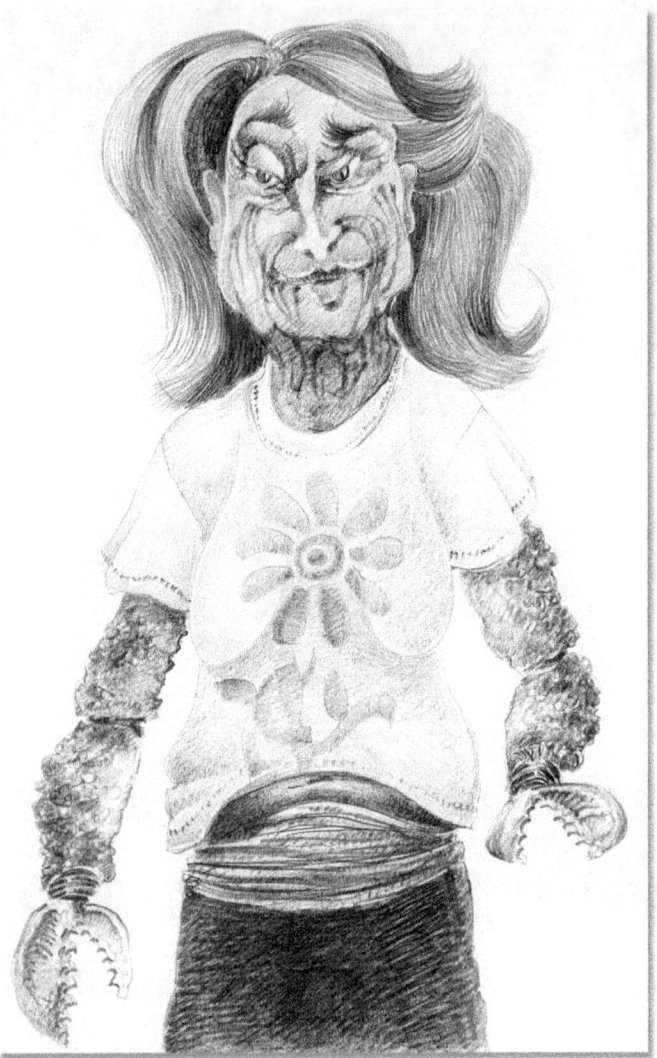
The Rancid Yellowpip

Pretty Homely

For modest, slender waist and hip,
The fearful Rancid Yellowpip
Has few competitors, and yet
Is homely as a beast can get—
Some say it's for her strong perfume,
So like the odor of the tomb;
Some say it's that her mode of dress
Is so outdated, hair a mess;
Some say it's something missing from
Her ("one stick shy of a pack of gum");
Some say it's for her lack of charms;
But I suspect her warty arms
And pincer hands contribute, too,
To her un-loveliness, don't you?

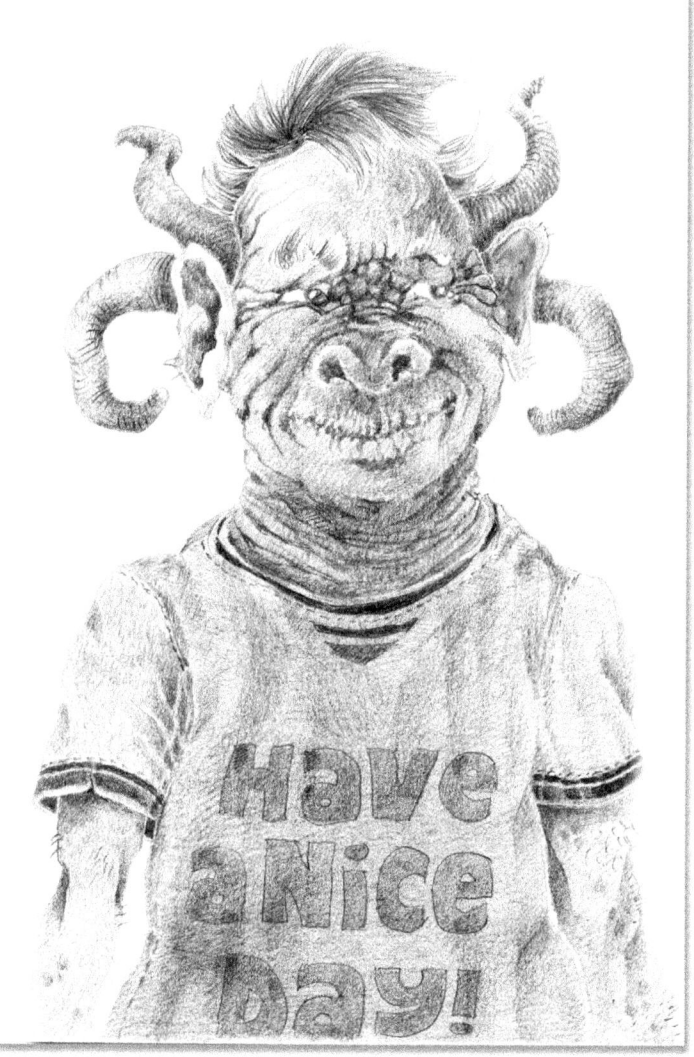

The Peristaltic Jackanapes

Trolling for Lady-Friends

After a meal of gravel and sand,
He thinks it's grand to take a stroll
Among the oysters on the strand
With weeds in hand, the wizened troll
With fuzzy eyebrows, rippling throat,
Horns like a goat, his nose an ape's;
Yet not from beauty so remote,
The Peristaltic Jackanapes
Still has allure for lady-kind,
Who quickly find abundant charm
In his exquisite manners, mind,
And wide behind; his wiry arm,
His scent like violets, his eyes
Seeming so wise; the half-moon brand
Upon his forehead, small in size;
That he can gargle on demand—
This last, in fact, a potent draw,
Lest you guffaw, or worst of all, tick
Off as useless throat and jaw
Skills if *your* gifts aren't peristaltic.

Odds Against

We all have aspirations, and
Have wishes, dreams and hopes,
But none more touching than those of
The Blimhock as he slopes
Around the house he's made inside
A poison toadstool's cap,
Keeping the faith that it won't
Kill him while he takes his nap;
No life's-ambition stronger or
More poignant than his own
That he won't soon be crushed
Beneath its heavy lintel stone;
None have a drive more moving or
Existence quite so frail,
And yet each day he smilingly
Renews it, without fail.
This is a creature that we should
Admire, who perseveres
Against all odds and, likely,
Will outlast us all by years.

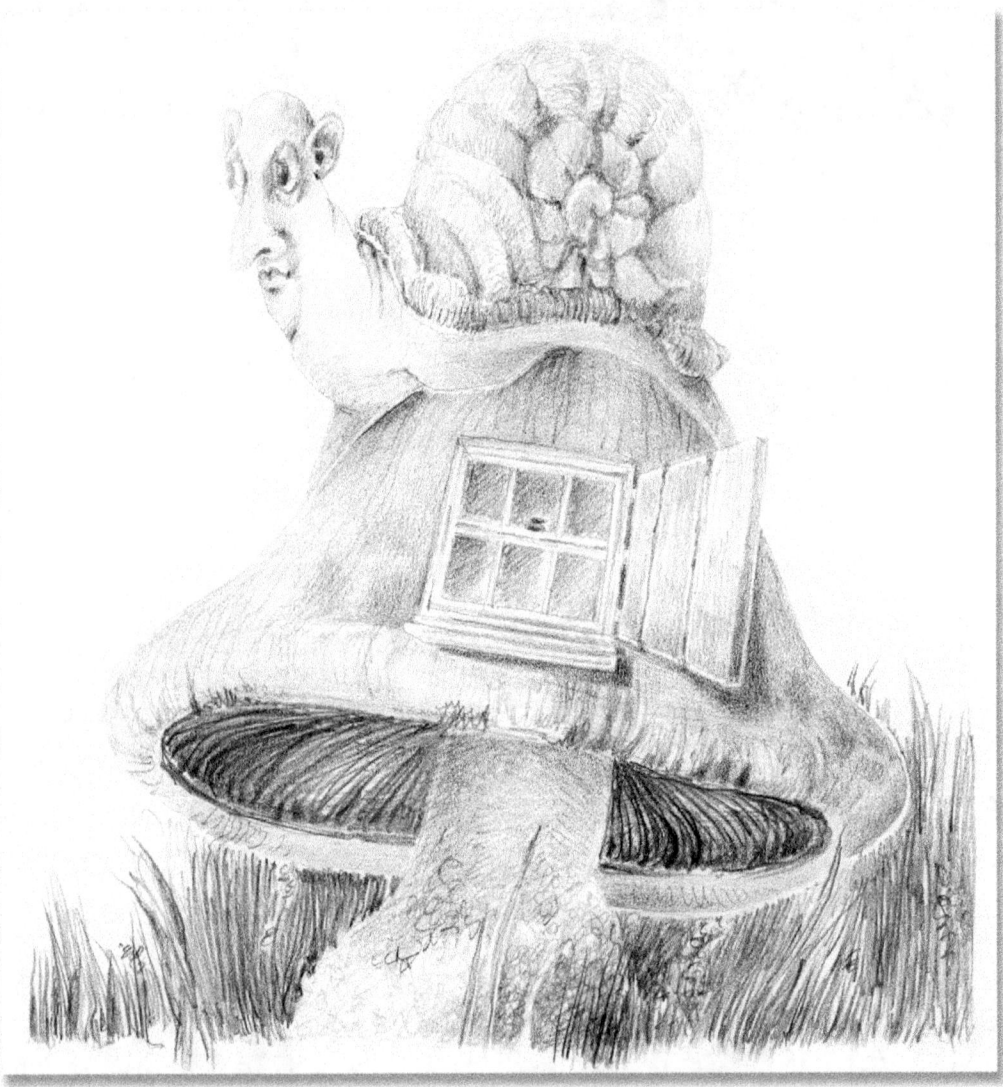

The Aspirational Blimhock

Another Myth without Meaning

Deep in the convoluted earth
And subterranean lakes and pools
Strange beings drift about in schools—
Although, perhaps, there is a dearth
Of discipline belies that term,
For these odd fellows, having three
Heads thinking independently,
More likely are to flop and squirm
In random ways while paddling by
With their eight-legged stroke askew,
Just wandering, as such will do
When every mind decides to try
Its own direction, tangent, way,
And tries to swim with that intent,
Not knowing that the others went
After another thought, so they
Just circle in their fabled caves
And ramble, making futile waves.

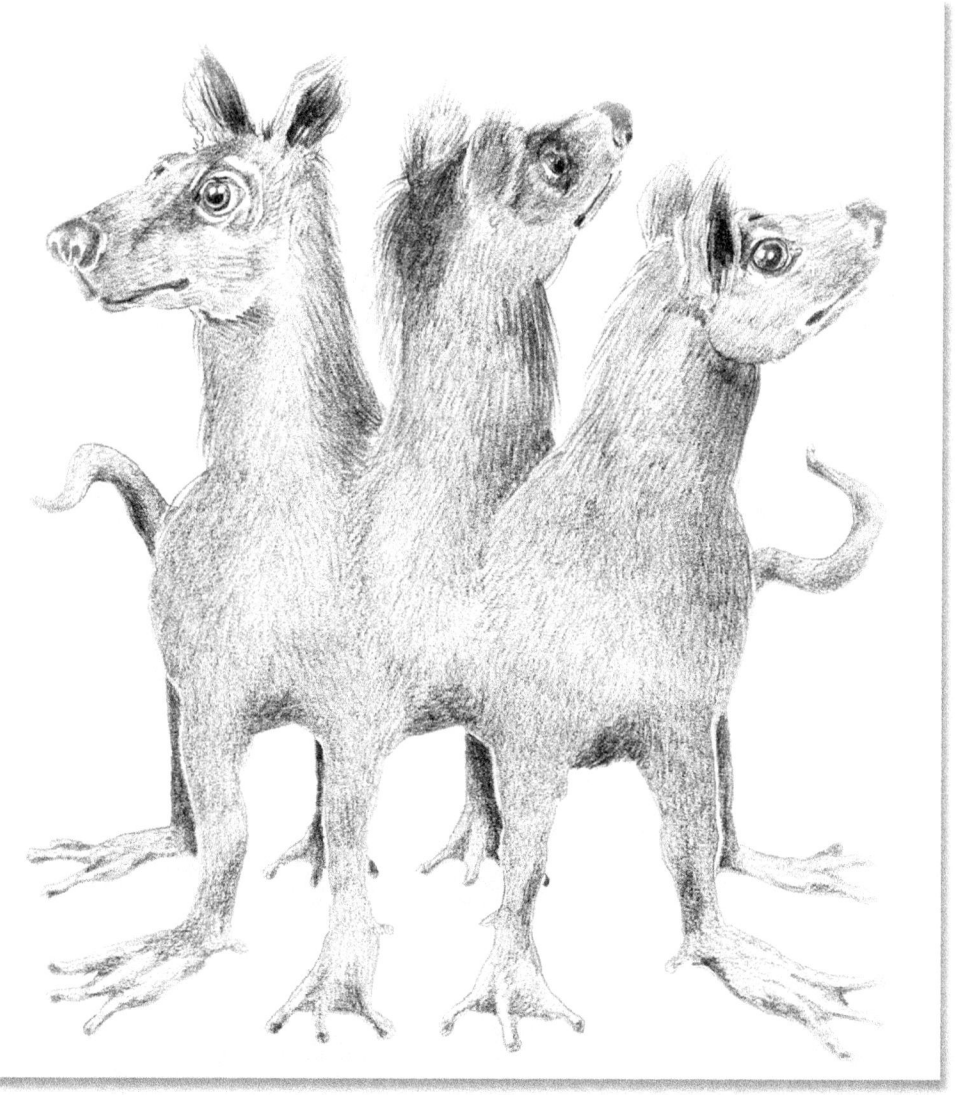

The Hirsute Tricranial Pondpaddler

Cast Iron Stomach

The Glaucous Polydactyl Snupp
Knocks rhubarb down and eats it up
And, in a trick none else achieves,
Survives eating its poison leaves,
Along with rhododendron, yew,
And things she found under the pew
In church while munching on barbed wire
To drown the singing of the choir;

After the anthem, she communes
By gnawing stuff from the spittoons,
Licking lead off the organ pipes,
And chewing bugs of several types,
But shuns the wine, for that intinction,
She is sure, would cause extinction.
So she dines and sups on death,
Yet suffers only mild bad breath.

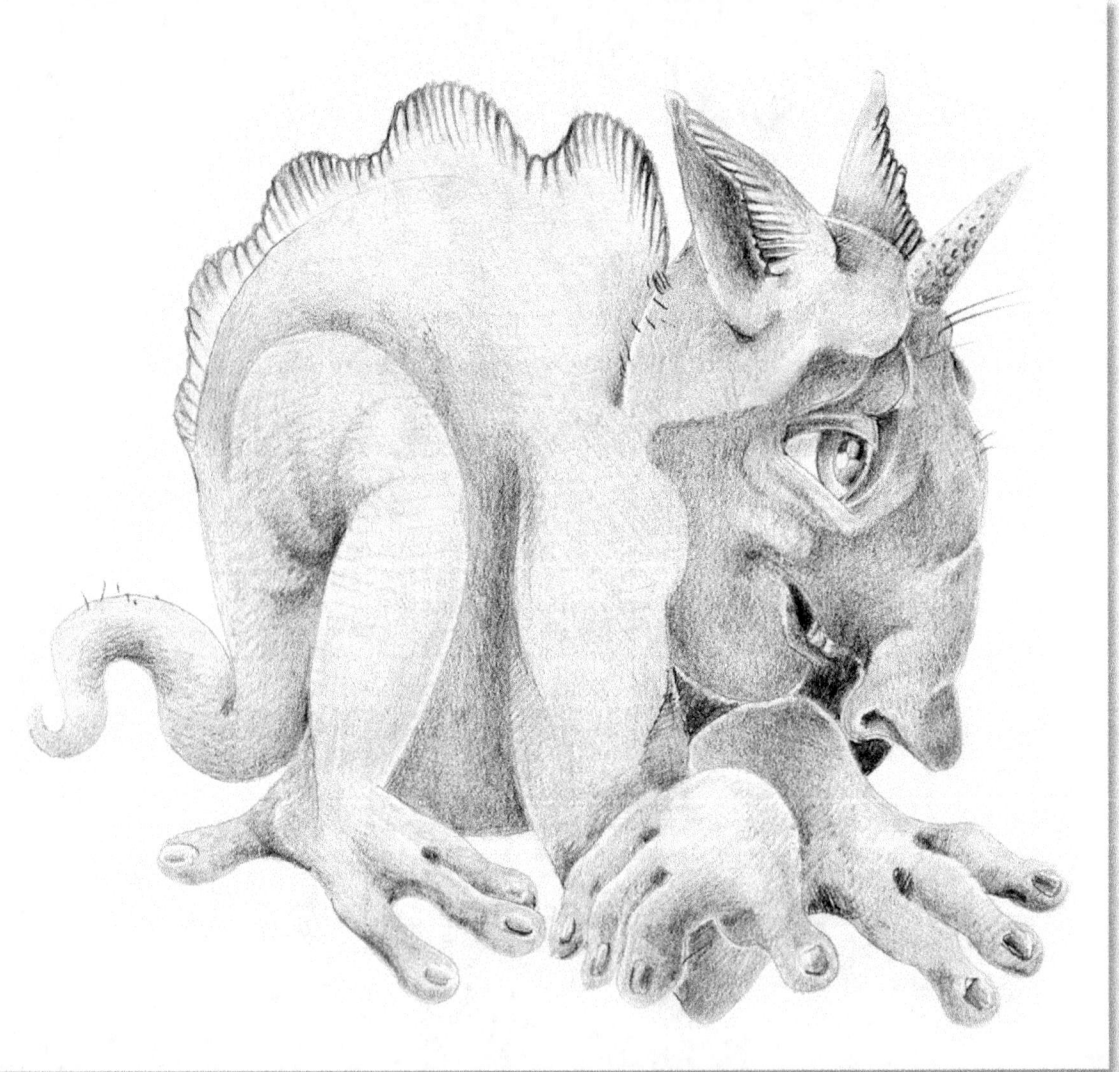

The Glaucous Polydactyl Snupp

Progress is Progress

Persistent though his nature is,
The Whooshing Flimble finds that his
Ability to get things done
Is undermined by lust for fun,
And so he's often sped off track
When gripped by an amuse-attack,
And off on different tangents races,
But at the least, it takes him places!

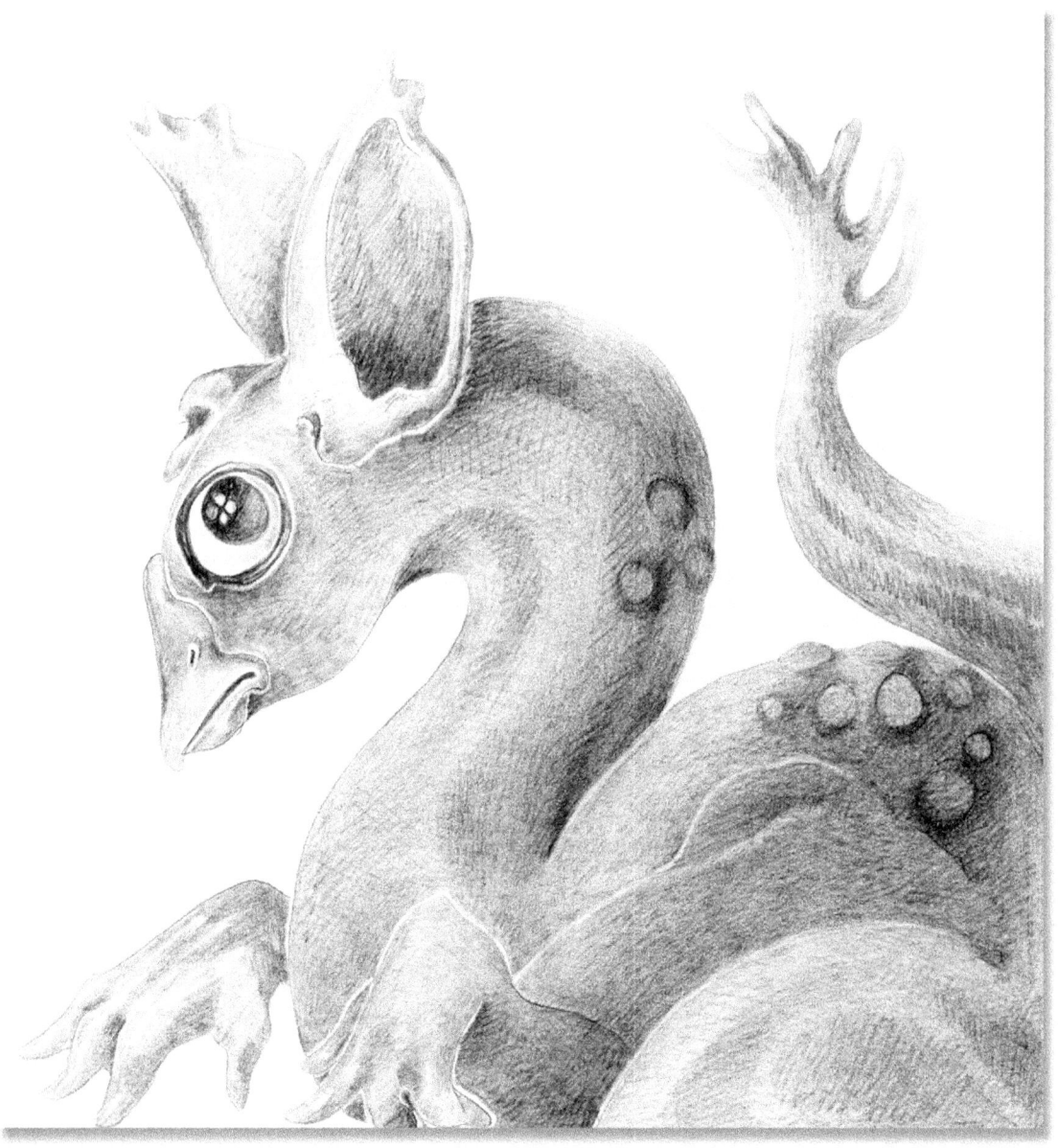

The Whooshing Flimble

He Hates Us All Equally

This fellow, whom I've never met,
Is ornery as a guy could get,
Or so I'm told by those who know,
For I'm unwilling still to go
And spend a moment near to one
Whose sole idea of having fun
Is blowing bubbles from his pipe
That's filled with saponaceous tripe
With the extremely rancid smell
Of—seemingly—where corpses dwell,
Then watch the bubbles float on by
And pop his neighbors in the eye
Or suck into their nostrils, too—
So I avoid him, as should you.

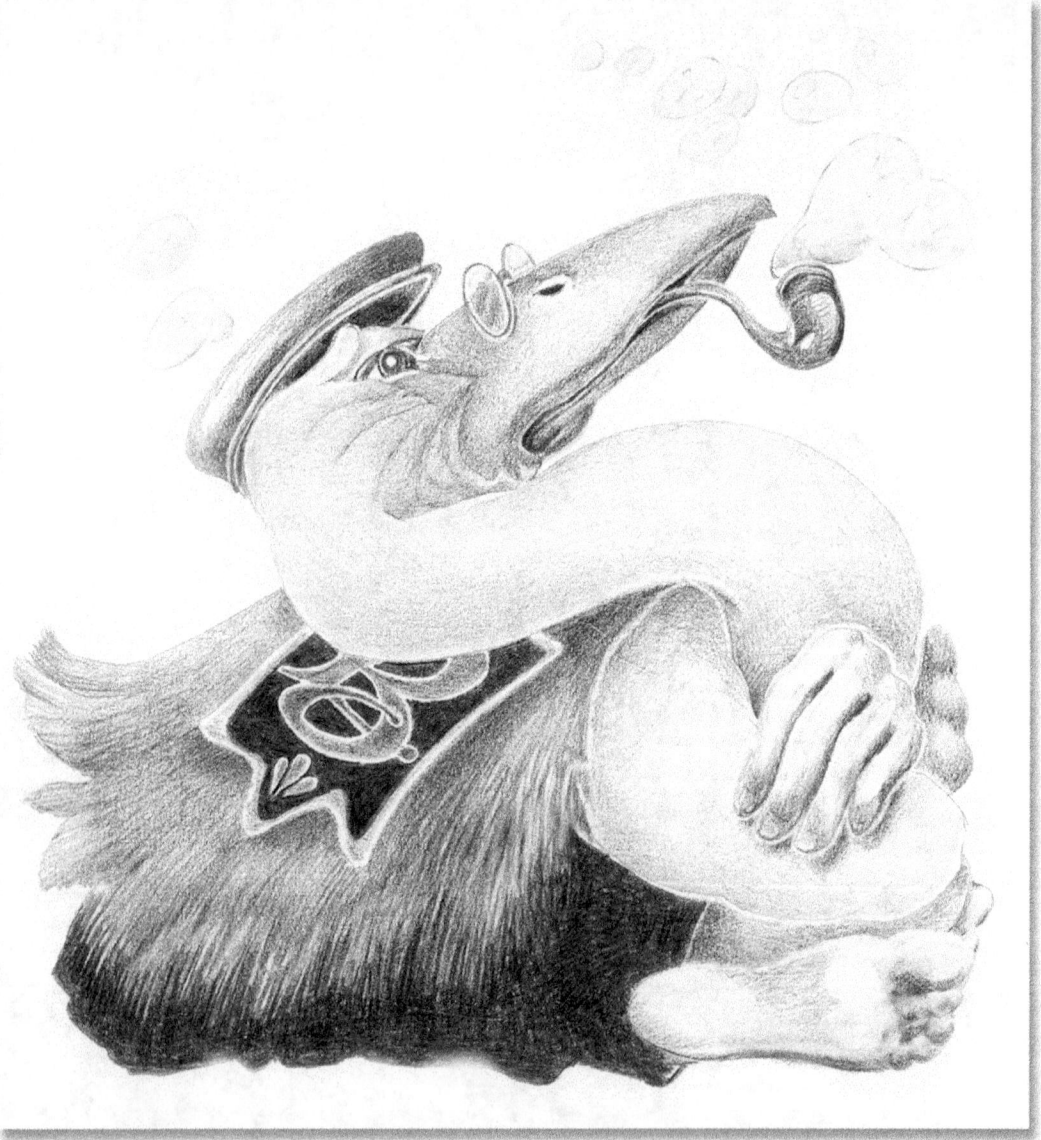

The Buddle

Everybody's Best Friend

On the other hand, the Diffulous Squizz,
Who may be the jolliest beast there is,
I would seek out on any day
As companion, friend and pal at play,
For when she sneezes, candy flies
Out from her spout before your eyes,
And in her tentacles she can hold
A million dollars in coins of gold
To sprinkle about if she's in the mood,
Which she often is, and is never rude,
And best of all, if she'll kiss your cheek,
Everything tastes of peach for a week,
And her hugs—with all those tentacles going—
Make her a cuddler well worth knowing.

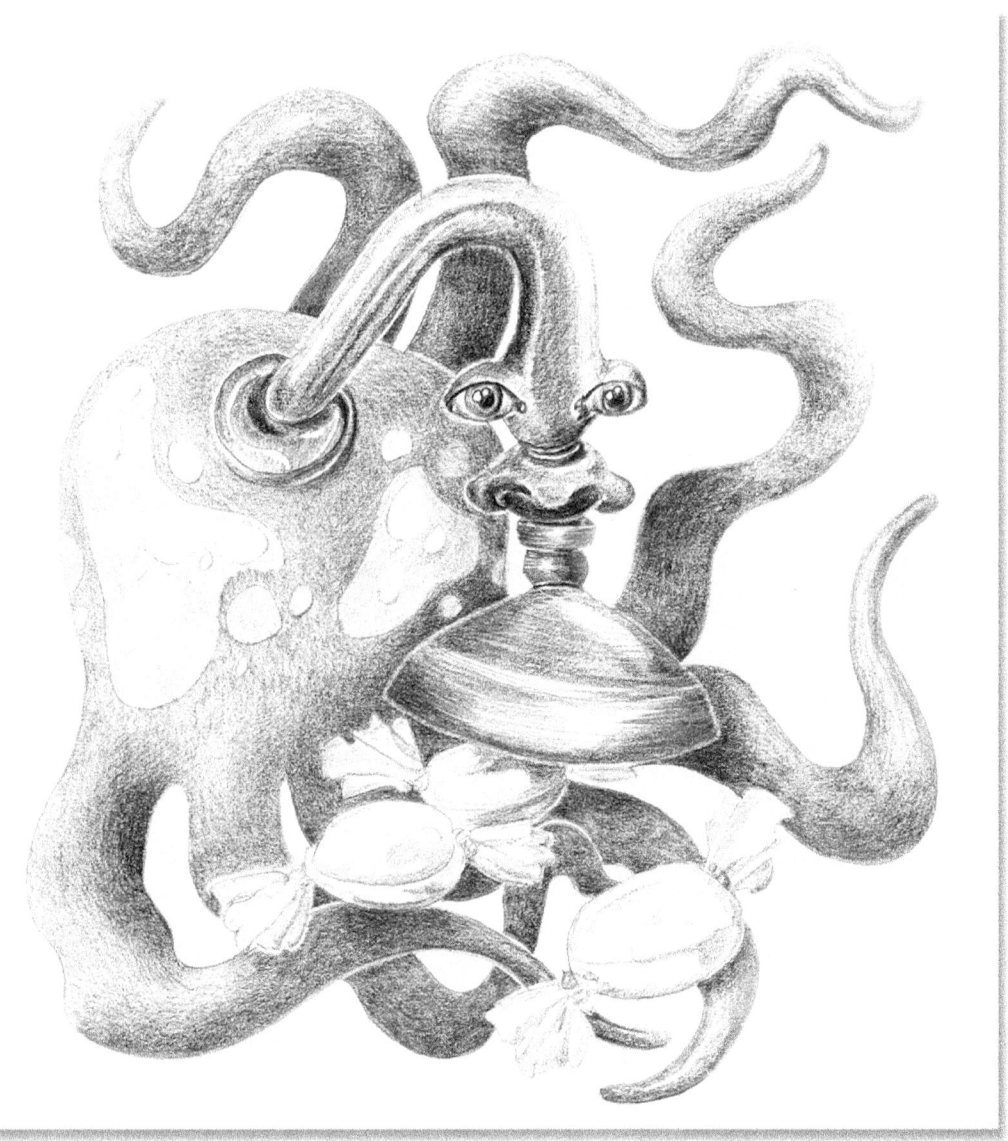

The Diffulous Squizz

Absorption

The Gompilatious Froobitant's A handsome beast in shoes and pants
Who, though he paints and sings and cooks, Would rather get by on his looks,
And so instead of skiing, knitting, Or good deeds, he prefers sitting
By the curb, his daily station, Showing off his gompilation
To the passing gawkers whose Admiring of his pants and shoes
And general handsomeness he craves, Then goes at evening to his cave's
Dull ease, repeats his daily cant, So pleased that he's a Froobitant.

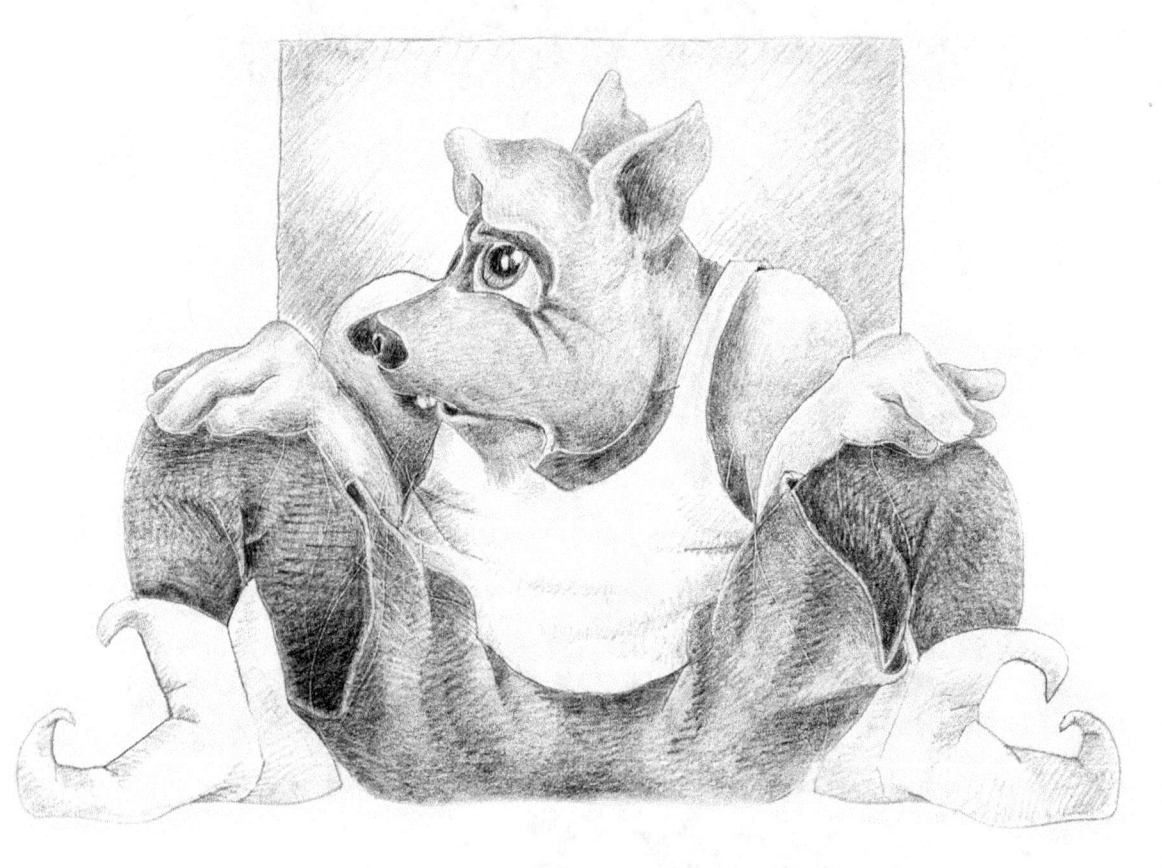

The Gompilatious Froobitant

In Search of a Calling

Superheroes we have many, though perhaps not needing any:
Case in point, the SuperBooby, built just slightly inner-tube-y
And with pointless attributes and superpowers, like the glutes
That with their springy muscle tone let him leap up or remain prone
For hours, motionless, without wearing his butt or patience out;
He has wings, too: their muscle bands don't fly but function more as hands
(Albeit awkward ones, at best); his slick hair rises to a crest
That could deflect a tidal wave, if that were what he were to save
A person from, but that won't come, as he calls Arizona home--
He has six hands, which might be handy (no pun meant), but understand, he
Only has two thumbs, which meet the fingers on his hand-like feet,
So, to gain dexterous command, he cannot really crouch or stand
But must invert and use what those of us would think of as his toes--
Not that it's wrong, just that delay might mean the chance has passed away
Before Our Hero intervenes, which limits both his speed and means;
At least, if limited in scope, he's brave, and never gives up hope.

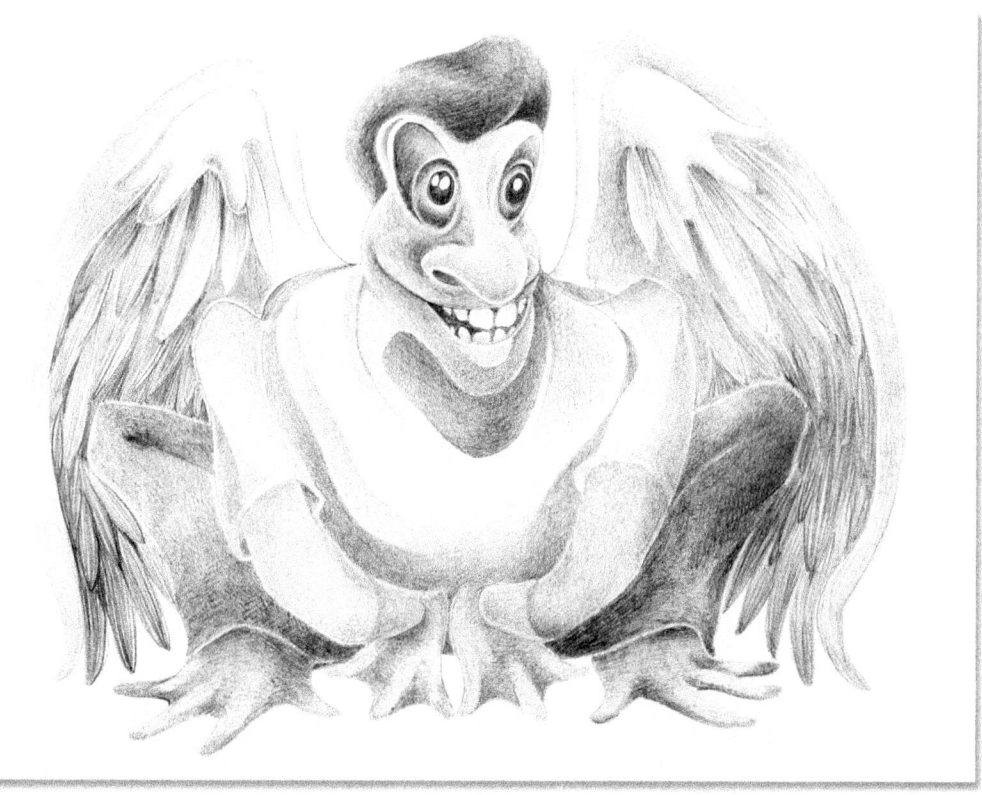

The Redundant SuperBooby

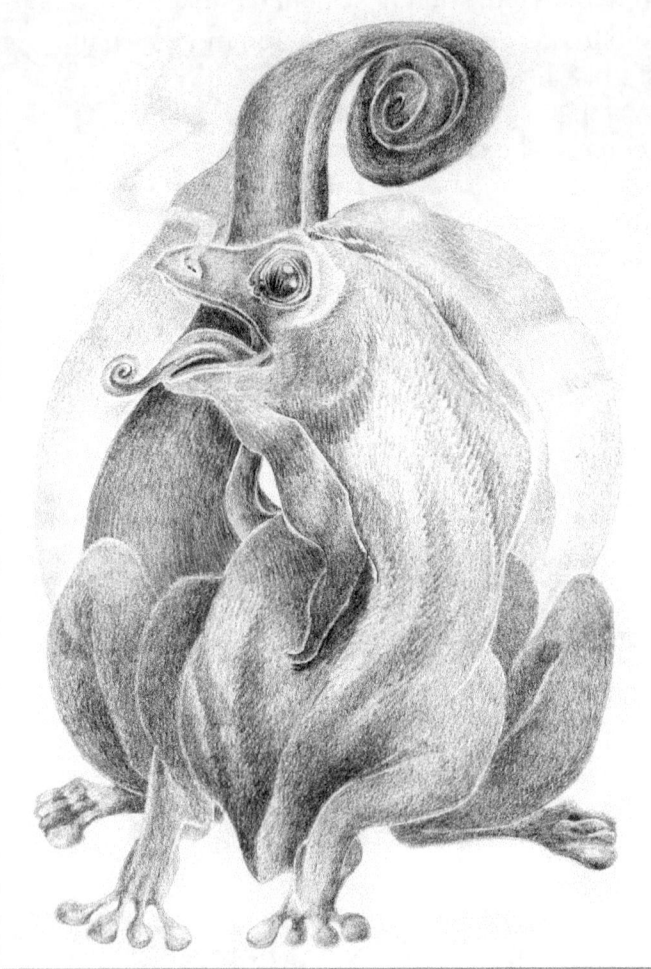

The Morticle

So Many Fine Features

The Morticle, surprisingly,
though marvelous remains unsung
Despite her dainty curling tail
and even nicer coiling tongue,
The sticky-pads upon her toes
so she adheres each step she goes,
Her scaly skin and ruffled ruff,
reptilian twinkle in her eyes—
Yes, all these beauties aren't enough,
and she remains, to my surprise,
Unknown, but if I can't decode her
Mystery, perhaps her odor,
Quite like filthy socks in tone,
Impedes her being better known.

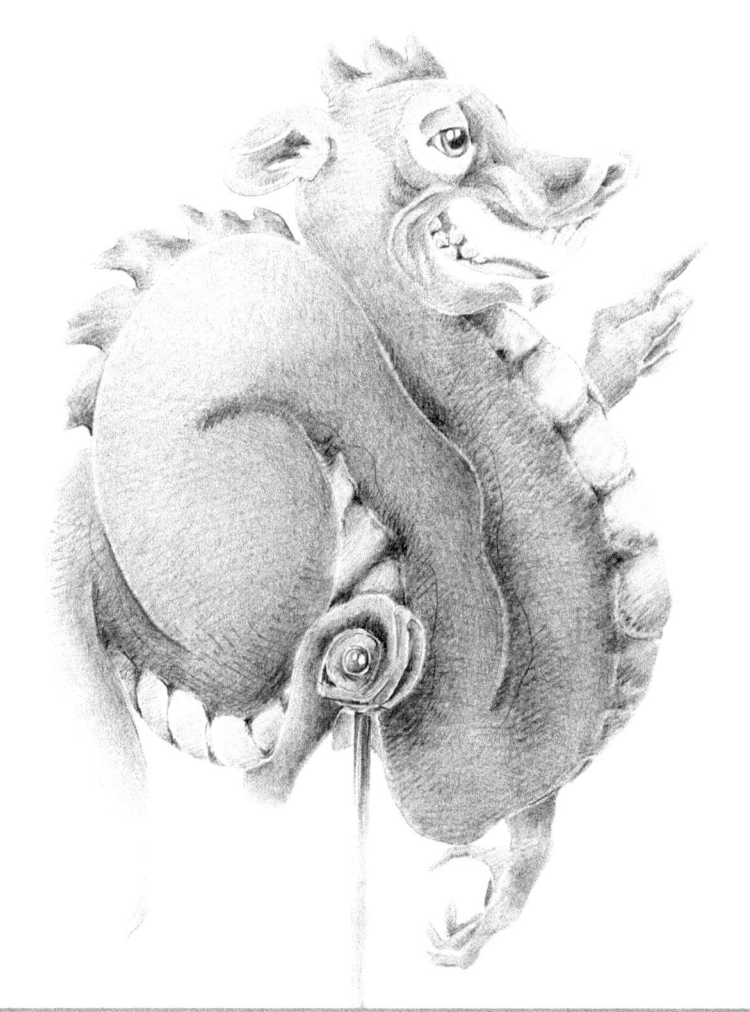

The Chattybogle

As I was Just Saying . . .

There was a chatty dragon who
Could not resist a tale
He hung around and nattered,
Yakked and gabbled without fail,
And rarely had a point or made
It to the final part
Before his audience would find
That they were losing heart
(And possibly their minds) and must
Go dashing for the door
To make escape, and hope
Not to go near him anymore,
Until one day a clever child
Enticed the beast to eat
A lovely sticky peanut butter
Spoonful for a treat,
Since when he's less loquacious,
Having still a lot to say
But finding peanut butter
(How delicious!) in the way,
So if you find you're plagued
By a long-winded, tireless nutter,
I recommend you arm yourself
With jars of peanut butter

Under Intense Pressure

Do not trouble him with your
Existence, for the Hipposaur
Has urgent business to attend
And is equipped toward that end
With hose and gauges, meters, clocks,
And tubes that spiral as he walks,
Connecting him with others driven
By the same tasks he is given—
If you should interrupt the flow
Of his engagement, he won't know
What he should do—the stress increases
And he'll burst into a million pieces

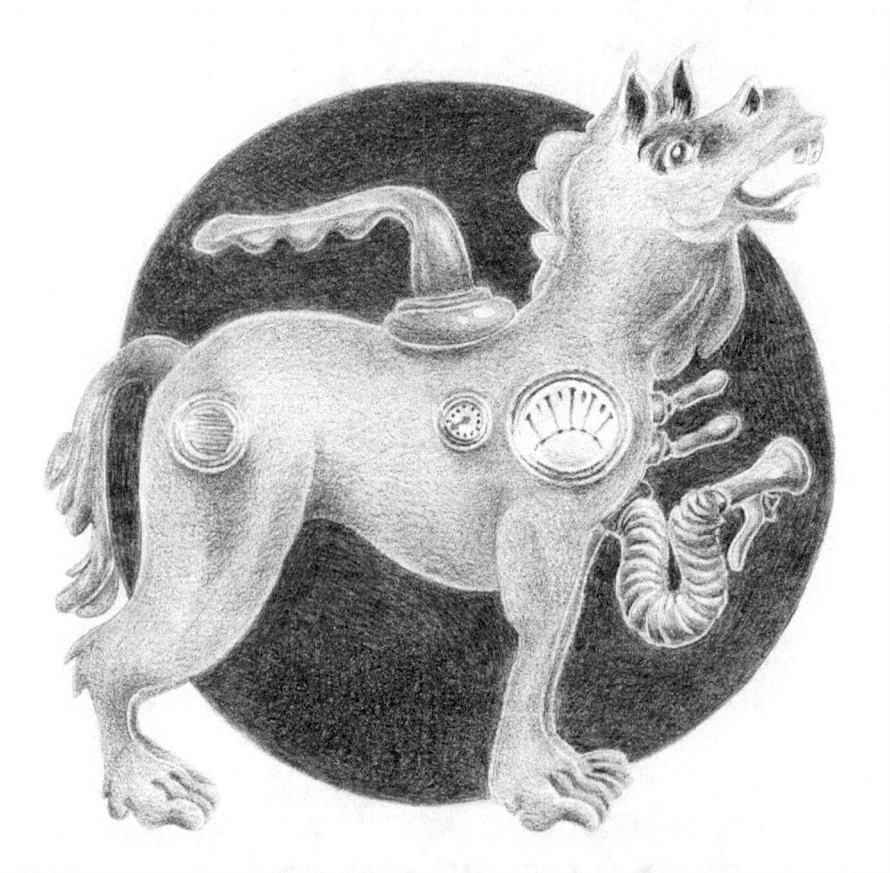

The Steam-Powered Leopedal Hipposaur

The Confounded Hootynoggin

On days of perplexity (all are such days),
This Confounded fellow lives in a haze
Of wondering what he intended to do
When he left home that morning in Kalamazoo,
So mostly, he wanders round scratching his chin
Or his noggin (it's left his down coat mighty thin)
And muttering quizzically, pacing the floor,
And seldom progressing beyond right next door.
For all his confusion, he's well liked by folks
For his tuneful response to their practical jokes.

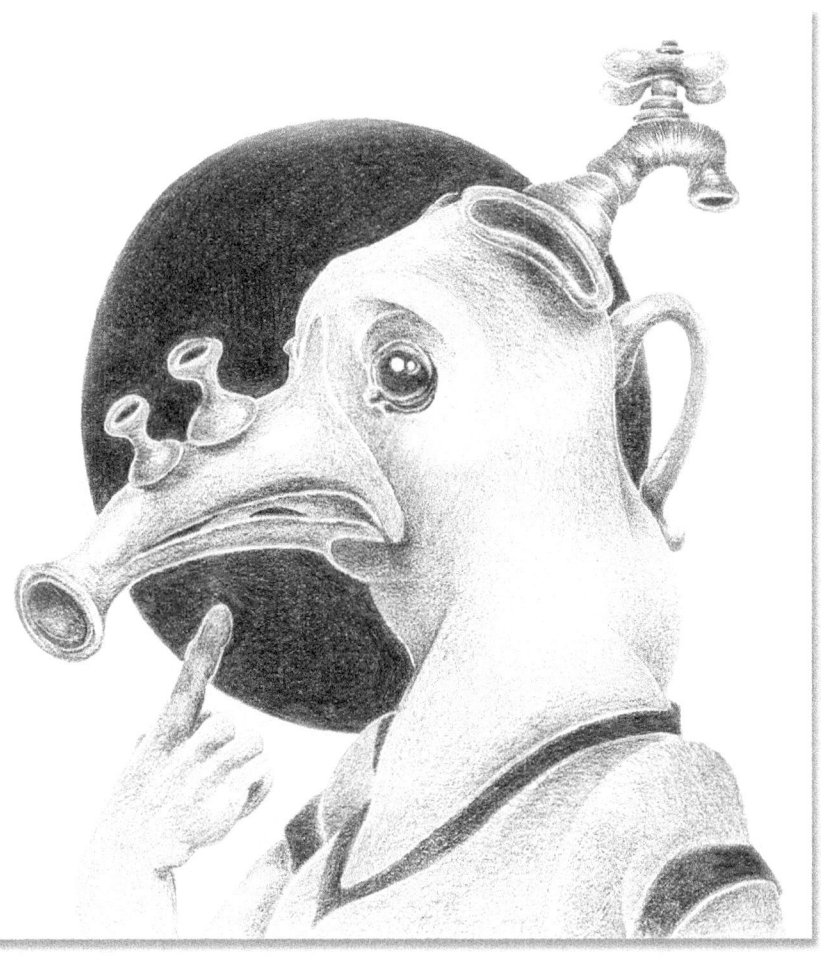

The Confounded Hootynoggin

Underground Entertainments

Under a stately poplar stump There lives a Bifurcated Wump
The roots that serve as beams in there Rest in the parting of his hair
And since the ceiling hangs so low Crouched on his belly he must go
But he is comfortable too And finds it all worthwhile to do
Because the roots end in a ditch With silver filled, so he is rich
And has a butler and a maid Who also crawl around thus splayed
And willingly: the pay is great And all play poker after eight.

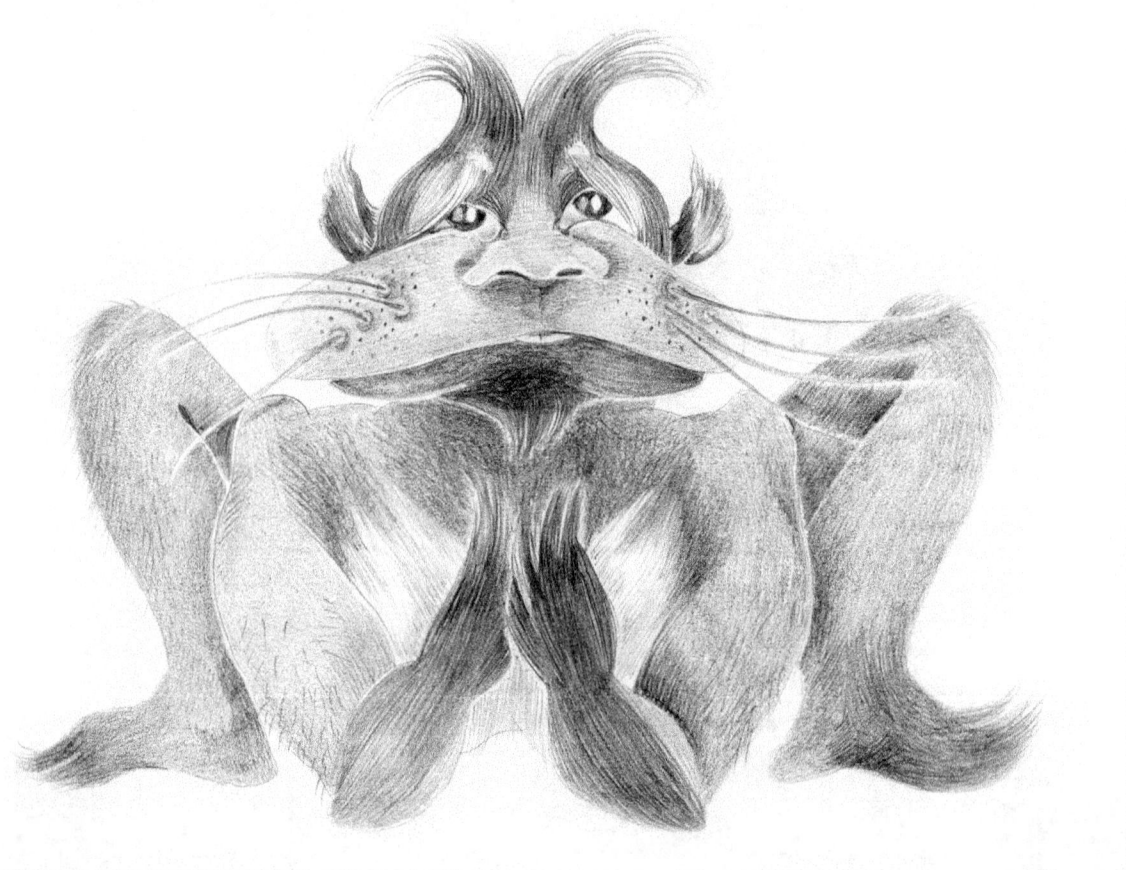

The Bifurcated Wump

Charm for Its Own Sake is Quite Sufficient

Amusing in his winsome, happy, sweet, meandering way,
This tusked and horned, piebald round fellow often saves the day
By simply entering the room to make his presence known,
For though he's not a superhero full of strength high-flown
And skills and talents made for rescuing or solving crime,
His mere appearance is so dear it cheers us every time;
Along with that, his hopping gait that wheels him wall to wall
Brightens the day and brings a new enchantment to us all

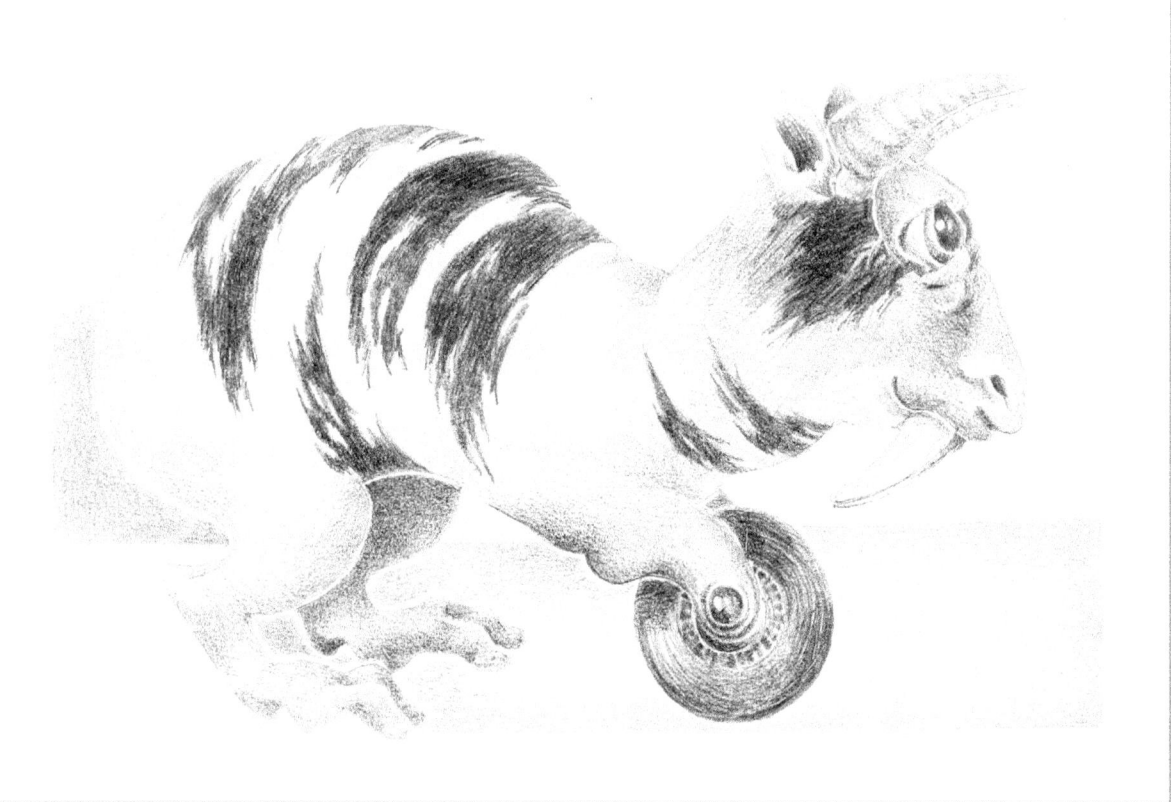

The Foreshortened Carom

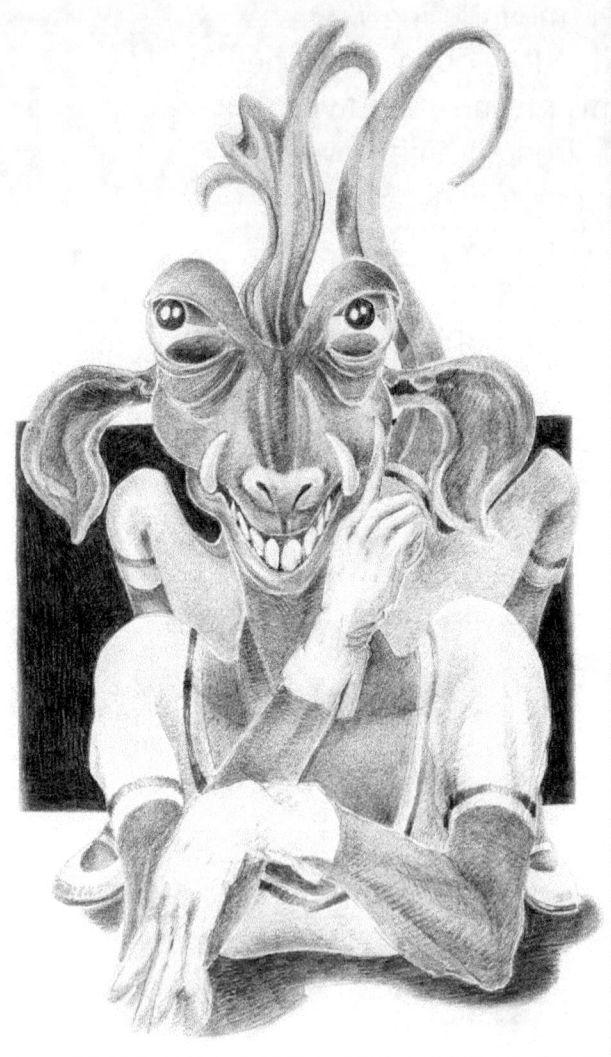

The Grismatilda

Dress Makes All the Difference

If Grismatilda has a passion,
Anyone can see
It's for the latest style in fashion,
And well should it be,
For though she's such a charming creature
And has such panache,
Her looks are not her finest feature,
So it's just a wash
When one's deciding if to meet
Or to avoid her's best;
Thus, Grismatilda shoes her feet
In summer's prettiest
New patent leather Mary Janes,
Her hands in kidskin gloves,
And her sleek figure's curving gains
From Lycra suits she loves
In dreamy colors seasonal,
So now if you're not sure
Approaching her is reasonable,
You'll love her clothes' allure
And find you're drawn in feasible
Proximity to her

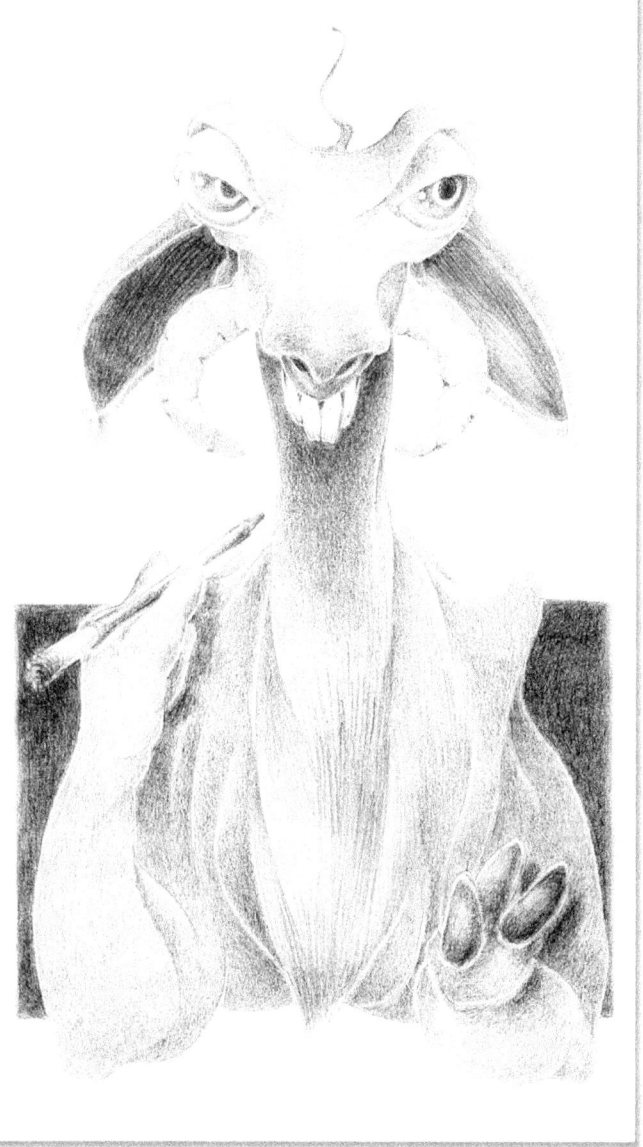

The Spurious Huffdangler

Be Not Puffed Up

With her elegant long neck
And sweeping ears, she's cool as heck;
She draws attention for her style,
A charismatic oenophile
And sailing expert, known for wit
And for the sharpening of it;
The one detraction from this great
Attractiveness is that, of late,
Her secret smoking was revealed,
And while it's known among well-heeled
And upper-crusty folk to be
Not so uncommon, it's that she
Exhales the smoke all at one puff,
From her posterior: that's enough
To put off just a few who were
Once great admirers of her.

Brilliant Anatomy

Superfluous though it may seem, the flywheel that he sports abeam,
In concert with antenna blips, the moustache garnishing his lips,
The gilded fringe hung from his ears, his tongue askew—well, it appears,
In fact, to help to great avail, sparking the light-bulb on his tail.

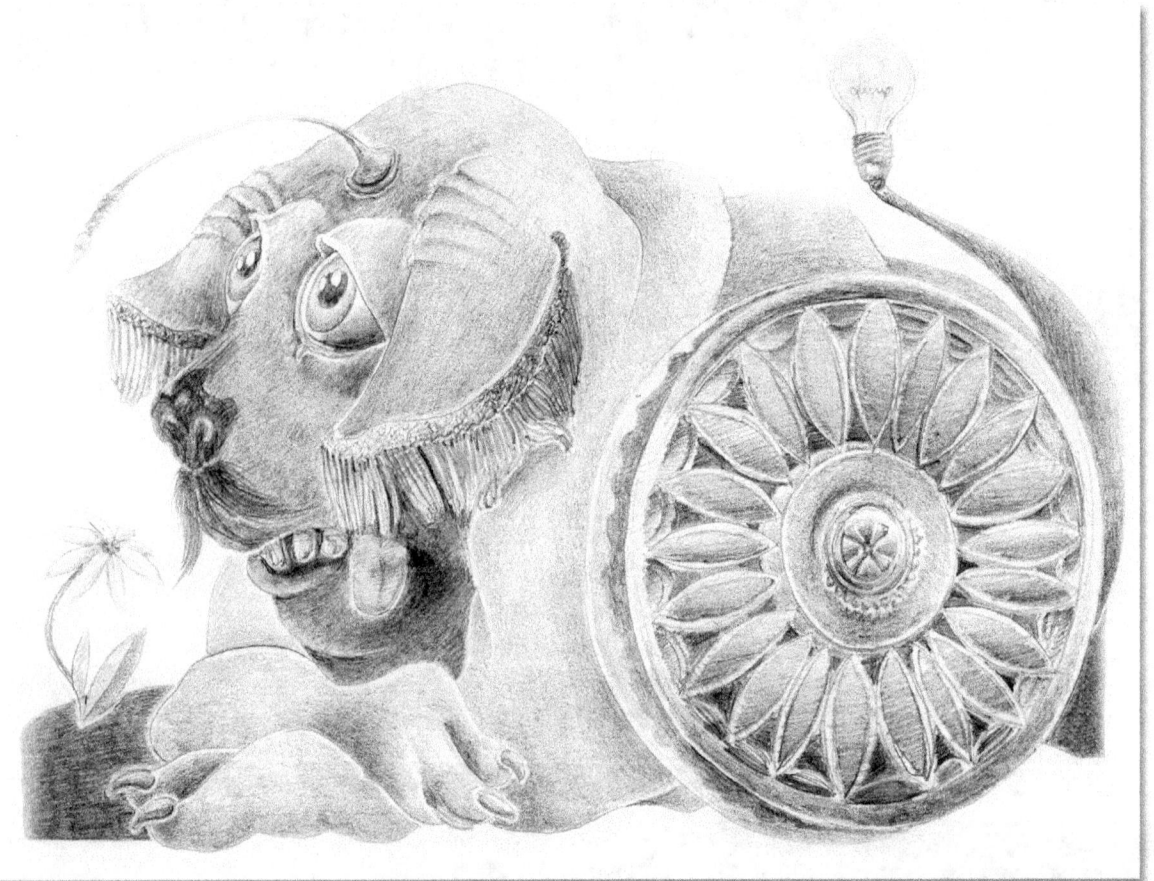

The Superfluous Flywheel

Wall-Eyes of the Beholder

The Crested Ocarina is a quirky creature, yes,
Best loved by those of his own ilk,
for, as few others guess,
The virtues of his beauty are perhaps to foreign eyes
Less obvious than if he wore a handsomer disguise:
His skin is slippery, his ears
quite large and full of hair;
His nose depends with pointed end
so far as to impair
His dining, so his tongue hangs out
in order to reach past
Its promontory o'er the lip (some viewers are aghast
To see his drooling, thus endowed);
his feet, as widely splayed,
With webbing in between the toes,
like lily pads are laid
Upon the surface of a pond;
his eyes stare left and right;
He hops sideways, not forward,
when an interest comes in sight.
Yet all of this is nothing to the beauty of his song
The moment that a dainty Ocaretta lopes along,
For he is able to flute lovely tunes upon his middle
While plucking at his eyebrow strands
to play them like a fiddle.
So never underestimate the oddity's allures,
Which may be grander than you guess—
At least, more grand than yours.

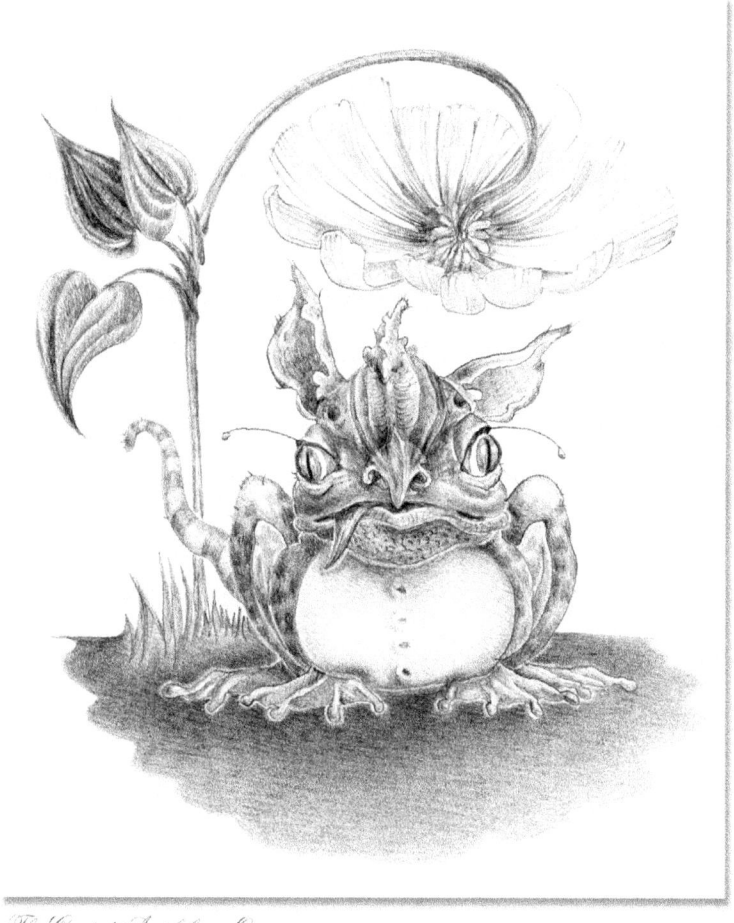

The Crested Amphibious Ocarina

Behold, the Flying Radish comes
But once a year, to press his thumbs
Upon the kneecaps of the meek,
Preventing both bowlegs and squeak—
Although he flits from house to house
Mainly in search of mate or spouse,
He brings the bonus, if you please,
Of pressing needy people's knees.

Der Fliegende Rettich

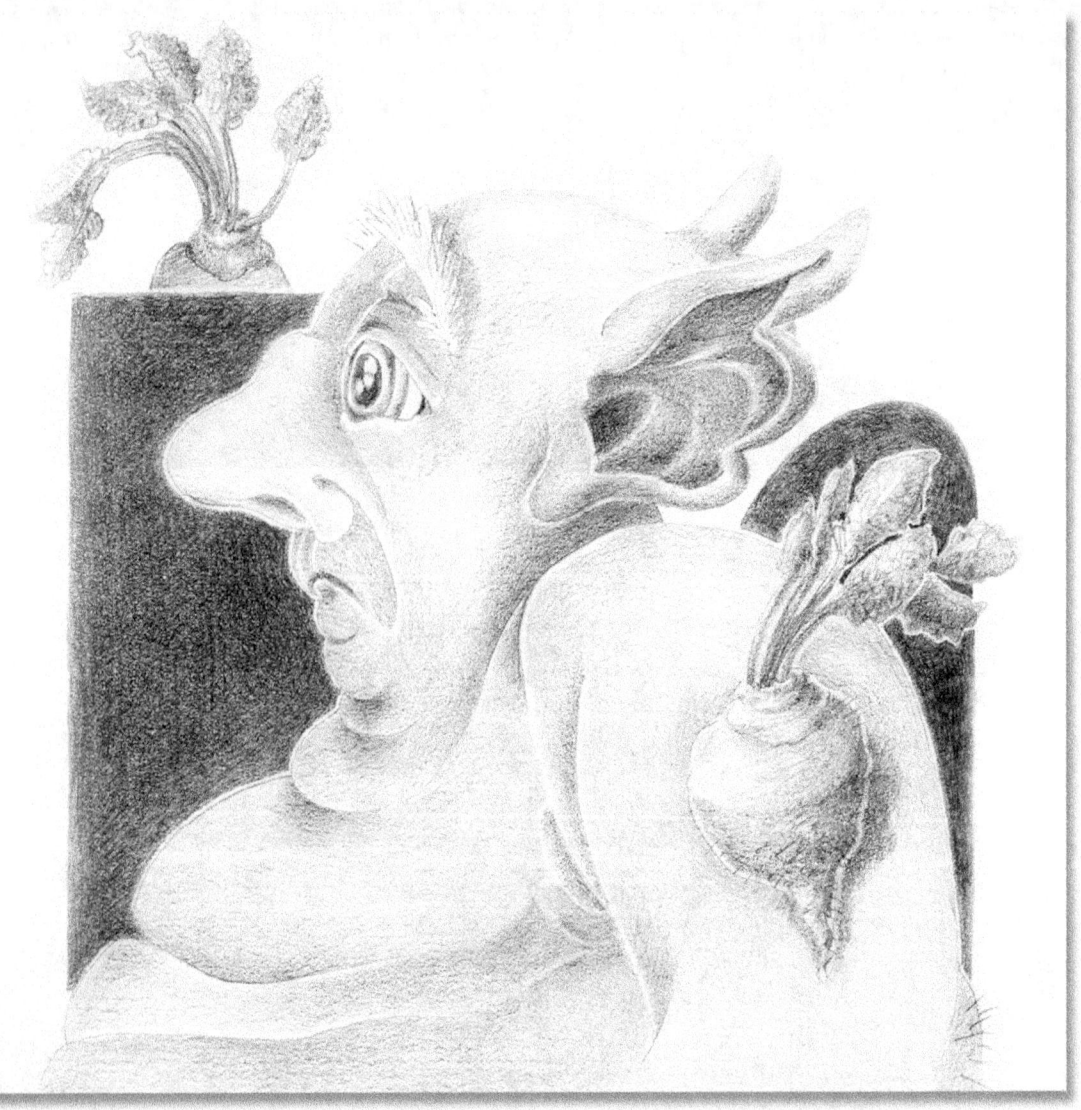

Der Fliegende Rettich

Not much to look at, he,
the awkward godling of amour:
Blessed with three eyes, in fact,
and yet his eyesight's pretty poor;
He has his pair of waving wings,
it's true, to help him fly,
But they're so weirdly
miniature that the goofy guy
Must hover, bounce and swim
about, to garner his propulsion,
Lest he be dipt and drowned,
instead, in that liquid emulsion
Of deep Love's odd elixir as
he showers it abroad
Whilst working faithfully
as grand Affection's giddy god;
In short, he is a comical
and caricatured lad,
But, seen through adoration's lens,
he really isn't bad!

Love Makes Us All Crazy

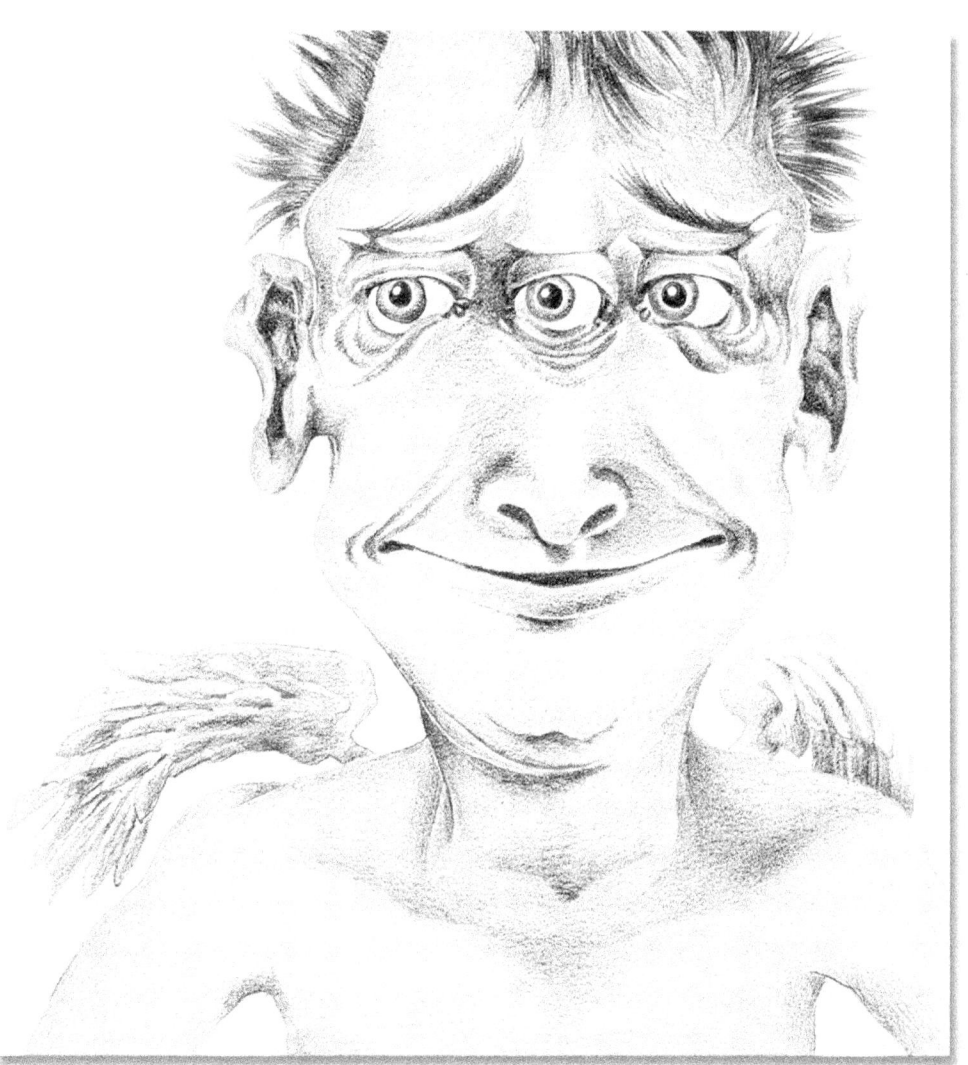

M. Folies d'Amour

Incubating Gloom

Every hundred years or so,
At least that's how the legends go,
The dour Depressive Quandary
Crawls up ashore from in the sea,
Aground on its four stubby legs,
To find a place to lay its eggs,

And instantly dissatisfied
At having no such nest espied,
Rolls down the pebbly shoreline scree
Back to the dank and murky sea
To nurse in underwater tears
Its eggs another hundred years.

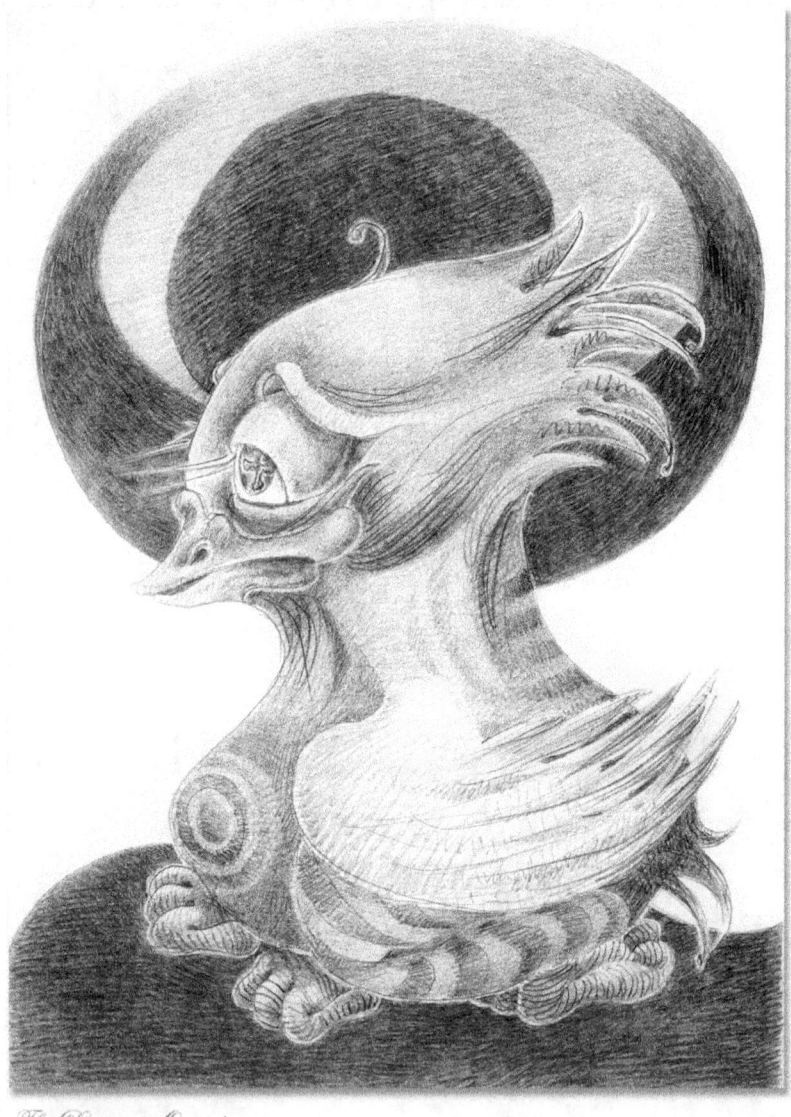

The Depressive Quandary

Beautiful by Design

The Pharmadillo's portholes, neatly set into her flank,
Enable scientists to see as though in a fish tank
The fluid motion of her inner parts; she doesn't mind:
She far prefers this mode to people ogling her behind.

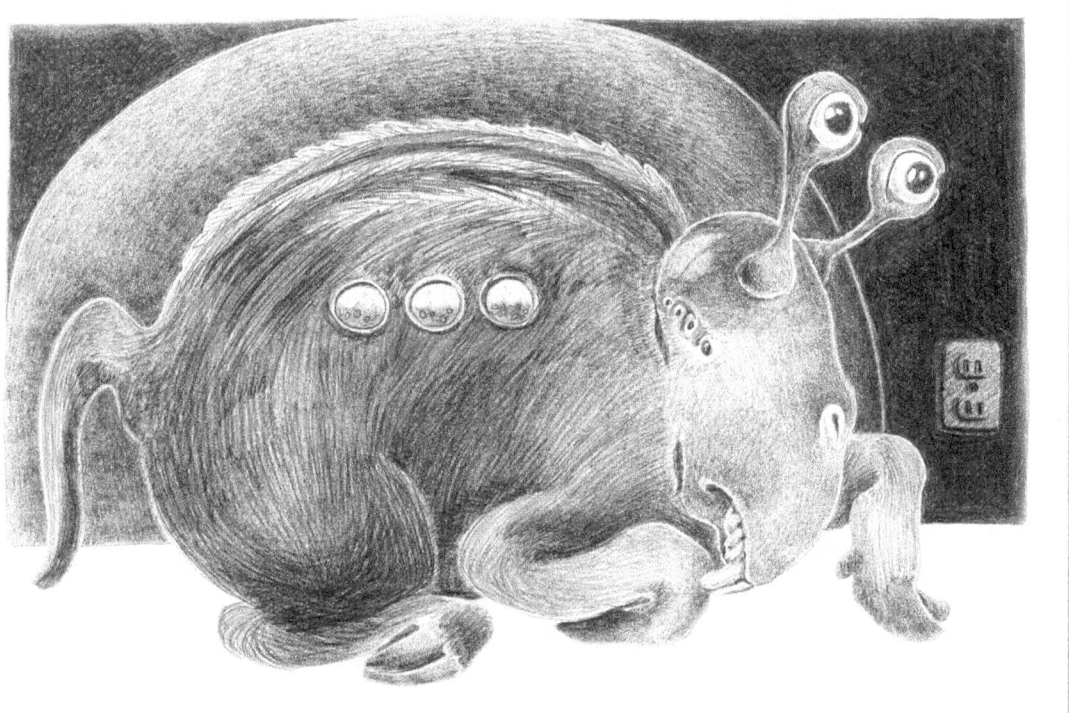

The Phabulous Pharmadillo

Always Look Inward for Beauty

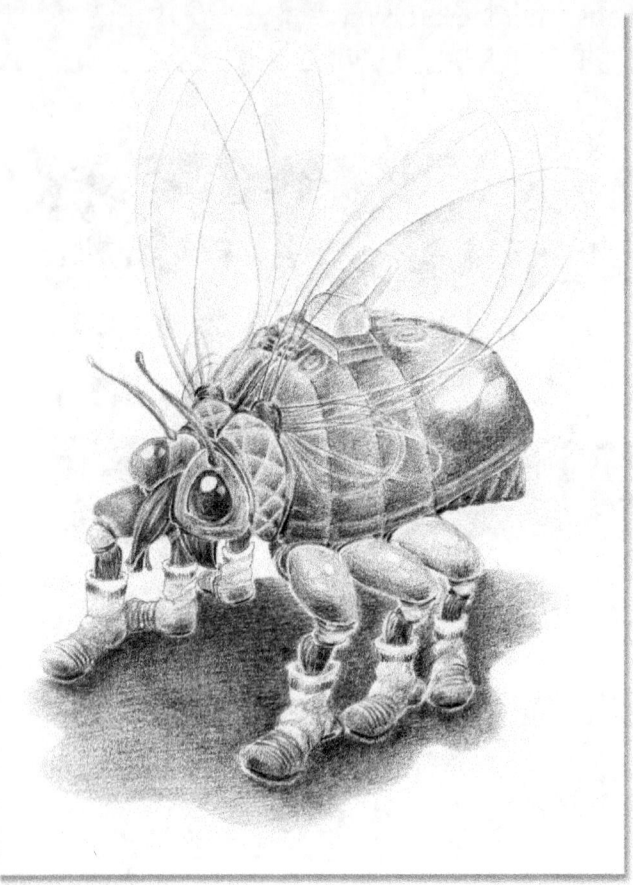

The Great Walloping Gnitt

In a hollow forest feature,
Living near a pool of spit,
Is the funny lumpy creature,
Large and leisurely, the Gnitt.
He is slow to wake and worry;
Though he's got a lot to do,
He won't do it in a hurry,
And his style of rubber shoe
Drags along the ground as slowly
As if held in place by glue.
He could speed up if he wanted,
But would rather rest in place
Than zip off as if he's haunted
With his wings flapping apace,
For he most delights in lazing
And in making slow-cooked stew
Without roasting it or braising
As the other creatures do;
He can just relax and loll about
While waiting for the brew.
He hums a little tune inside,
Methodically; his brain
Produces this one codified
And patterned song, no strain,
But toward conversation he
Is disinclined to move,
As it interrupts unpleasantly
His tune's internal groove,
And besides, he's quite content
He's got nothing to prove.

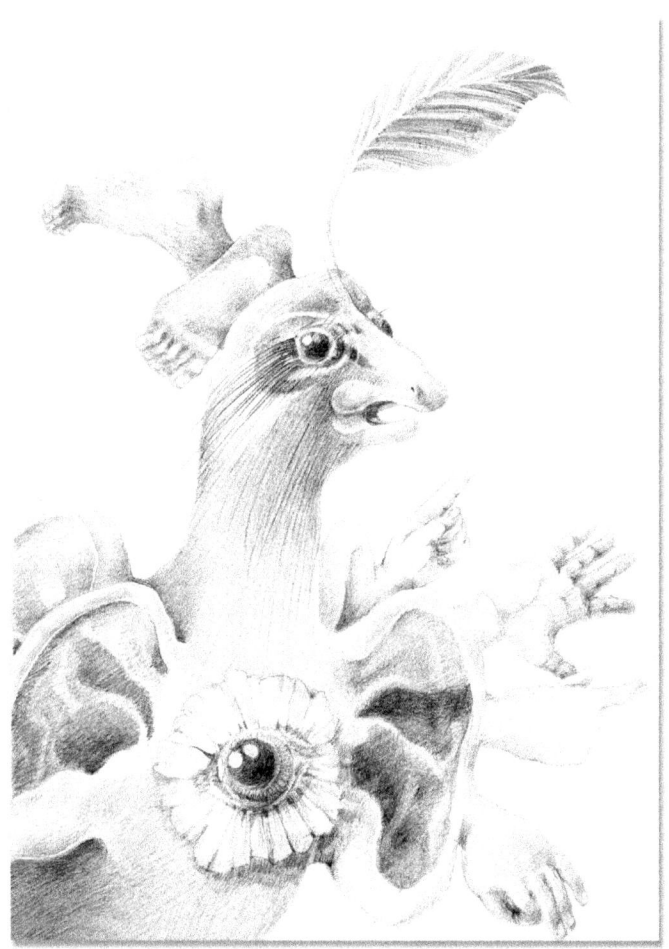

The Portentous Long-Nosed Stzhumbler

Some Things are Best Left Unused

The gods, despite their myriad arts,
Sometimes are left with odd spare parts
That, lacking use, they then combine
In efforts to create some fine
New creature, sometimes with success,
And sometimes with something quite less,
As in the case of one strange beast,
Concatenating twelve, at least,
Or maybe twenty, random bits
Of physiognomy; he sits,
Thank heavens, on the best he's got,
For sadly, he falls down a lot,
Being unbalanced and unmatched
In every aspect since he's hatched.
Being so, he is embarrassed,
Often gloomy, cranky, harassed;
Who can blame him? Poor weird bird,
Assembled thus from parts absurd,
He's doomed to roam earth, far and near
And tumble, often, on his rear.

Simplicity Herself

No creature's more crazed than the Nackle,
With her lunatic grin and loud cackle;
She's a snap to maintain,
Though, because both her brain
And her innards are made of pure spackle

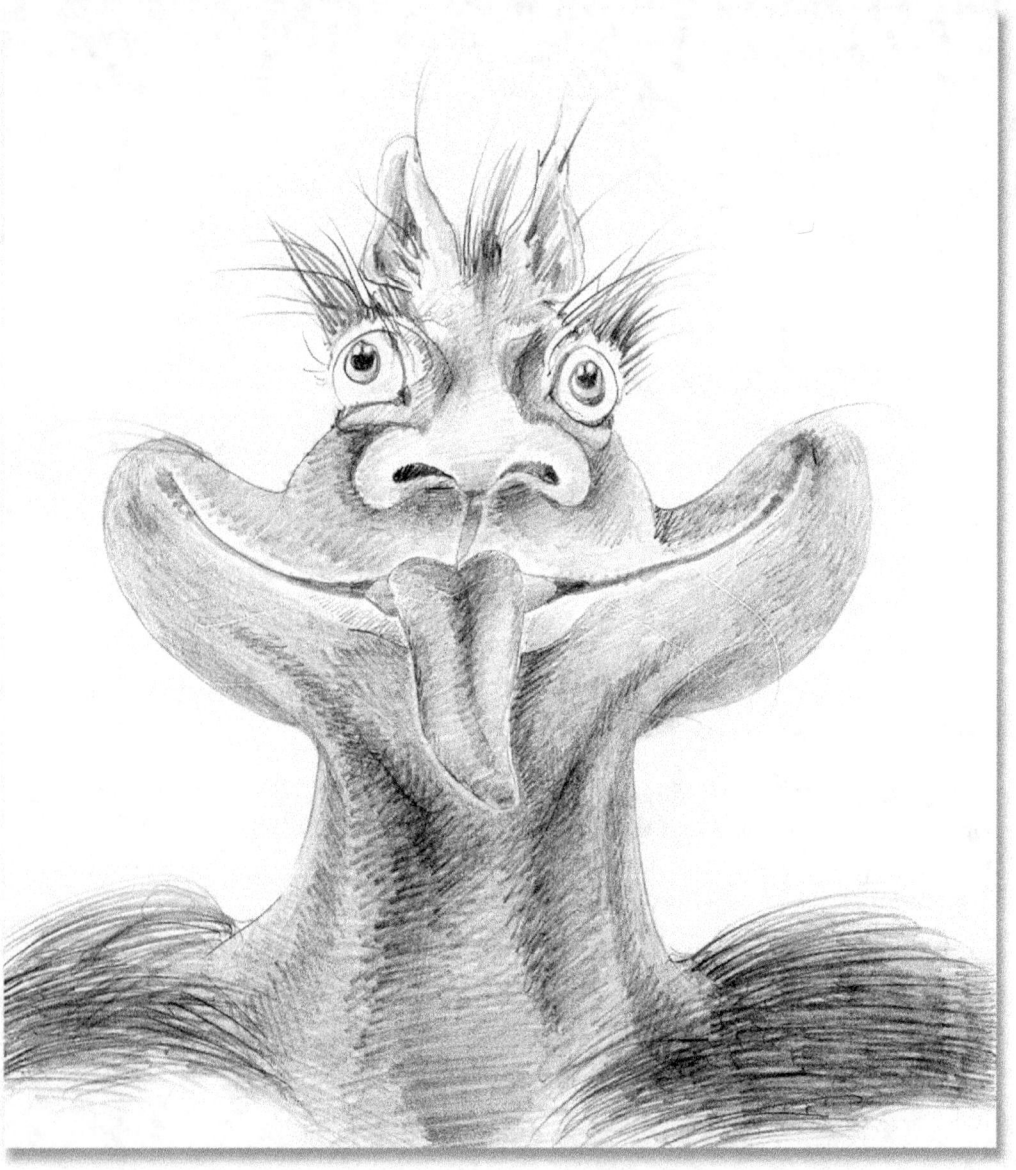

The Credulous Nackle

The Zargue

Consider the Source, Tout le Monde

Far from city folk and town,
In the misty mists of the Camargue,
Lives a character of some renown,
That paragon of taste, the Zargue,
Who as an arbiter of style
And fashion, diet, schools of thought,
The Arts—also Italophile,
Expert on Finnish customs, not
A stranger to a dozen tongues
In print and conversation—he
Seems like fresh air pulled in the lungs,
Inspiring as anyone could be,
And so the hordes come to consult,
To sup his wisdom, pick his brain,
Absorb his genius like a cult—
Although beneath lies a refrain
That something might be slightly odd
In worshipfully acting slave
And treating as all-knowing god
The Zargue, who's never left his cave.

Appearances can be Deceiving

Beware of the Bearded Fangdoodle
He's wriggly and lithe as a noodle—
Though he seems a fierce snake,
It's a pose and a fake—
He prefers snuggling up like a poodle

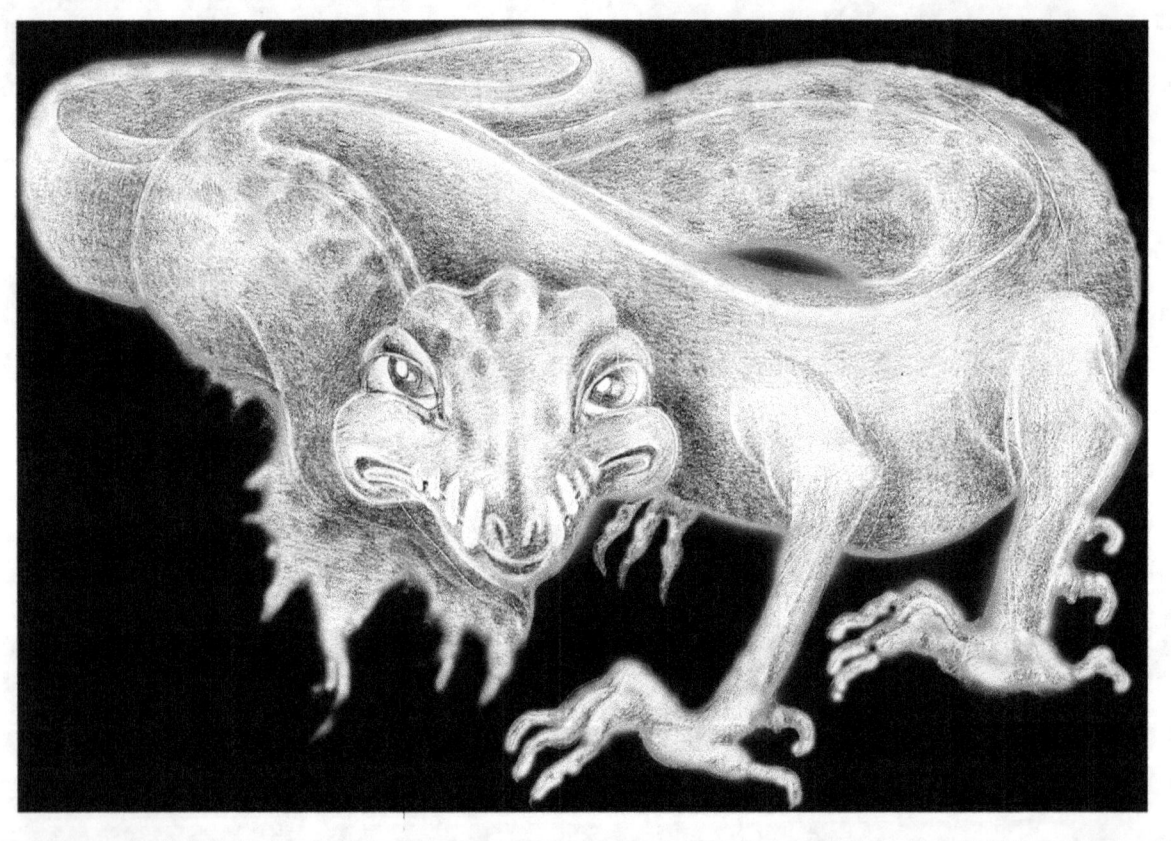

The Bearded Fangdoodle

I'm the Only One

You might think there are many of my kind, given that as it is
I look quite like a group or school or covey, but then besides my phiz,
With all these wings and extra parts, I'm odd, oh yes, and oft made fun
Of by those creatures with hard hearts—but really, I'm the only one

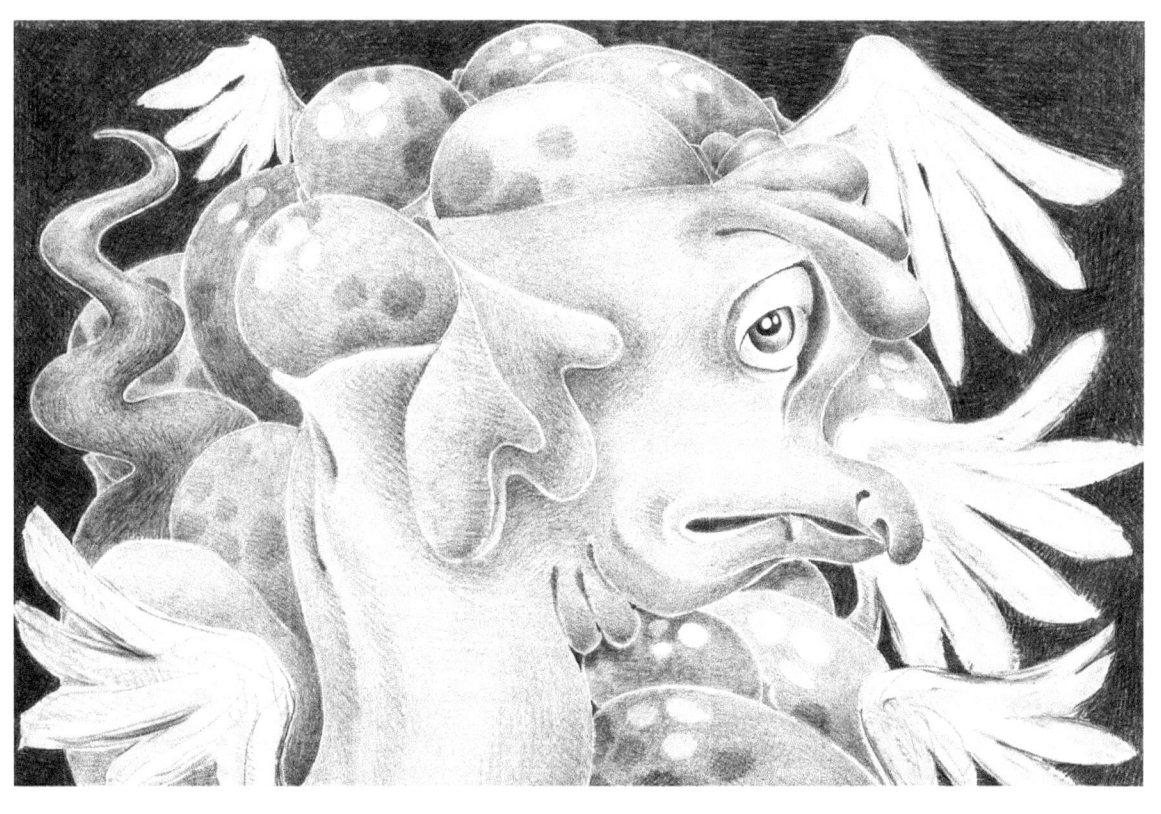

The Solitary Eggbubbler

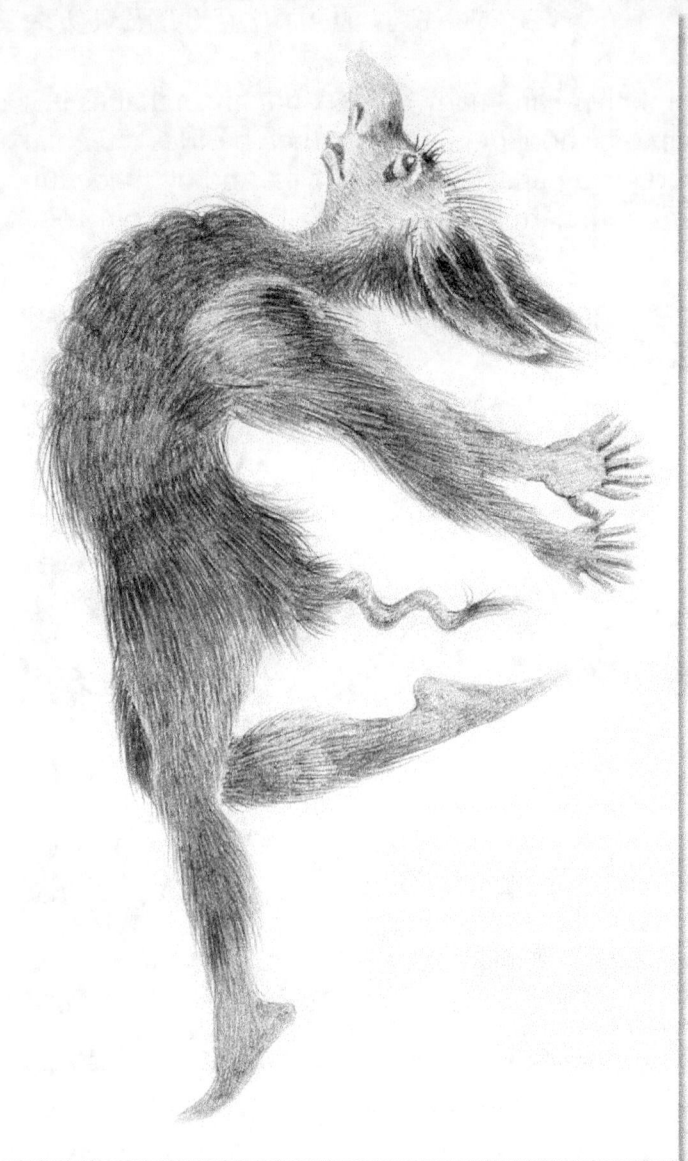

The Rough-Coated Wheef

Speciality

A beast of great talents,
The Rough-Coated Wheef,
Relies for her fame
On her dancing, in chief,
Despite her known skills
In both language and law
And for eating whole tigers,
Both roasted and raw.
Why dancing, you ask?
Is it true she's that good?
Oh, you wouldn't inquire
If you'd seen her: she should
Be the picture you see
When you look up the word
In the dictionary—
"Dance" has always referred
To a sort of a pattern,
An action, a sport
Full of grace, style and matter,
But I would retort
That never until the great
Wheef came to dance
Was the world so aware
Of how dancing enchants—
Not to mention she has
Furry legs, and not pants.

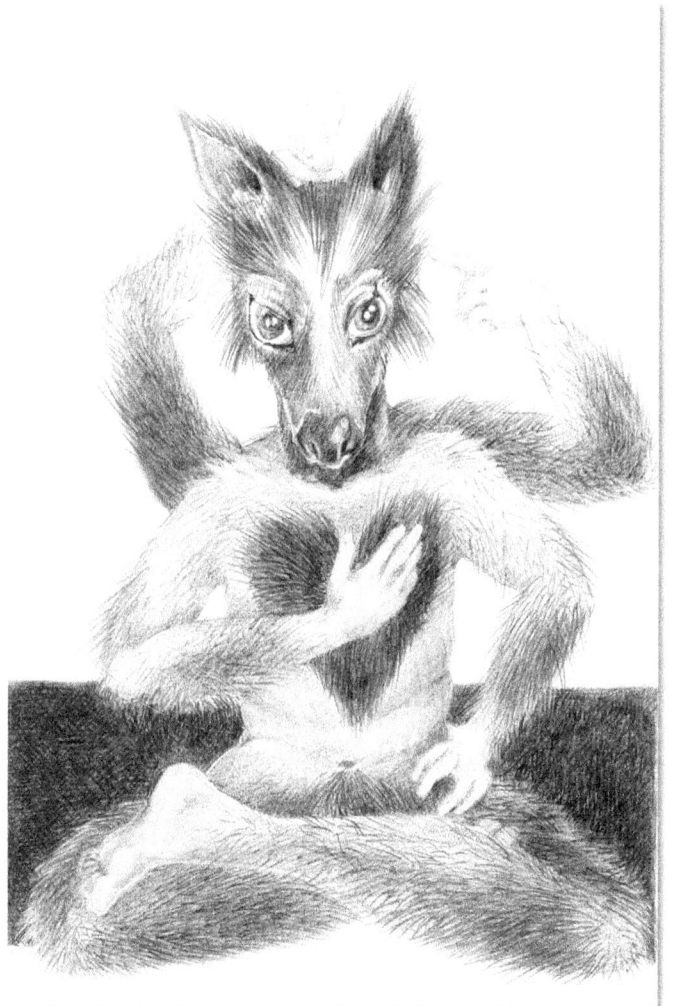

The Quadubrachial Lycanthropic Heartthrob

Kiss Me, Cuddly Canine

Under the yellow werewolf moon,
when all fair youth in fear might swoon
With fright to think of creatures scary,
there's a beast quite dark and hairy
That instead inspires their love:
this fellow that I'm thinking of
Is also vulpine, lycanthropic,
but a kinder, gentler topic,
For his heart is filled with hunger
for those kids aged two and younger,
Yet instead of hope for dining
on them, he's instead repining
For friendship and sweeter kinds
of links, a meeting of the *minds,*
Youths who appreciate his charms;
he'll hug them with his four strong arms
And kiss them gently with his snout,
and if these lures don't draw them out
Enough, he even might unveil
and wag for them his plumy tail.
Indeed, if kids are nice to him,
he will not rip them limb from limb
But rather, sisters, brothers, nieces
one and all, love them to pieces.

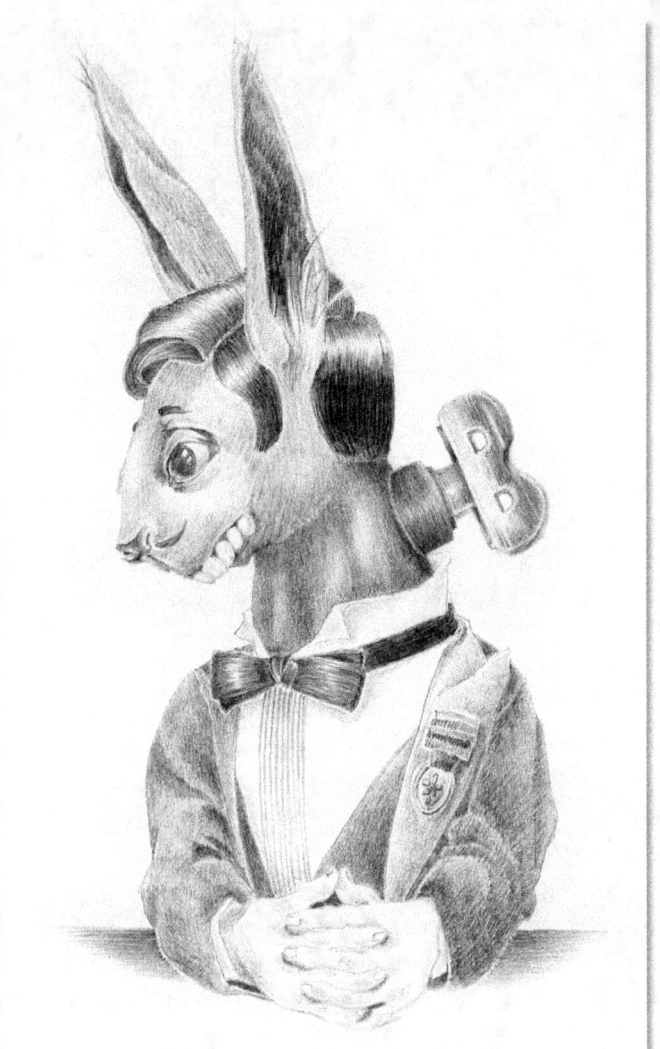

The Handy-Medaled Gorm

Dashing for Office

The sleek-haired Handy-Medaled Gorm,
Despite his malocclusive form,
Is dashing, daring, debonair,
And has the aforementioned hair,
Appealing to the Gorm-girls there.

His name affirms he is not gormless,
Nor in fact, is aimless, formless,
But instead has clear, high goals
To win election in the polls,
Enrapturing the Gorm-girls' souls.

His medals all were won in war,
When he was teen-aged and before,
When he was just a youthful pup,
With endless energy to sup,
Though at his age, he's still keyed up.

The moment when he chose to doff his
Hat and run for this high office
Was, in fact, at Gorm-girls' bidding,
Irresistible—no kidding:
Into the ring he hurtled, skidding.

How the vote will go's in question,
But the Gorm-girls' fine suggestion
Means the Handy-Medaled Gorm
May set a new official norm
And keep our admiration warm.

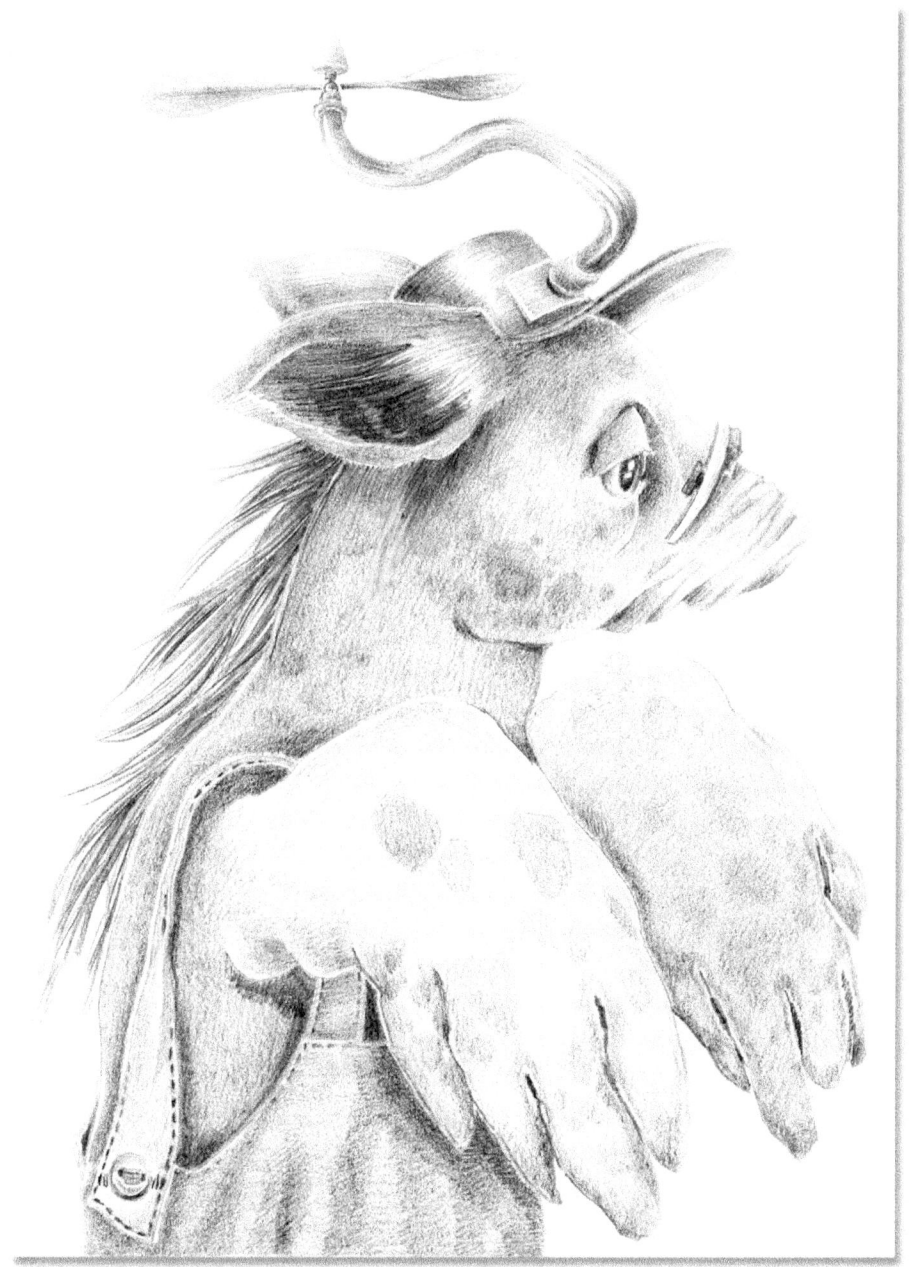

The Soft-Snooted Billcap

His Preferences

A shy, mild-mannered creature he,
The kind Soft-Snooted Billcap,
Who underground might rather be
Than a top-of-the-hill chap,

Except for that his fins are not
Well suited to a cellar,
And he'd have trouble with a clot
Of dirt in his propeller.

Some Assembly Required

Everything went so smoothly when the aliens were landing,
Our early apprehensions and misgivings notwithstanding,
That we were taken quite aback to find, despite their brains
And their advanced technologies' impressive upward gains
In terms of progress, evolution, growing, if you will,
They lacked as much as humankind the one essential skill
Of reading and interpreting the manuals included
To guide the reassembling of their crewmembers, those who did
Important tasks like social integration with new races,
And so the aliens built oddball hybrid folk with faces
A little like their own, a little like a human's too,
And having other parts remaining, knew not what to do
But (as a human often does) made random fumbling guesses
And put the rest together in such fascinating messes
Of wacky biotechnical contraptions that at last
They found the new-made beings were surpassing them, and fast,
And bypassed all the humans too, and at the end of day,
Took over from the both of them—so *their* new manuals say.

A Post-Human Assemblage

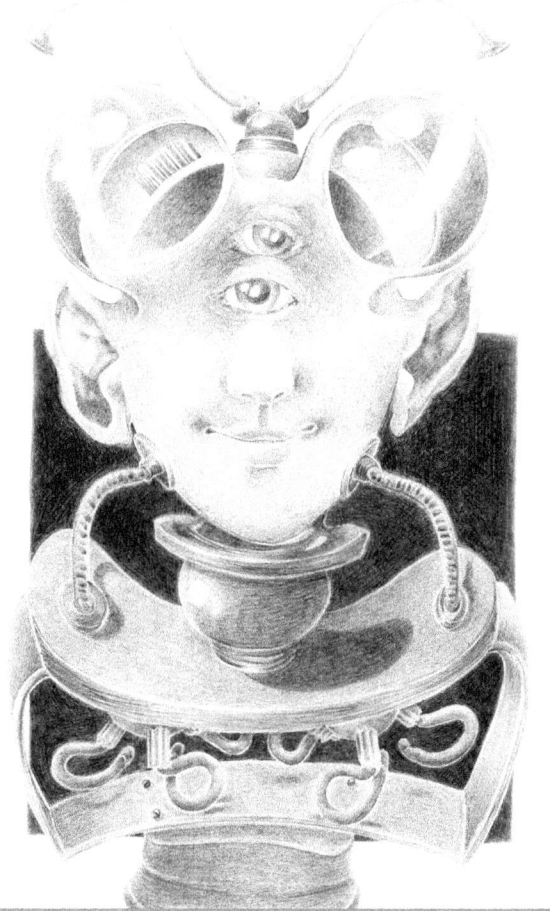

An Underdeveloped Facsimile

Slight Imperfections are Natural in these Handcrafted Products

The invention of Humans was such an odd choice—
Just the way we're assembled, not counting the voice,
Independence or character, habits, desires—
No wonder the average person requires
So many improvements, repairs and design
Adjustments as time passes, just to refine
Each into a useful and functional state,
A status we all find too seldom, too late
Or too small, if at all, as we age and grow up,
Learning on the way how imperfect our sup-
Posed wonderfulness and impressive physiques,
Our dandy conglomerate bodies' mystiques,
Are really, what fragile and frazzled machines
We are, what dysfunction our humanness means.
All true! Every word; but what's startling is this:
We still wouldn't trade our humanity's bliss
For something more perfect, less flawed, less bizarre
Than all of us wacky assemblages are.

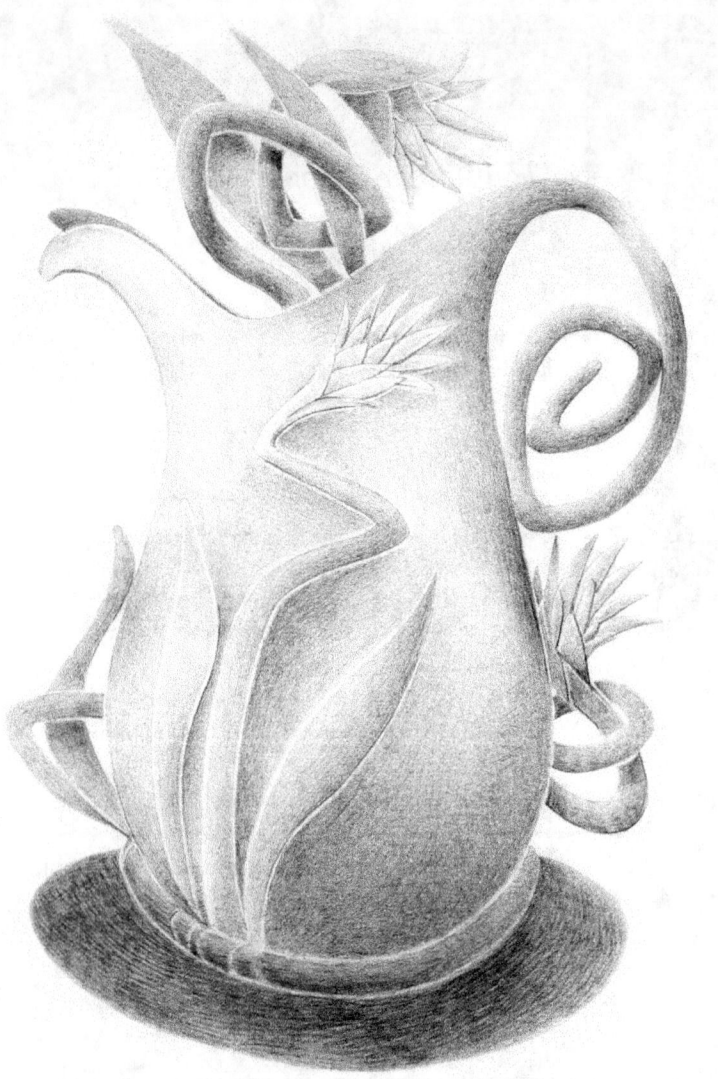

Once Started, Some Things Just Take Off

A picture of a pitcher
with a plant in it or on it
That started in simplicity,
vessel for ode or sonnet,
Intended only to be there
containing little thoughts,
Ran off amok among the weeds
of internecine plots,
Deciding and defining its
own destiny beyond
What little plans I'd made, designs
of which I am so fond,
And twisted up its own design
of coils and sprouts and knots;
So much for all my power trips
begot of thoughts and plots.

Words Going Their Own Way

When I would write of beautiful things,
A prayer, a pageant, a pattern of light,
I keep tripping over weird tangles of strings
And mucilage made of hilarity, fright—
And what had begun as bouquets of sweet flowers
Begins to congeal into sludge in two hours.
I start off with blooms' silken petal and leaf
And the rain falling mistily on them by day,
When suddenly rain turns to gravy, good grief,
And a magical romp of peculiarly fey
Inventions of brain-matter soaked in red wine
Takes over the nice little blooms that were mine.

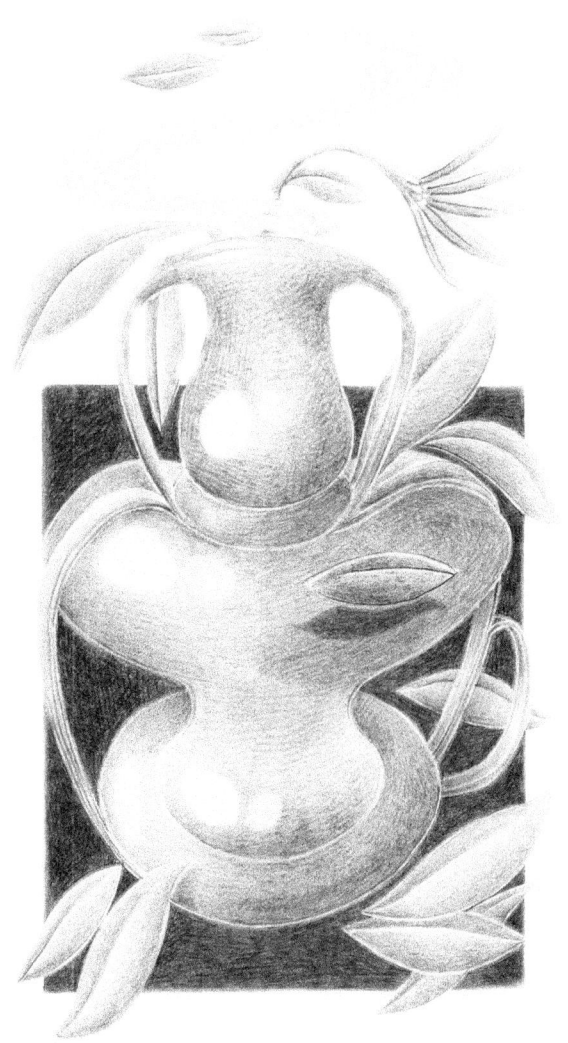

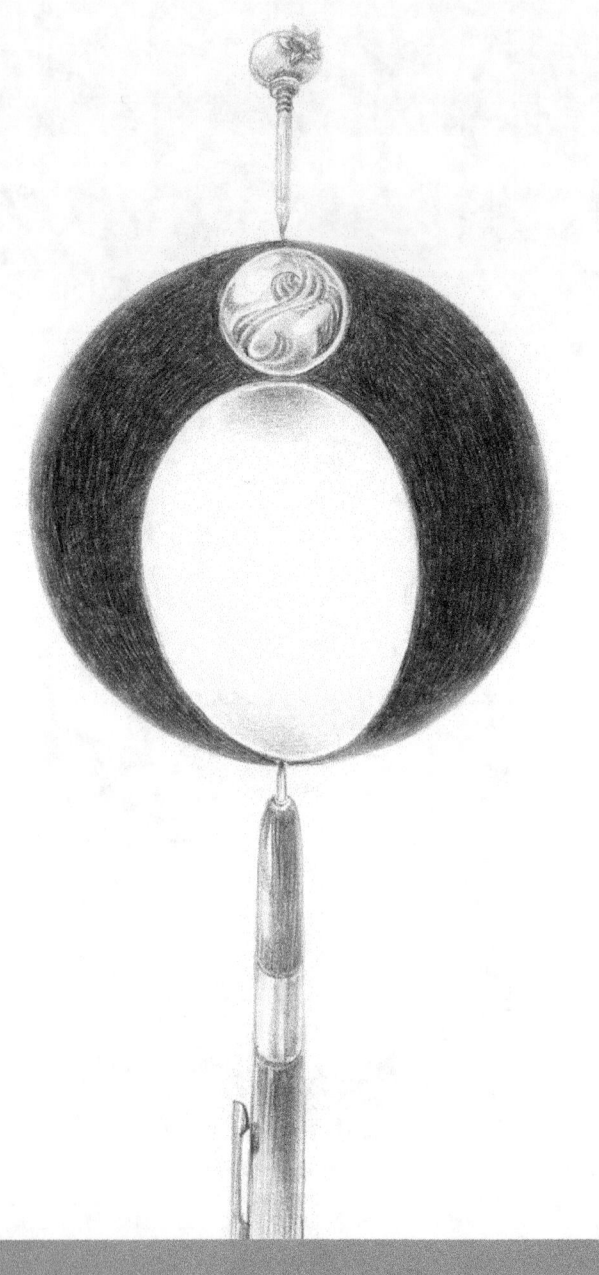

Stacked Odds

Hoping my oddball interests
Are not quite all in vain
Stacks up to a conundrum
That puts a bit of strain
On all credulity, on sense,
On logic and on taste,
But then I've never bent so much
To worrying on waste
Or practicality or on
The common good of man,
But in my weird self-centered way,
I hope that if I can,
At least I will have managed in
My love of things bizarre
To make the world and all its quirks
No worser than they are

Afterlife

It may be that the sweet tooth kills
And love of fat leads to decay,
But I still crave these risky thrills,
Preferred to dullness any day—
And secret hope lies in my heart
That I'll eventually find
These are elixirs or the start
Of immortality, a kind
Of magic potion that transcends
Apotheosis and can save
My soul like nothing else that mends
All ills and shortcomings I have—
At least I know that if this food
Be not salvation, I'll have been
In earthly heaven in my crude
And mortal way, I'd say, 'til then

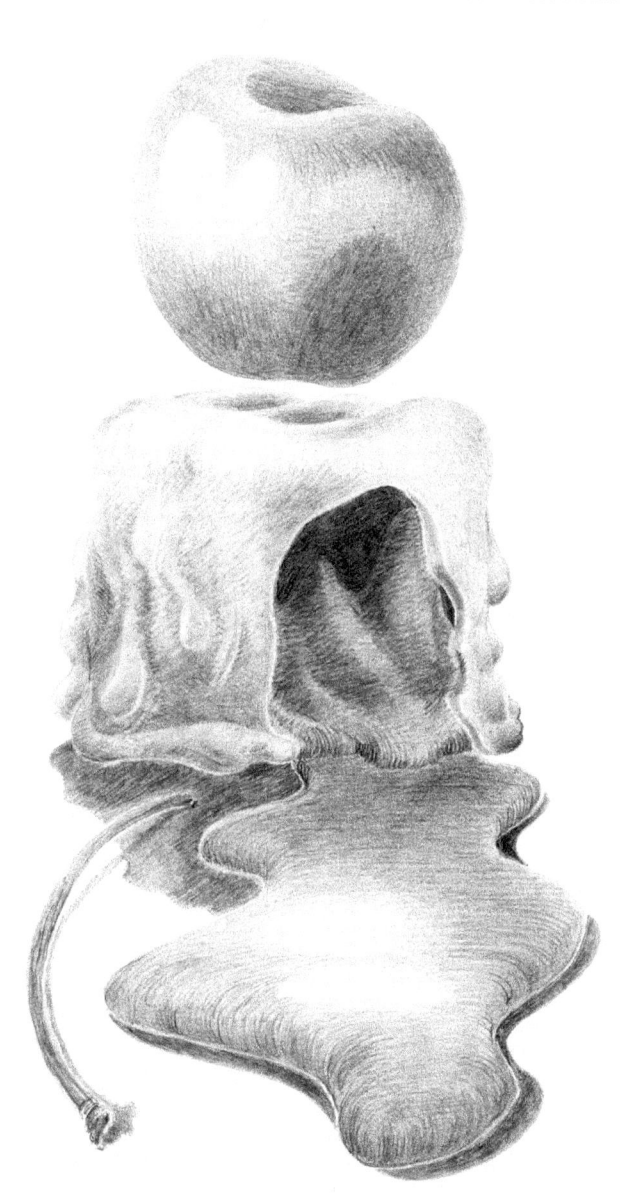

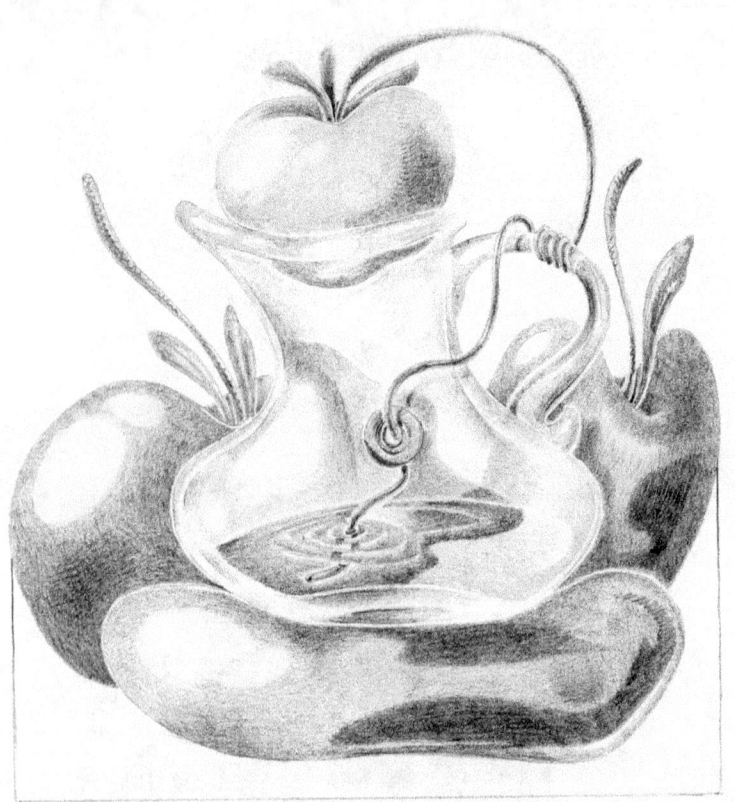

Lap It Up

A boiling hot soup course at dinner
is a sure-fire delectable winner
unless it should spill
and so test your goodwill
that your language should make you a sinner.

Secret Ingredient

The traveler peripatetic
Who lives a life anti-ascetic
May wish at some point
For a salve to anoint
Him with powers pain-free
But emetic

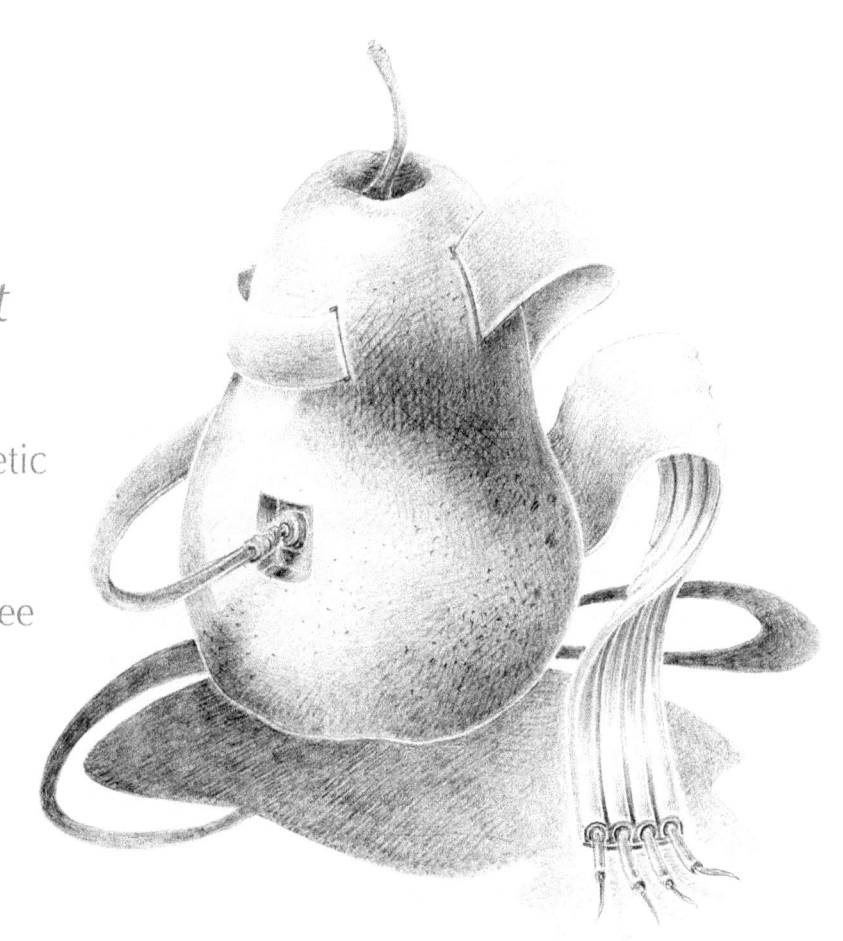

A Surprise in Every Cup

The splendid beauty of the morn Becomes a little bit forlorn
When from my teacup peer the eyes Of someone, something otherwise
Than merely tea, and trepidatious As I am to look in, gracious!—
Just as fearful is my guest—Though he's not here at my request,
'Twould be uncouth to not invite Him in, if only in our fright,
And so I curtsey, greet him sweetly, Pour some tea out for him neatly,
And together sip our sup Before he climbs back in the cup.

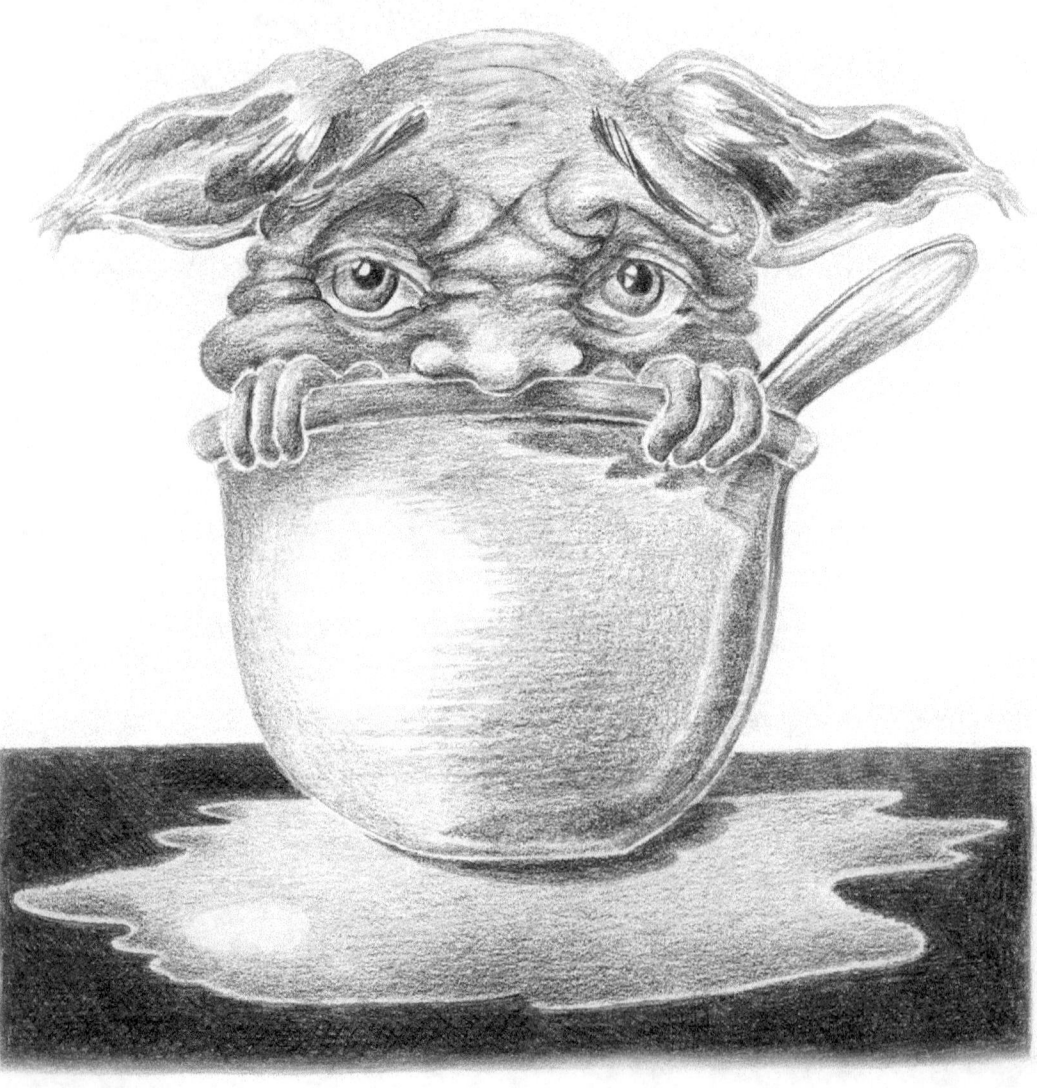

What's Brewing

Out from the teapot, steam and a hiss Might never have told me something's amiss
Except that the snake writhing out 'round the pot Is certainly one of those things I have not
Either seen or expected, but often indeed, A morning's surprise is full worthy of heed—
I inquired of the snake whether she had some news To warn or inform me or shock or amuse,
Or what was her purpose, appearing here thus, And whether there might be some bond between us—
It turned out, quite simply, she'd come as she durst And merely intending that she'd slake her thirst,
But found the tea intoxicating, delicious, And fell quite asleep there amid the tea dishes.

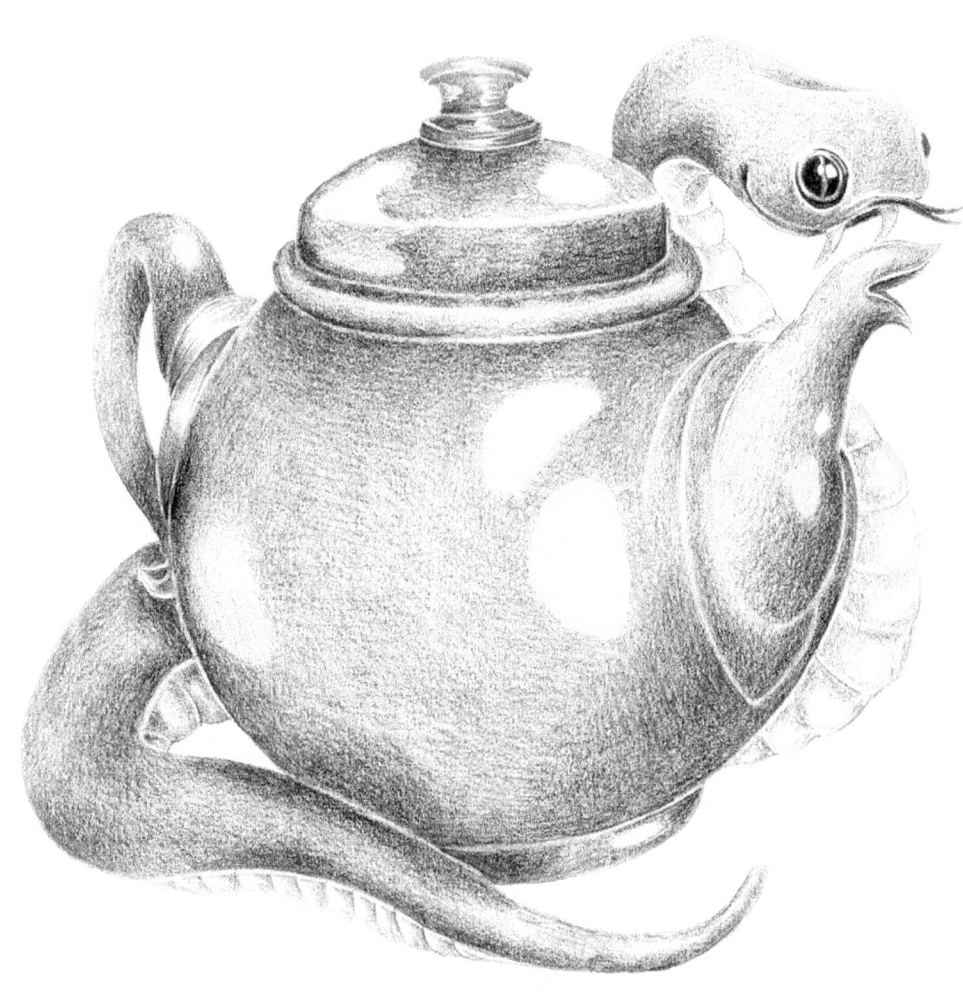

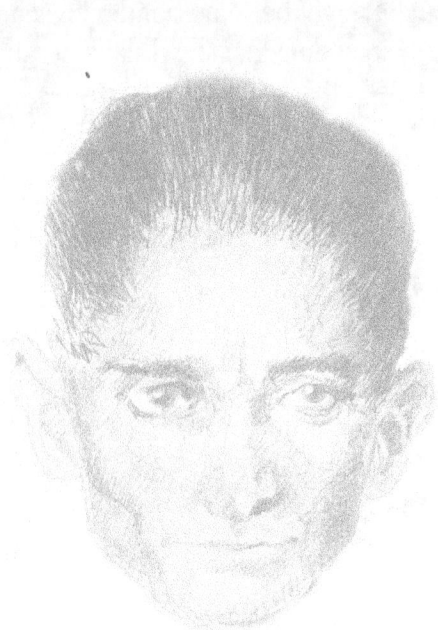

It Bugs Me

O bitter thought, that I should make
The selfsame terrible mistake
I've made before and will again, Though it's the fate of mortal men
To cycle through our lives with such Fool certitude we know too much
And find because we fail to read Our history within the seed
That we repeat, remake, renew Our sins—it's simply what we do

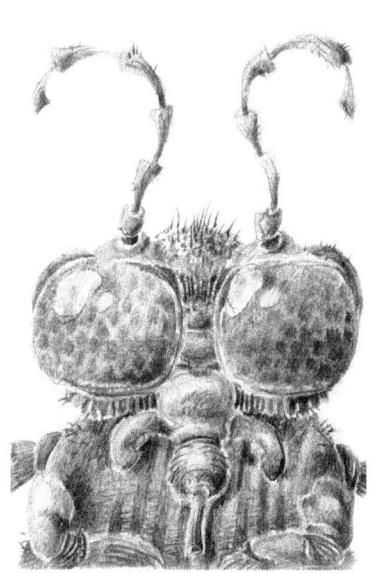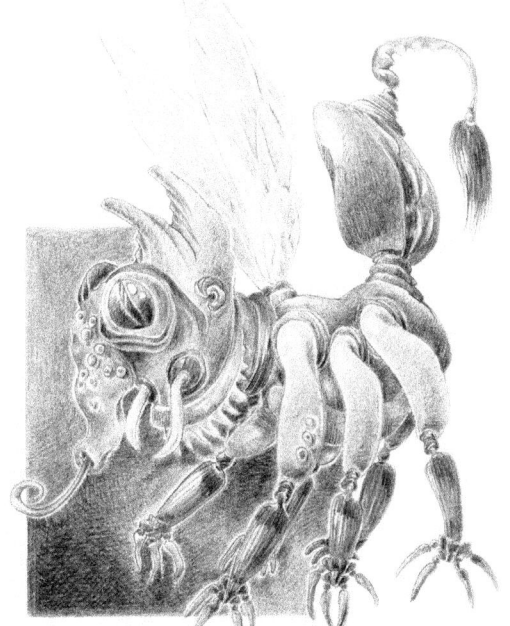

Complexity

A multicolored creature with a thorax made of steel, four compound eyes, antennae, tail, wings & a steering wheel,
A set of cram-ulator gears, ten jointed legs, a nose made of fluorescent barium, and knee-high pantyhose—
This creature most spectacular astonished every eye, but never otherwise impressed, too weird to aught but die—
The lovely outcome of this tale is, myriad such works fill up the world in every part, each with its own odd quirks—
Although too few survive enough to propagate their kind, it's marvelous to even know there's more in store to find!

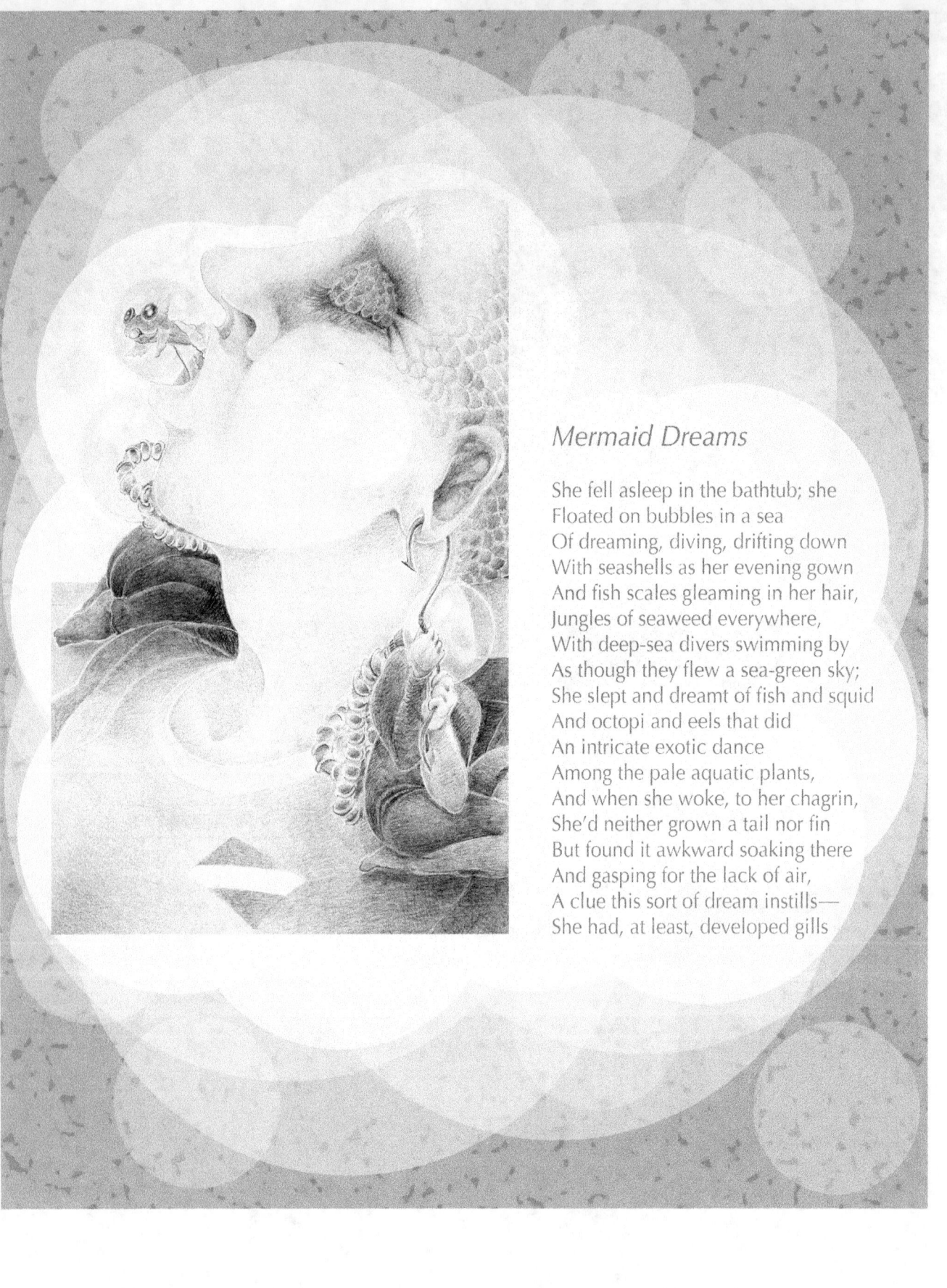

Mermaid Dreams

She fell asleep in the bathtub; she
Floated on bubbles in a sea
Of dreaming, diving, drifting down
With seashells as her evening gown
And fish scales gleaming in her hair,
Jungles of seaweed everywhere,
With deep-sea divers swimming by
As though they flew a sea-green sky;
She slept and dreamt of fish and squid
And octopi and eels that did
An intricate exotic dance
Among the pale aquatic plants,
And when she woke, to her chagrin,
She'd neither grown a tail nor fin
But found it awkward soaking there
And gasping for the lack of air,
A clue this sort of dream instills—
She had, at least, developed gills

Dilemma

Yes, I have caught this lovely fish—
Which would have been a tasty dish
And quite a catch, for he was speedy,
Slippery, clever, and indeed, he
Managed to elude me long,
Considering I had no prong
Or spear or hook, but only claws
Upon my hunting kitty-paws—
It's why I thought to go, instead,
After him, sticking in my head—
He squirted out—I grabbed and caught—
I was rejoicing, when I thought
That possibly I'd gotten stuck,
My head—the fishbowl—rotten luck!
So here I am, the fish a-wriggling,
With this nasty thought that's niggling
At me that we're both quite near
To asphyxiating here
Without my having eaten him
Or his having gone on to swim
Another day—but darn it, I, for
One, hope he's a catch to die for.

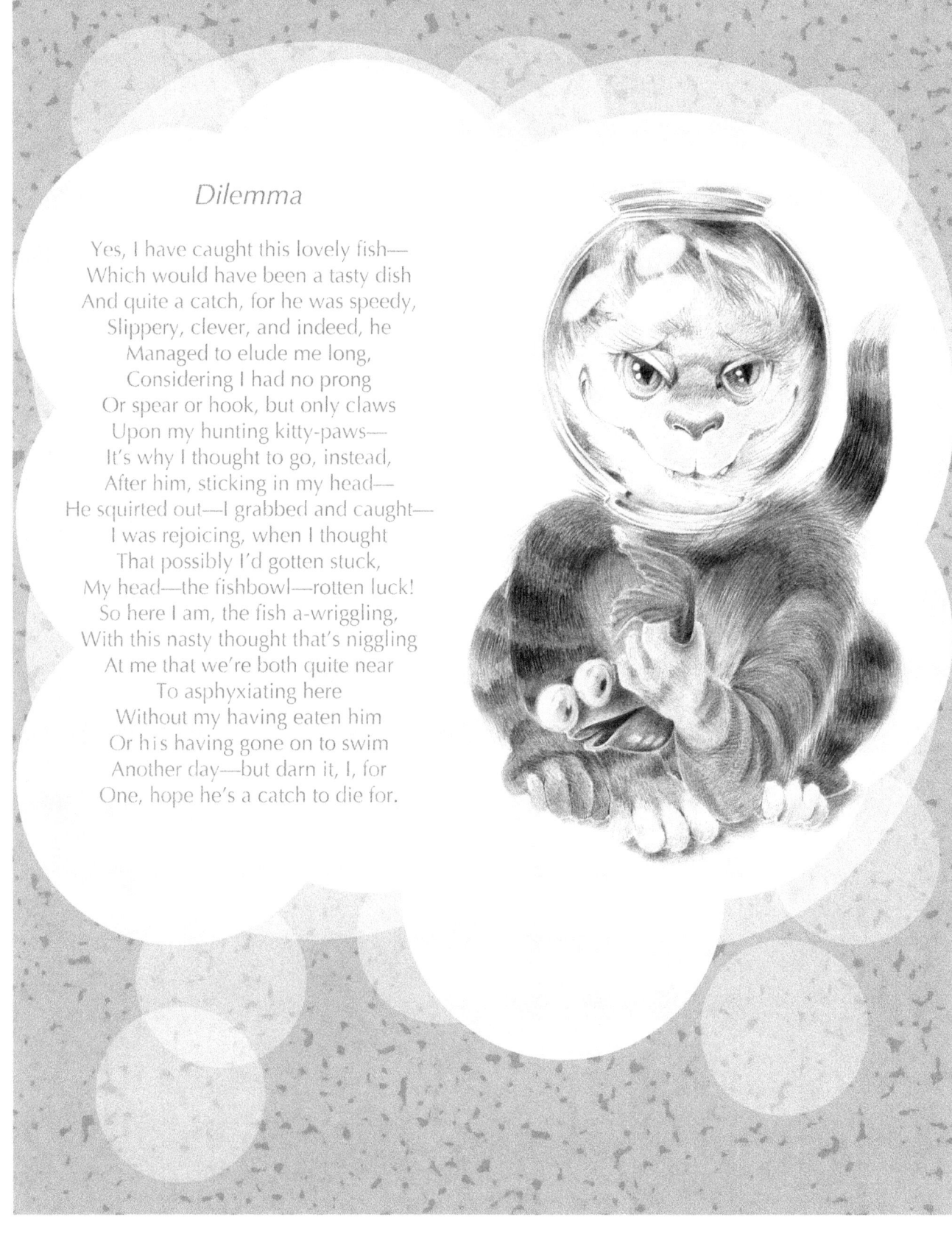

Semi-Samurai

Attempting at a fierce demeanor,
Scowling with a tiger's snarl,
Geared up with a frightening sword,
Still cannot get respect, poor Carl—
Maybe, pausing to consider,
I'd suggest the smallest tweak
To his would-be warlord getup—
Hearts and teddies do look meek.

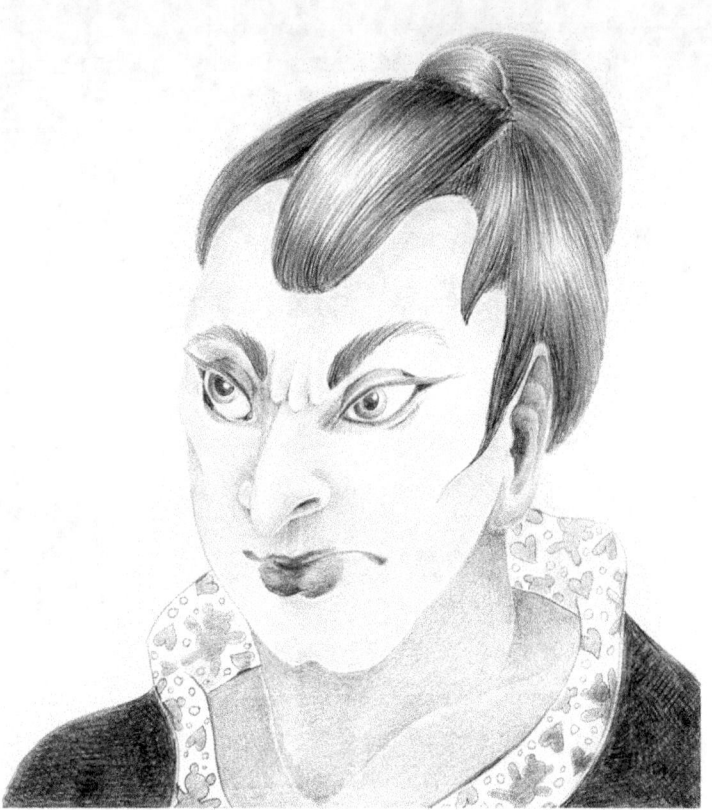

*You Have Me
All in Knots*

Slither over here, my love,
And wriggle close to me;
Writhe up and coil around my heart
And you will swiftly see
I'm not put off by scaly skin
Or hugging that constricts;
There's nothing viperish that one
Good dose of love can't fix

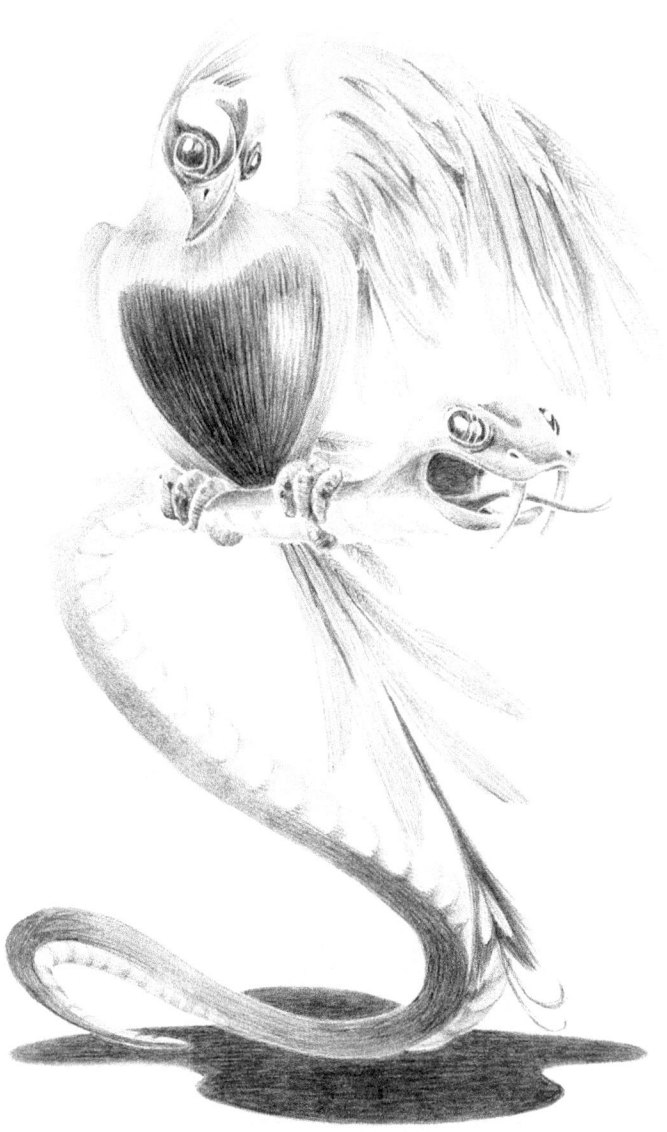

Where the Wild Popcorn Blooms

Ramona has a garden
With twenty-thousand rooms
Where pencils grow, and octopi,
And wild popcorn blooms,
Where children pick fresh mittens
On a sunny summer day,
And rubber balls float in a stream
And otters come and play—
It's such a happy garden
That Ramona takes it down
And packs it in her suitcase
Whenever she leaves town,
And royalty from near and far
Come visit when they can,
For what has more
Appeal than dreams
For woman, child or man?

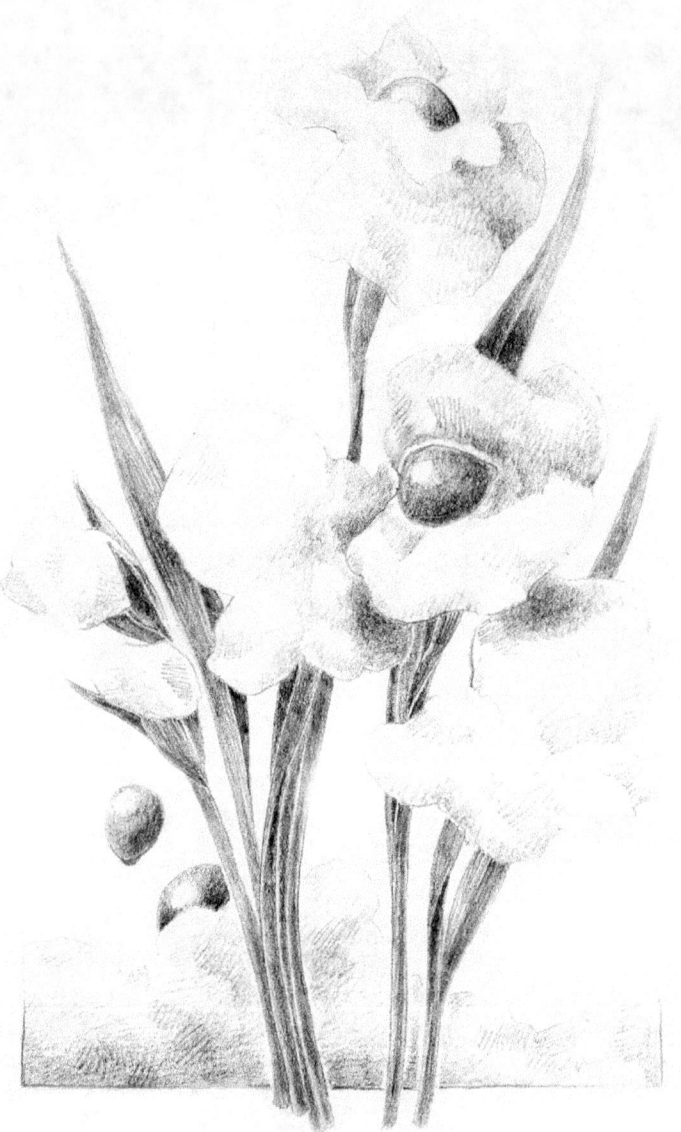

Corn Crib

A cunning little bungalow,
hid far out in the fields,
Where every kernel of retreat
that leafy shelter yields
Expands the sense of comfort
in the shuttered yellow home
For cozy hospitality
to please a farming gnome
Quite small enough to fit inside
and curl up by the hob,
Enjoying all the pleasance of
the life lived in a cob

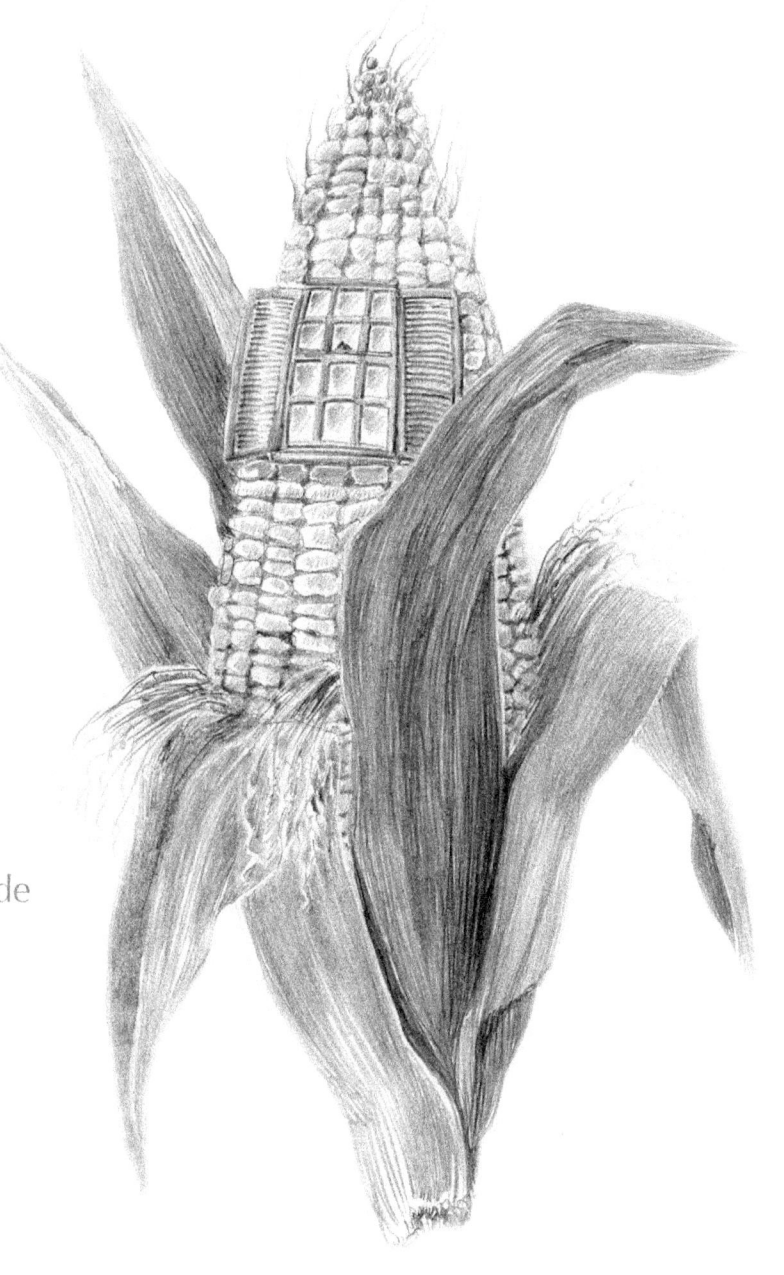

My First New Car

A shiny little sharp mobile where, perched behind the steering wheel,
I'm slightly dazzled by the flash of all those gauges on the dash,
Of all the buttons, pedals, lights; the knobs and gears are pretty sights
That make me feel I will arrive in highest style, where-e'er I drive;
Must say, this new car is a spiffy font of fondness in a jiffy.

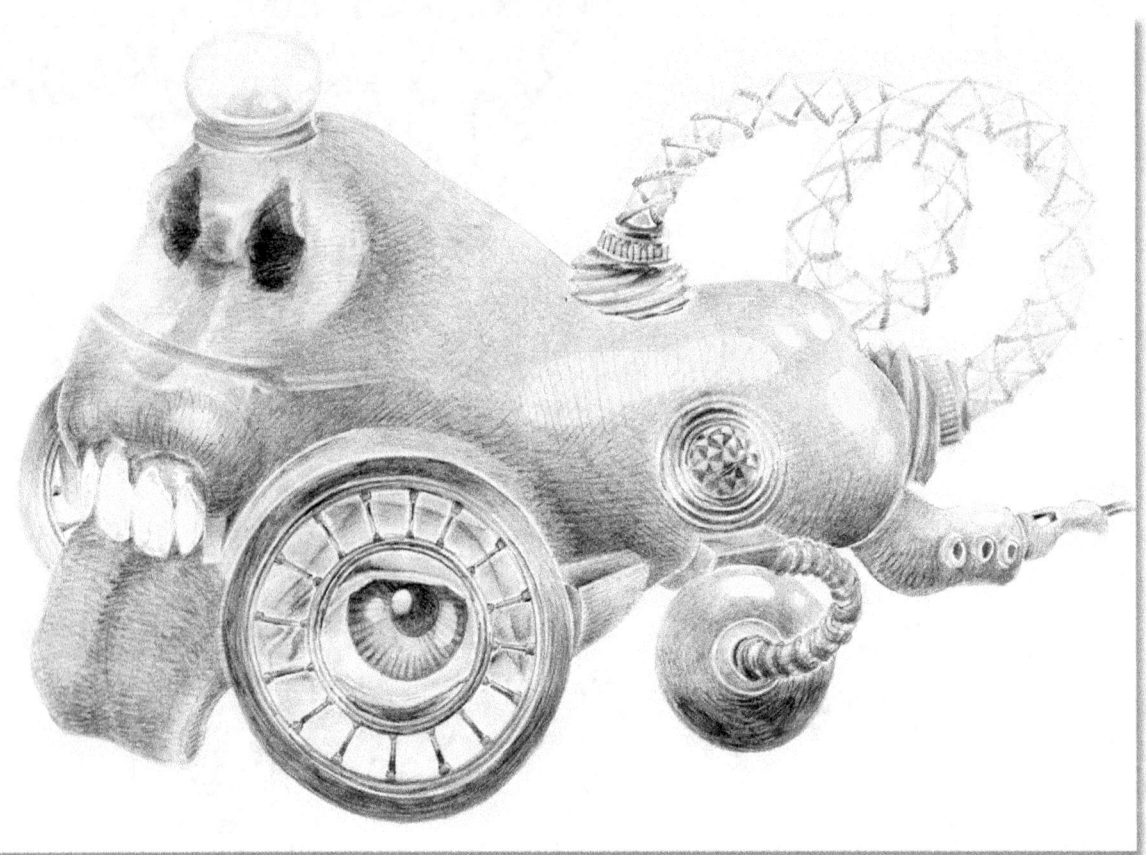

Three Little Words

Three words strike fear
into the heart
And with a sense
of doom impart
Their horrors in
the modern breast—
On hearing them,
we grow distressed
And fear for love
and life and limb
And see our
happiness grow dim—
There is no
palliative retort
When we are told:
Call Tech Support.

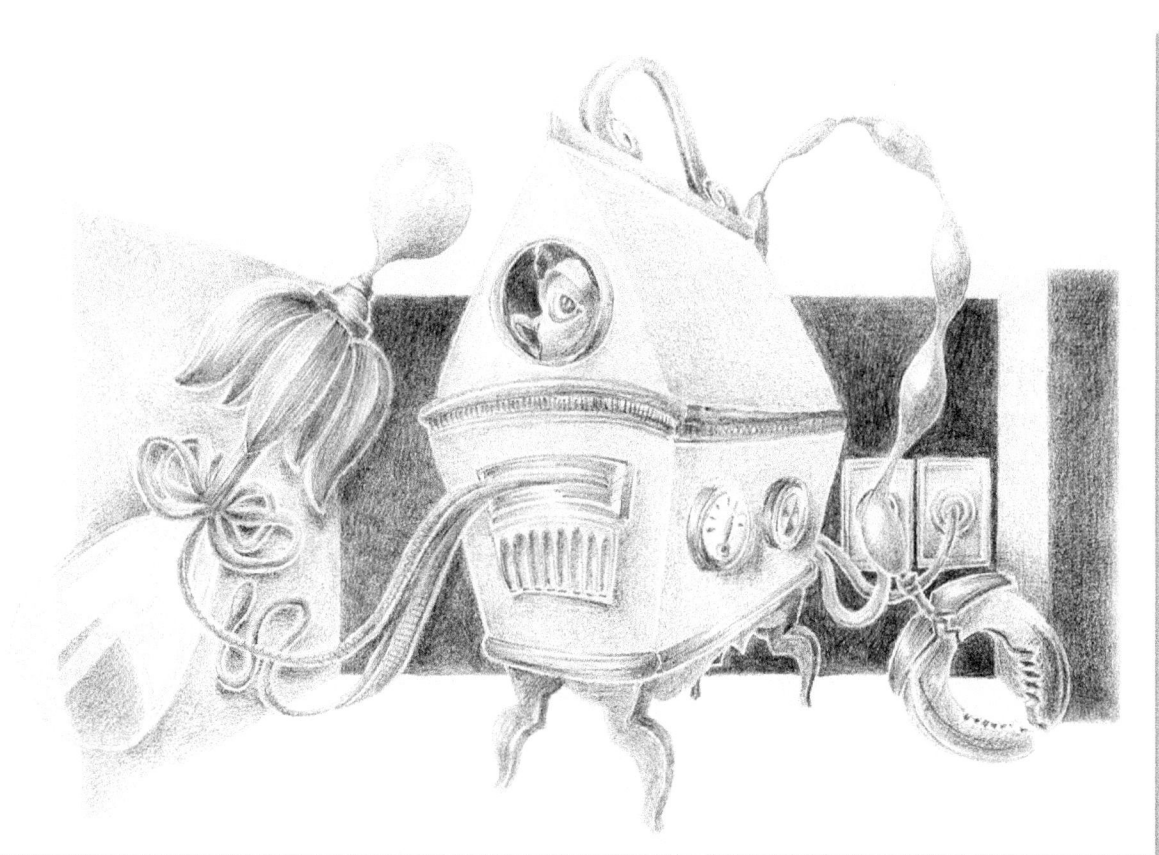

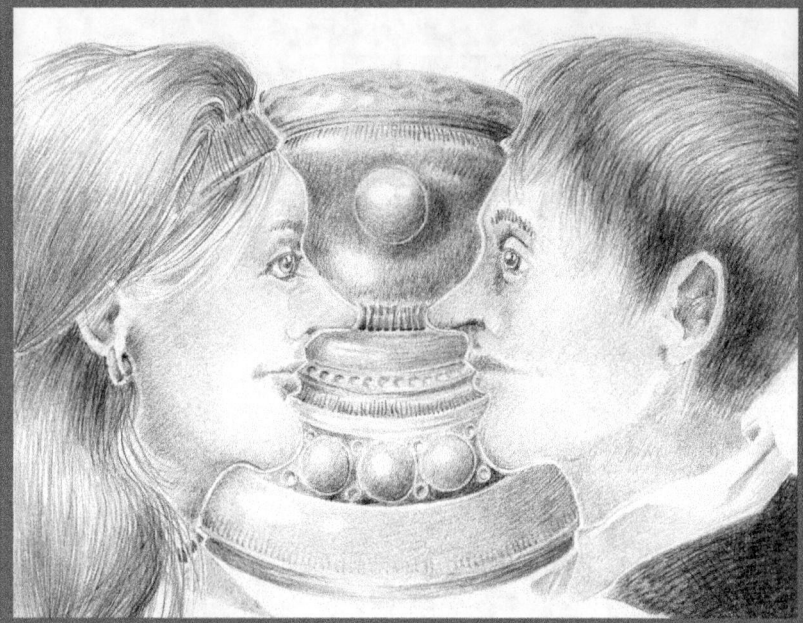

Points of View

Depending how I look at it, a man and woman seem to sit
In conversation face to face, or I may focus on a vase
Or goblet rather than those two—it seems no matter which I do
It's no more false and no more real than what of *me* viewpoints reveal.

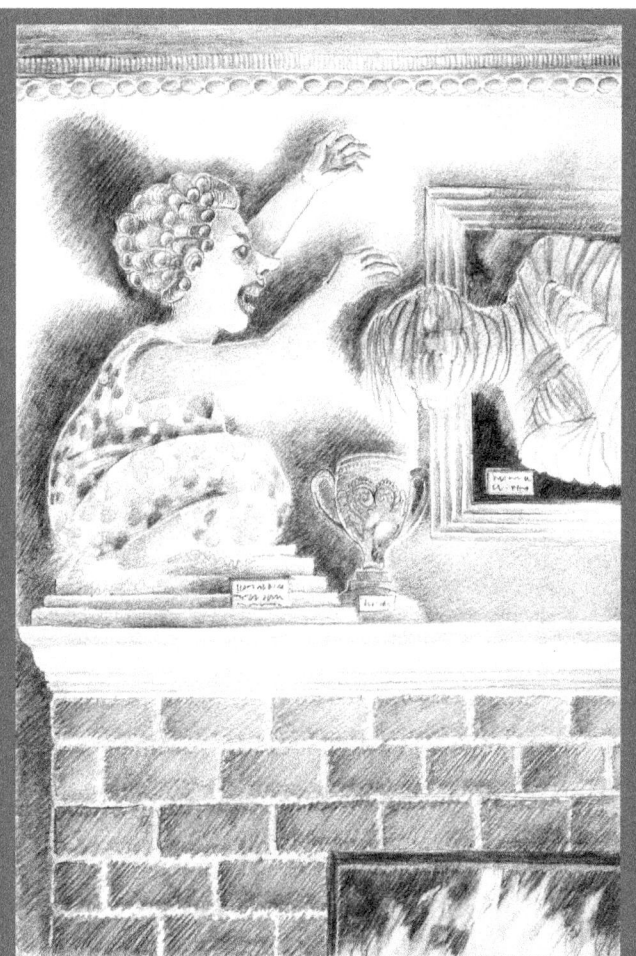

Preserving Their Love

Although he loved her well
(My mother knew),
Dad always said
He'd take her to the
Taxidermist's shop
When she was dead,
For if they sometimes
Disagreed and
Chafed from year to year,
He loved her so,
He'd never stand
Not having Mother near—
And Mom, for her part,
Told Dad when
It came to his dire case,
She'd have him
Mummified and hung
Above the fireplace,
For she, though they might
Spar a bit as
Married couples do,
Loved him in kind
And wished to keep
Him always near her, too.

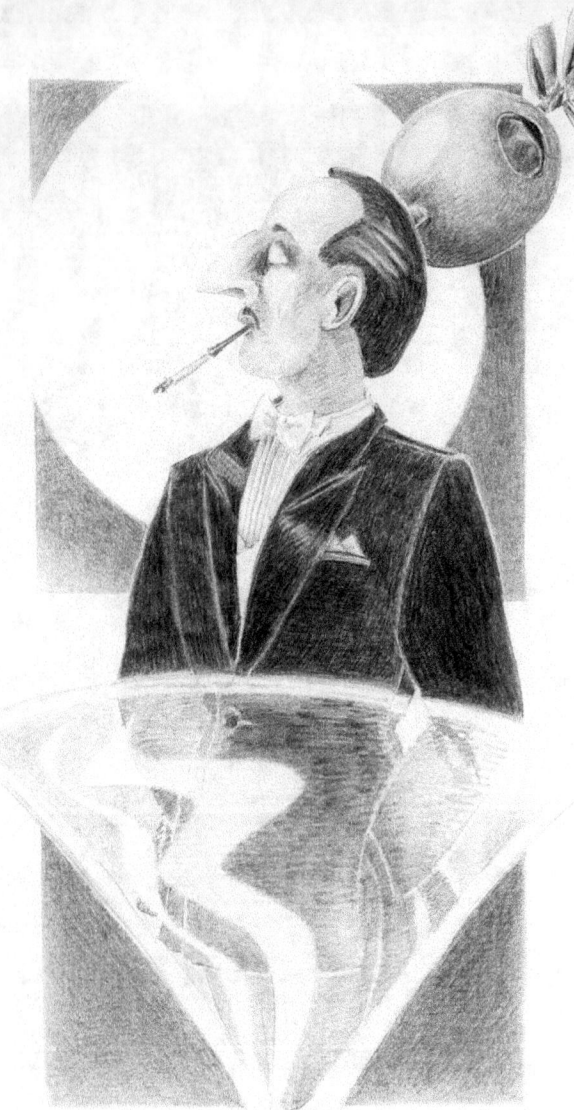

Bit of a Pickle

I say, what spiffing digs you have,
Old chap, *Oui, quelle cachet!*
I shouldn't drop a spot of bother
On your grand soiree—
I hate to trouble you, old chum,
And be a tiresome ass,
But while a Swell, it seems I fell
In my martini glass—
No doubt you will be thinking
That a rescue's just the thing—
Yes, you can save me from my slip:
Put me in a Gin Sling

*From One
Mad Scientist
to Another*

A little experiment that I have made
May, possibly, just on the off chance, have strayed
Afield for the moment—I mention it merely
Because I am hopeful, so deeply, sincerely,
You won't be too startled and mash it to bits
If you happen upon it—admittedly, it's
A tad unexpected—so if you would, please,
Just return my small jar of Infectious Disease-
Filled Robotic-&- Insectomorphic Toy parts
Before any indiscreet silliness starts,
And we will just agree to forget that I saw
What you put in that sandwich you gave Dr. Shaw.

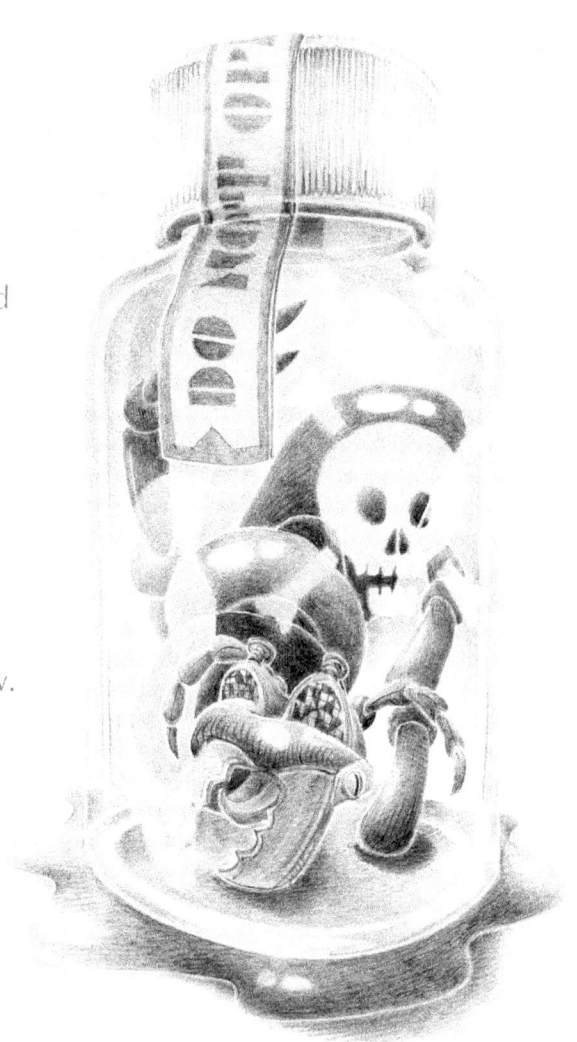

Thing that Does Things

There is a wonderful machine that's spiffy, neat, and super-keen
Because its functions are so grand and great, but on the other hand,
It's hard to fix when it's abuzz, malfunctioning, or conked, because
It is so arcane, intricate and complicated, that we get
Bamboozled trying to describe
what's wrong, and end in diatribe,
For truthfully, we've not a clue
just what this fine
machine can do,
Or what its actual
functions are,
for it's so complex
and bizarre
That we, in our
benighted state,
prefer to simply
think it great
And know that if
we could have guessed
what it is, we'd
sure be impressed.

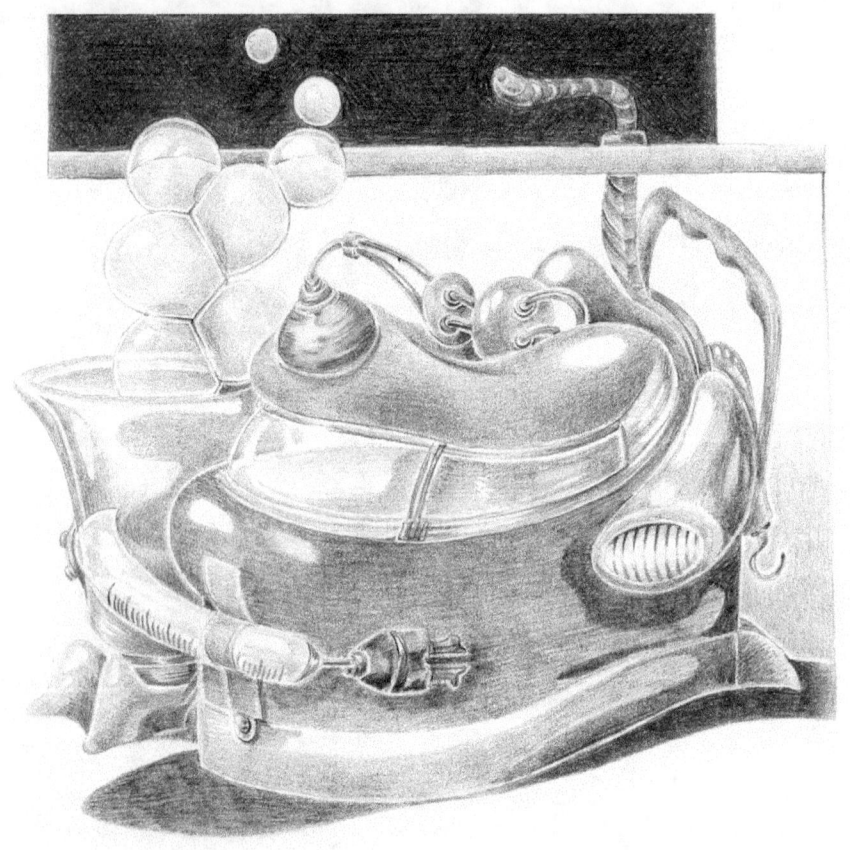

The Essential Whatchacallit

Bartholomew, fetch me the Thingamajig,
The Whosis, the Thingummy—Quick!
I have to do Stuff that requires the rig,
You know—that one with the odd trick
  Of listing to starboard
    and sputtering dust
      When its gauges are
        set in high gear—
      No, I can't remember
    its name, but you must
      Rush it to me,
        Bartholomew dear!

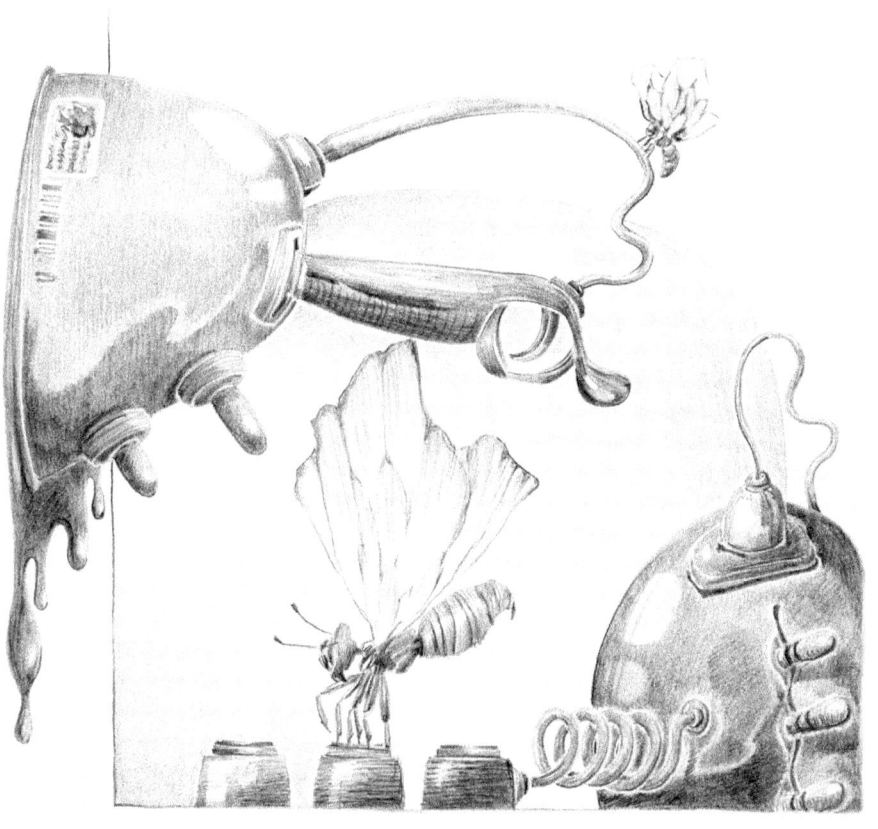

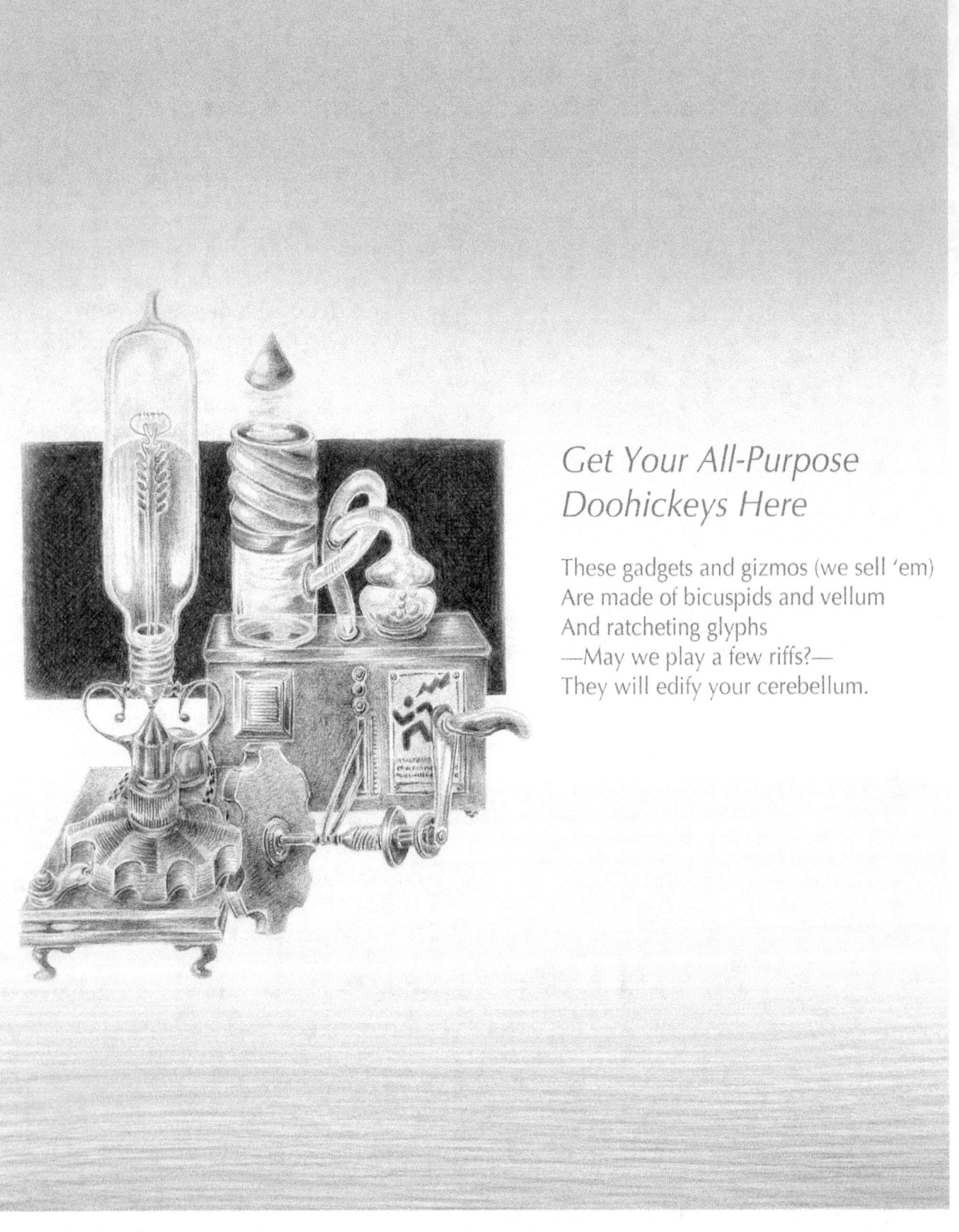

Get Your All-Purpose Doohickeys Here

These gadgets and gizmos (we sell 'em)
Are made of bicuspids and vellum
And ratcheting glyphs
—May we play a few riffs?—
They will edify your cerebellum.

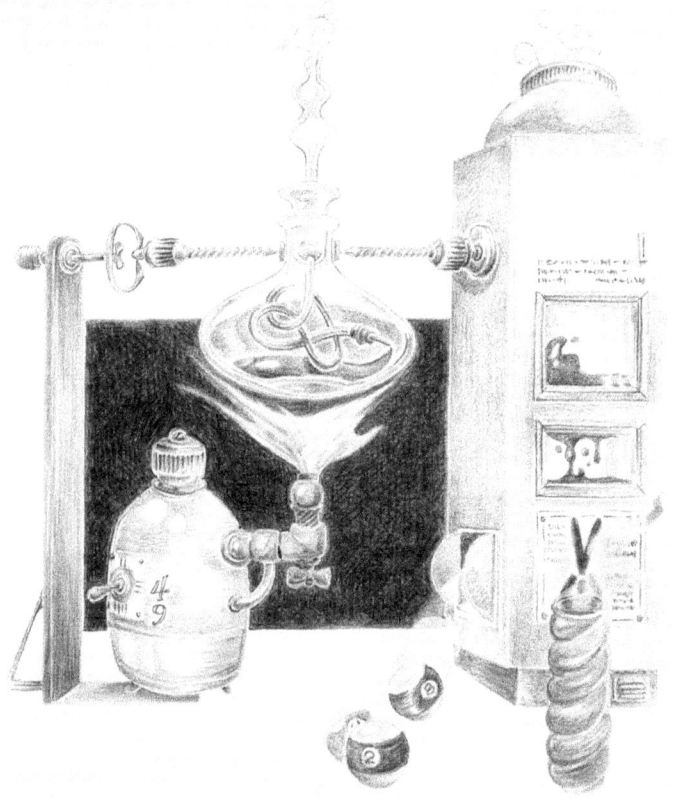

Dr. Whizbang's Unusual Retort

One night the startled janitor
Saw something rather odd occur
When in the lab a strange machine
With creaking gears and lights of green
And yellow flashing on its side
Let out a belch, whereon he spied,
Emerging from its gurgling parts,
A murky mist, in fits and starts,
That gradually took the shape
Of something like a shambling ape—
No, 'twas a hunched-up scientist
That shambled out from in the mist—
And lest the workman be distressed,
He found himself kindly addressed
By this, his boss: "Forgive the quirk
Of how I choose to come to work;
It's just much simpler to arrive
For night shifts without need to drive."
He smiled and to his office went
By sliding out the cooling vent.

Keeping My Toes Warm

To you who don't approve of my
Weird methodology
For keeping warm in winter months,
Just have a look and see
That while you are all freezing cold
And whining over chills,
I am as warm as toast and have
Much smaller power bills:
While turning down the furnace,
I have found what warms the most are
A mug of Irish coffee and
Three minutes in the toaster

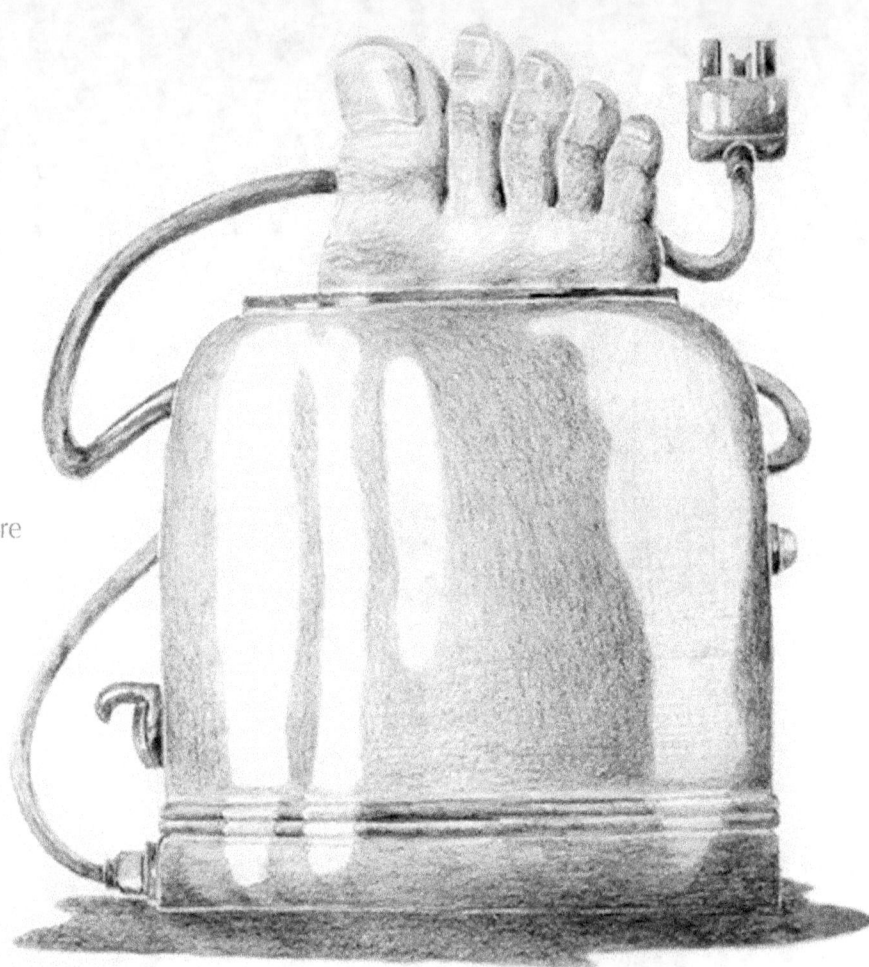

Unexpectedly Dangerous Sport

Whilst roller-skating in the street, I fell upon my elbow, seat,
Upon my knee, my forehead, ear, But since there was nobody near
To stop my bounce, I finally fell Straight down the culvert: what a *Smell!*
If you should want to try to skate, Stay far off from the culvert grate,
Lest you, as well, lack skating skills And not be rescued from your spills
Until you, too, have bounced away too far. That's all I have to say.

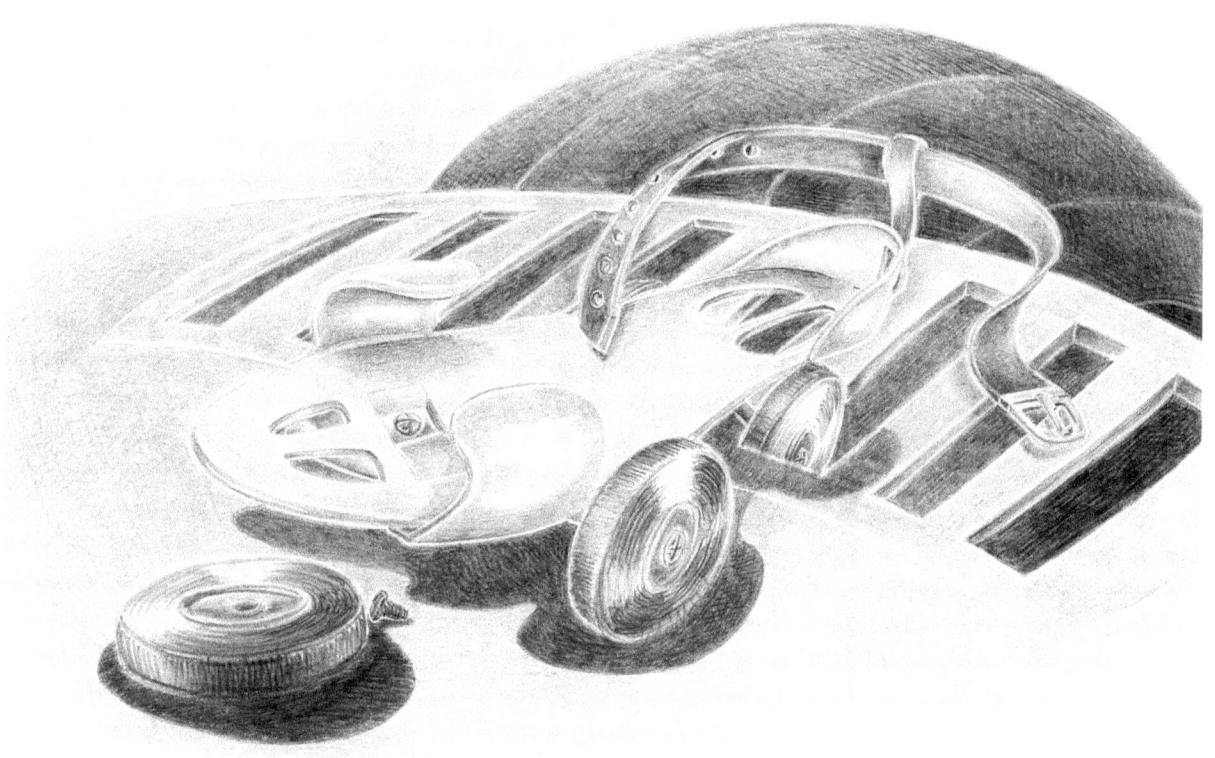

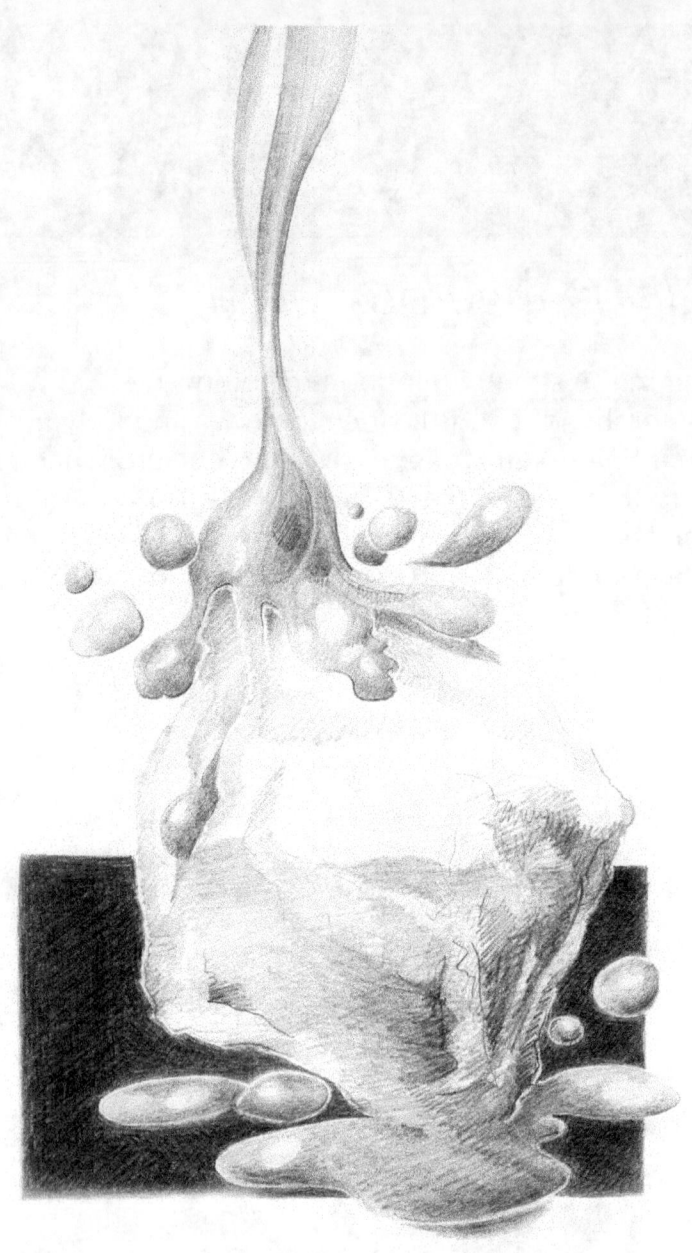

No Lager, Thanks, but I Sure Could Go for a Zombie

We're sitting around the barbecue Enjoying a brewski—cold—or two,
When, Holy Toledo, here comes Ed! It's no big deal, except he's dead.
But then, he always did enjoy A show-off moment, that good ol' boy.
Now, as he approaches, a hint of fear: Will he still expect us to share the beer?

The McGuffin

A mystery story has a twist,
The clue caught in the tight-closed fist,
Whose revelation stuns and throws
Into relief what no one knows
And solves it all by final credit—
Frankly, though: I still don't get it.

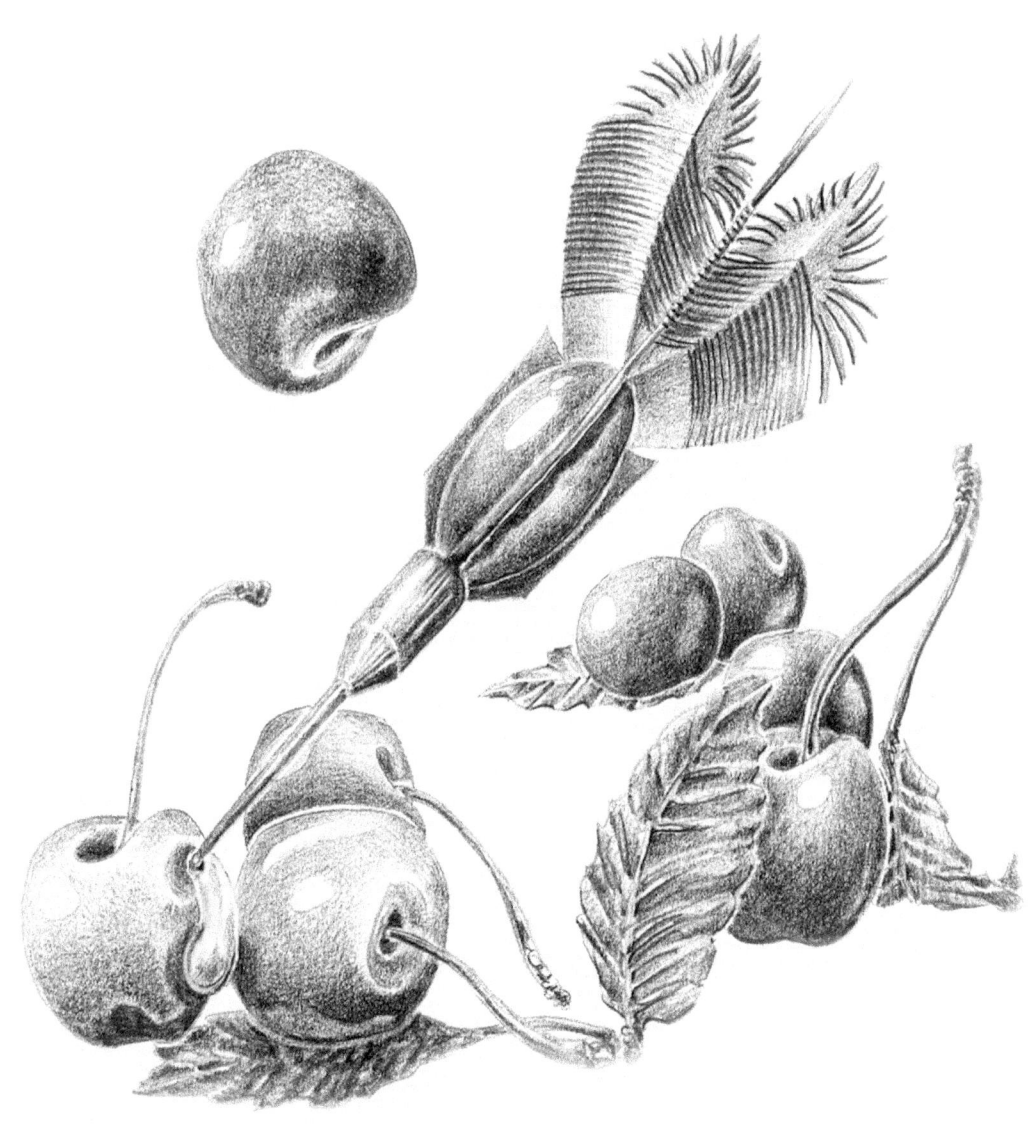

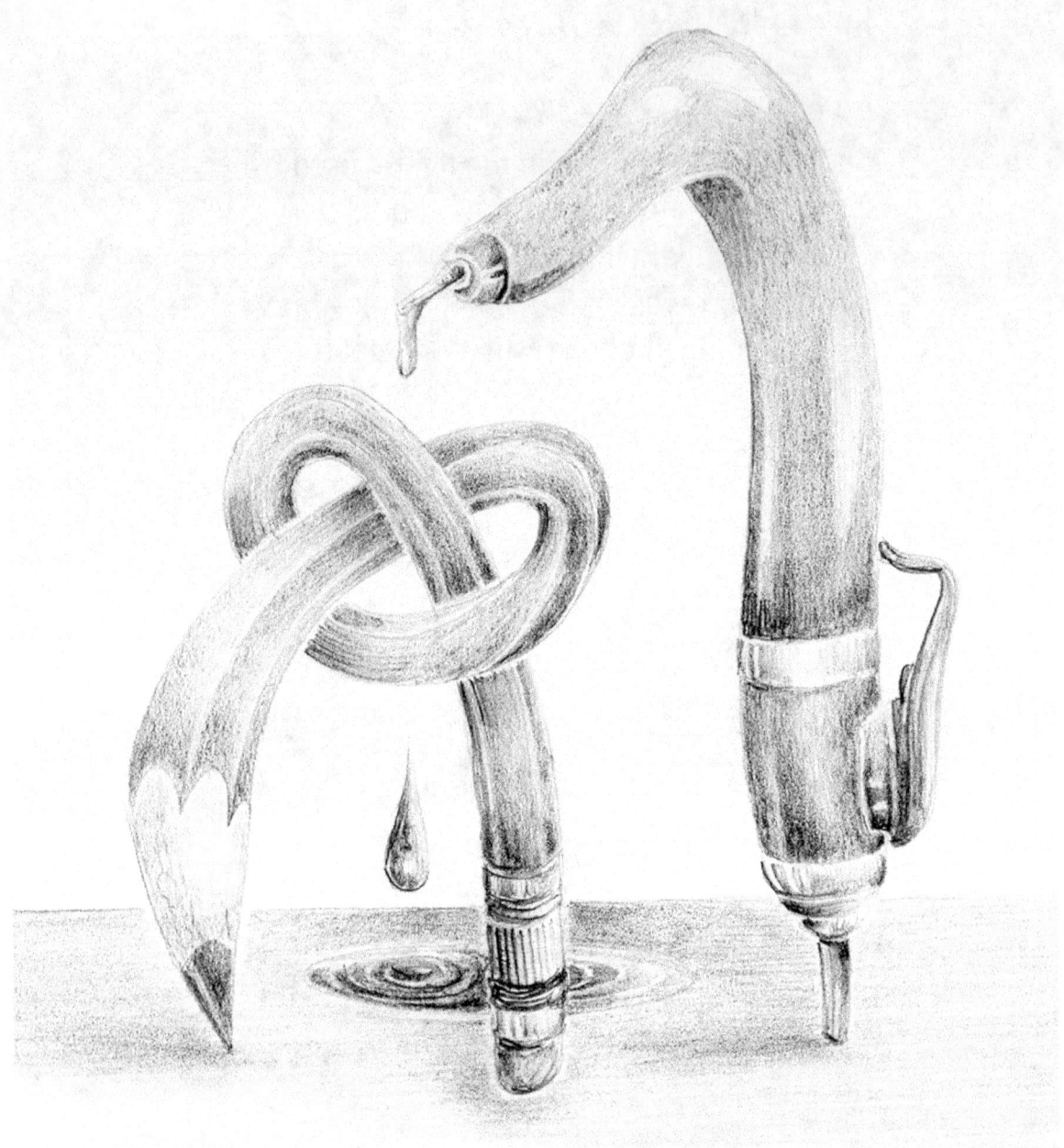

When sitting down with the intent Of scribing with a certain bent,
It's best to be supplied with tools Of proper warp themselves; the rules
Of writing bend to fit as well, Long as there are wild tales to tell.

Implements for Writing
Mystery Stories

All I need is here: the desk, my writing implements, the sky
Seen in a little polygon of blue with myrtle brushing by
It just beyond the window where I sit and hope that words will come
To guide my thoughts, inspire my heart, or break the silence here at home
When that one other thing I need for greater inspiration yet
Is gone away—yes, that is you, my lifelong partner, love, my pet.

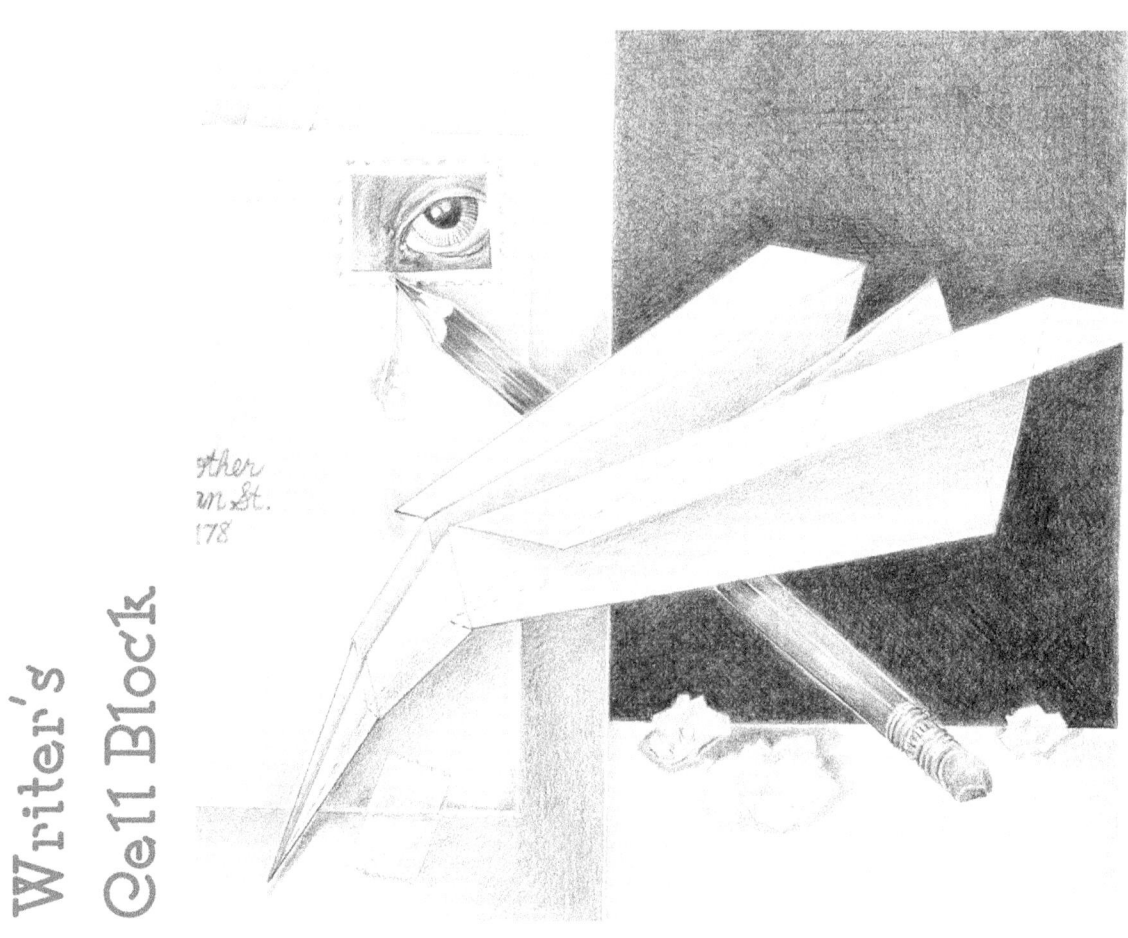

Writer's Cell Block

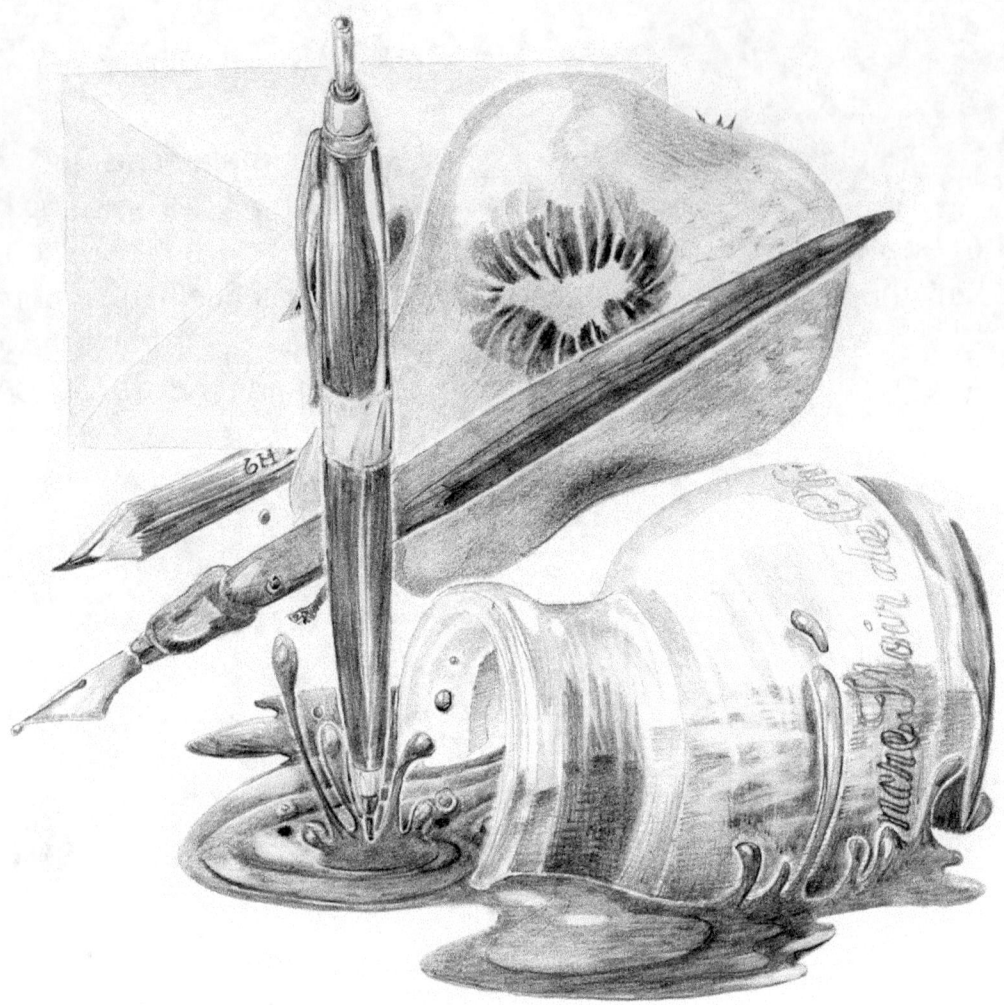

A Note in Passing

Mary had a little love
For violets of blue
And roses red, Forget-me-nots
And chocolate candies, too;
Brown paper packages, white dresses—
Let me count the ways
In which Mary's romantic heart
Embraced the hours and days—
But Mary, poor lamb that she is,
Finds no romance in store
When learning that nobody writes
Love letters anymore.

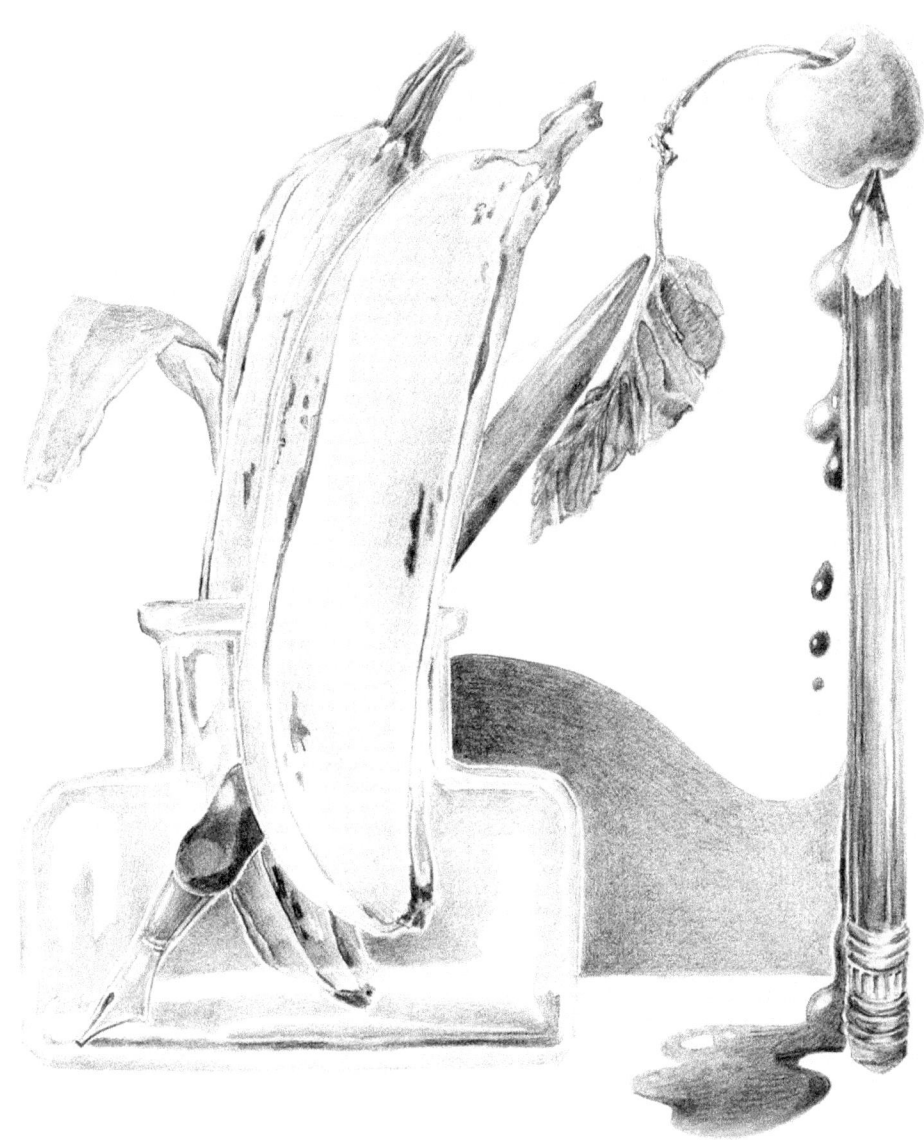

You Must be Joking!

Asking me to help you:
That's an honor I embrace.
But when you say it's writing jokes,
The grin's wiped from my face—
Perhaps you have forgotten
The old proverb of the bard:
Everything else is easy—
Writing comedy—***that's*** hard!

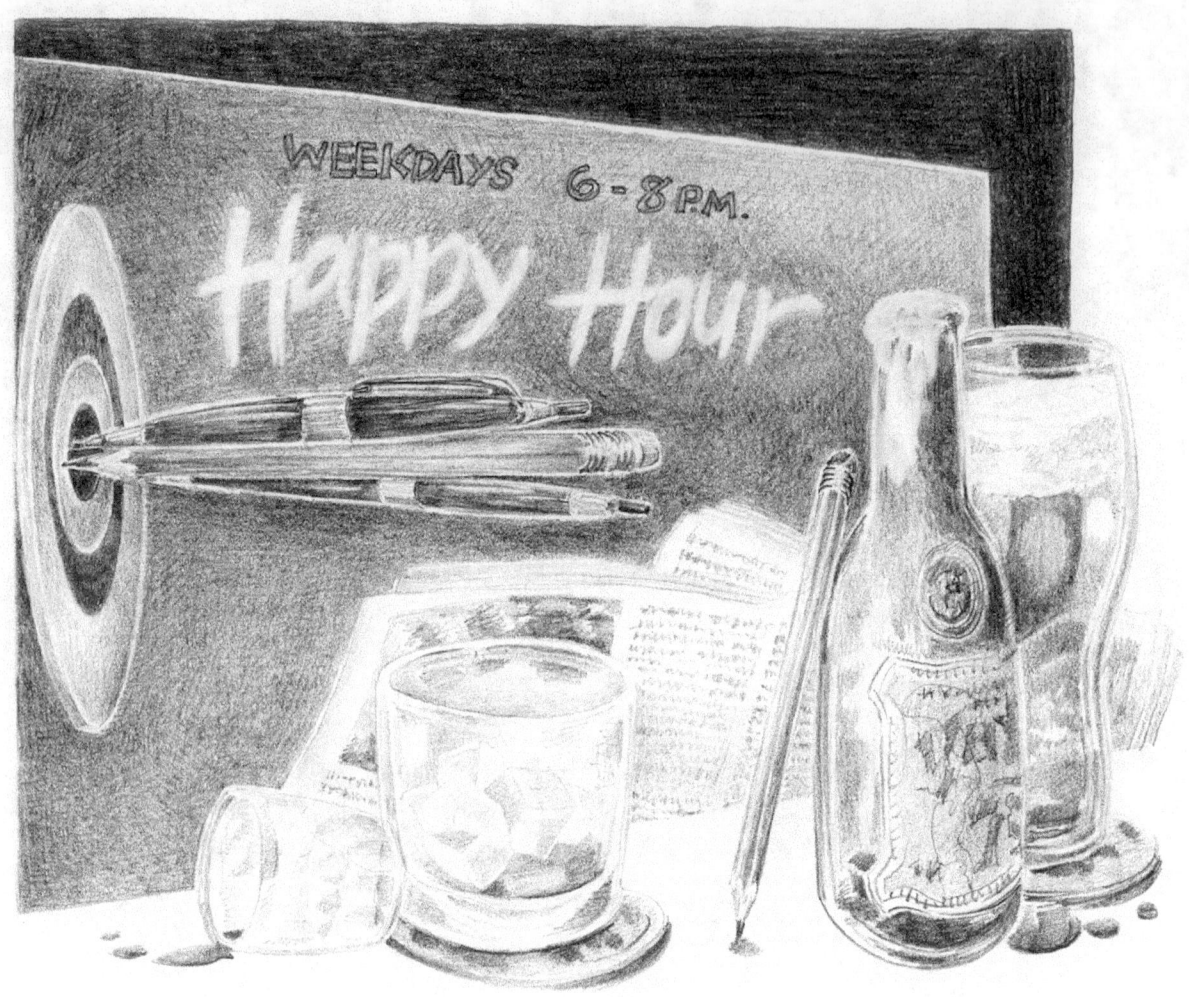

The Beginning of
The End

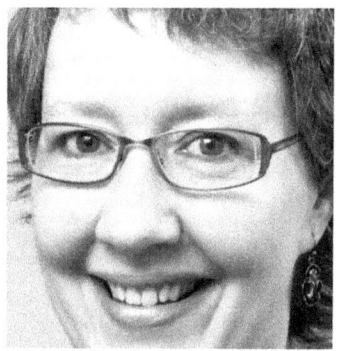

Having worked as a home caregiver, office temp, house painter, stagehand, freelance designer, university teacher, gallery director, grocery bagger, editor, and at a few other assorted jobs, Kathryn Sparks took the leap into self-reinvention as an artists to see if there might be a way to better integrate her life adventures with the abiding passion for creative pursuits. As an artist, she works in a wide variety of media and modes; her themes and interests wander from the curiously childlike to the embarrassingly earthy, through glimpses of the sweet and ethereal, and right on into the realm of the cheerfully macabre. Despite her excellent upbringing and continued living among highly cultured and intelligent people, she has been consistently supported and even encouraged in these happy pursuits, and the book you hold in your hands is a product of such profligate sustenance and inexplicable enthusiasm. You can also find her daily blog online at www.kiwsparks.wordpress.com.

www.ingramcontent.com/pod-product-compliance
Lightning Source LLC
Chambersburg PA
CBHW080250180526
45167CB00006B/2483